Kirtley Library
Columbia College
8th and Rogers
Columbia, MO. 65201

Henry Purcell and the Restoration Theatre

HENRY PURCELL
Portrait attributed to Kneller.

Courtesy of the National Portrait Gallery

ROBERT ETHERIDGE MOORE

Henry Purcell

& the Restoration Theatre

FOREWORD BY SIR JACK WESTRUP

HEINEMANN

LONDON MELBOURNE TORONTO

© 1961 Robert Etheridge Moore

First published 1961

Published by Heinemann Educational Books Ltd
15-16 Queen Street, Mayfair, London W.1

Printed in Great Britain by
Jarrold & Sons Ltd, Norwich

782.1
m786h
6163

TO MY MOTHER

Contents

Publisher's Note

Where English usage differs from American, musical terms are used in this book with their English connotations. For the benefit of American readers their American equivalents are given below.

English	American
bar	measure
minim	half-note
crotchet	quarter-note
quaver	eighth-note
semiquaver	sixteenth-note

The publishers would like to thank the Editor of the *Yale Review* and Alfred A. Knopf Inc. for permission to quote the copyright passages on pages 35 and 59 respectively. The musical illustrations for this book have been drawn by John Barkwith.

List of Illustrations

Foreword

BY THE CIRCUMSTANCES of his time Purcell was debarred from writing full-length operas for the professional theatre. This does not mean that his music for the stage is unimportant. Furthermore, the plays to which he contributed music, whether original works or adaptations, are important in the history of Restoration drama. It is a defect in many histories of opera that they do not sufficiently relate the music to the action. In the present book Mr Moore treats them both as equally important. I am certain that his discussion will be useful to those who are primarily interested in music, and I hope it will succeed in persuading students of drama that the music is something that cannot be ignored. It is hardly possible for us today to view these works through Restoration eyes; but the quality of Purcell's music alone is a sufficient inducement to take them seriously. To divorce that music from the stage is an error that does no credit to our admiration for the composer. Regret is sometimes expressed that Purcell did not live to play a part in establishing English opera on the Italian model. Such regret is understandable but hardly profitable. It is more useful to study what he has actually left us. This is what Mr Moore has done.

JACK WESTRUP

Preface

THIS BOOK is a study of Purcell's operas, works of great
musical stature which, with the exception of *Dido and Aeneas*,
are almost unknown. Since they are a genre of their own, part
spoken play and only part sung, they have been neglected by
literary historian and musicologist alike, each being hesitant to
encroach upon a field not his own. When one considers the
reputation of Purcell and, more important, the quality of the
music, this is an absurd situation which has long been in need of
correction. The book is therefore addressed as much to students
of literature and the theatre as to students of music.

The word 'students' is important. Specialists will inevitably
find a great deal here that they already know, indeed whole pages
that they will doubtless want to skim, but from the reports of
colleagues in departments of music as well as from my own
experience with even the most advanced students of English
literature, it is quite clear that literary and musical studies
seldom meet. A student of literature and a student of music are
virtually never combined in the same individual. Outside their
own field of study their ignorance can be described only as
sizeable. (Unhappily this generalization, not lightly made, applies
frequently to the podium no less than to the arena.)

Hence the opening chapter, a discussion of the origins of
Purcell's operas, is occupied largely with the nature of baroque
entertainment, a background which must be clearly grasped
before the operas themselves make much sense. The reader I
trust will not be offended if he sometimes recognizes familiar
signposts, inevitable I am afraid in this kind of summary.
The rest of the book attempts to analyse both libretto and
music in the light of their theatrical intentions and effectiveness. After *Dido and Aeneas*, each of the chapters discusses a
different kind of dramatic type and problem: *King Arthur* the

attempt to create a British national opera, *The Fairy Queen* the apotheosis of the masque-like opera, *The Indian Queen* the heroic play, *Dioclesian* and *Bonduca* the heroic romance, and *The Tempest* the Shakespearean adaptation.

Most of the chapters on the individual operas are divided into three parts, the first being background of one sort or another, the second musical analysis, and the third a particular problem that the opera at hand illustrates. *Dido and Aeneas* is, of course, a different kind of opera from the others, but, being the composer's masterpiece, it illustrates his dramatic powers best of all and stands as a rallying point around which the other works may be discussed. The *Dido* chapter must of necessity repeat a good deal that has been said by others—it is the only work of Purcell to have been studied extensively—but I hope that more is said here than anywhere else, and in new connexions. In the ensuing chapters each opera is discussed with considerable detail in both its musical and dramatic aspects, and finally a short conclusion attempts to place Purcell in perspective, both from the point of view of the seventeenth century as well as of the following Augustan period.

Certain things which have been done often before I do not attempt: an account of Purcell's life, a discussion of his religious and instrumental music, a history of seventeenth-century music drama, and so on. Instead the ideal of the book is to examine several fascinating and little-known works of genius in their proper background, and to have, in so far as it is possible, the theatre in our heads. The musical analyses, confined to the second division of each chapter, will be made practicable by as many musical quotations as possible, some of which I have included in the text, and even more by the recordings of the complete scores, all of which should soon be available. Music which is easily accessible, as in the case of *Dido*, or the excerpts printed by Professor Westrup, I do not reproduce. In literary quotations I have, except in a few obvious cases, normalized the spelling and capitalization.

For the help and encouragement I have received from various friends I am deeply grateful. Dr Nigel Fortune and Dr Neil Saunders have given me helpful advice on certain portions of the manuscript, and I am especially indebted to Mr Eric Walter White who at every point has been the wisest and most generous of critics. I wish also to express particular thanks to the University of Minnesota for granting me a sabbatical leave in which to complete my work. Finally two books, Dent's *Foundations of English Opera* (now out of print) and Professor Westrup's critical biography of Purcell, I have used so constantly for so long that I often cannot distinguish what is mine from what is theirs. These books first inspired me to make a full-scale study of Purcell's operas, and to extend and elaborate their work has been my highest aim.

ROBERT ETHERIDGE MOORE

London, 1960

CHAPTER I

Backgrounds

THE ENGLISH, like other peoples, can provide an almost limitless selection of gross miscalculations in artistic and critical judgment. In the same generation with Blake's confident dismissal of Rembrandt and Dr Johnson's of *Tristram Shandy* ('Nothing odd will do long'), Dr Burney composed a gloomy epitaph upon the genius of Henry Purcell. 'Unluckily for Purcell,' said Burney, 'he built his fame with such perishable materials that his worth and works are daily diminishing . . . and so much is our great musician's celebrity already consigned to tradition that it will soon be as difficult to find his songs or at least to hear them, as those of his predecessors, Orpheus and Amphion, with which Cerberus was lulled to sleep, or the city of Thebes constructed.' Though this may have looked like a good guess in Burney's day, it has proved happily unprophetic. In the past few decades the efforts of musical scholars have revealed that the materials are far from perishable, and the present spate of recordings has safely removed Purcell from the position of his two celebrated predecessors. 'Orpheus Britannicus' he was called in his own time, and as such he is securely re-established today.

The pull has admittedly not been an easy one. Until the formation of the Purcell Society in 1878 his works nearly all existed only in manuscript, and even now the work of the Society is incomplete. To make matters worse its early editors inherited from the eighteenth century a zeal for emendations and improvements in Purcell's harmony, popularized and perpetuated by inexpensive 'arrangements for the pianoforte'. Modern musical scholarship is still in the process of undoing some of this misrepresentation, as well as of finding out more about the nature of contemporary performance of his music. It is certain that soon we shall have good editions of virtually all of his many-sided creativity—instrumental compositions, church music, welcome songs, secular odes and cantatas, rounds and catches, and, richest of all, his scores for the theatre. Furthermore they will become generally familiar. The enthusiasm which greeted the recent tercentenary celebrations showed that the potential public for Purcell is wide and strong. What he has needed all these years is simply to be disinterred.

We may also expect for most of the categories of Purcell's music adequate performances. Unfortunately not quite all. The ominous cloud in this bright picture is that category which reveals his genius more fully than any of the others, his operatic scores. These elaborately beautiful works, almost totally unfamiliar to the general musical public, pose a great many problems which we are now to investigate. That their difficulties will ever be sufficiently overcome to give the operas the popularity they deserve admits of no certain answer. All attempts at least must begin with knowledge. Highly sophisticated products of a baroque culture that is not always understood by modern taste, these operas must be approached in their proper setting. Each will in due course be considered separately, but first we may look into the background from which they sprang, and thus discover what they share in common.

I. THE BAROQUE IDEAL

Music and poetry have ever been acknowledged sisters, which walking hand in hand, support each other; as poetry is the harmony of words, so music is that of notes; and as poetry is a rise above prose and oratory, so is music the exaltation of poetry. Both of them may excel apart, but sure they are most excellent when they are joined, because nothing is then wanting to either of their perfections: for thus they appear like wit and beauty in the same person.

These words Purcell wrote in the introduction he appended to his score for *The Prophetess, or the History of Dioclesian*, which he published in 1691. The opera had been staged with such great success the year before that the few remaining years of his life Purcell devoted principally to composing music for the theatre. His words were by no means original; he was merely echoing a humanist ideal that had been widely popular in England and on the Continent for well over a century. His statement is in a sense a summary of a long tradition of which it stands at the end, for though Dryden in *Alexander's Feast* (1697) was still to celebrate St Cecilia as a symbol of the higher union of poetry and music, the early years of the eighteenth century brought into England a very different kind of vocal music wherein the text is largely irrelevant. Addison could write contemptuously that 'nothing is capable of being set to music that is not nonsense'. The ideal of a sublime union of two arts to produce a yet higher art reaches its culmination in the seventeenth century; by Addison's time it was dying. It is significant that Dryden's more extravagant praise of St Cecilia had appeared in his earlier ode of 1687: an angel hearing her song had mistaken earth for heaven. A half-century earlier still, Milton had written:

> Blest pair of sirens, pledges of heaven's joy,
> Sphere-born harmonious sisters, voice and verse,
> Wed your divine sounds, and mixed power employ...

These are but a few expressions of a persistent idea running through late Renaissance musical theory that music is the combination of poetry and melody. Remembering the remarkable effects attributed to music by classical and Biblical authority—Orpheus, Timotheus, Arion, King David are the names most frequently invoked—musicians could not help feeling towards the end of the sixteenth century that something was wrong with their elaborate polyphonic music in which contrapuntal intricacies obscured the words. Music could not be the exaltation of poetry if the poetry was inaudible. A group of musical humanists appeared whose ideals found a rallying point in Jean de Baïf's Académie de Poésie et de Musique instituted by royal decree in France, and the more widely known Camerata founded by Count Bardi in Florence. The Camerata invented opera, which they described as *dramma per musica*, under the impression that they were emulating classical Greek tragedy, the highest form of dramatic expression. Although the actual works that they produced may have had an appeal quite limited even among the snobbish coterie for whom they were written—no one wanted to listen every night to a Greek tragedy sung—these operas supplied models and techniques that revolutionized Western music. In the masterpiece of the type, Monteverdi's *Orfeo* (1607), the composer aimed to make the words the mistress rather than the servant of the harmony. England had no academy devoted to discussing the problems of poetry and music, but for roughly a hundred years from the appearance of John Case's *Praise of Musick* in 1586 the number of humanists who published treatises on the subject is very large.[1]

In England the supreme champion of music as the exaltation of poetry was Purcell. His lamentably brief career culminated in a series of works called dramatic operas dedicated to this principle. They are by no means what we should today call dramatic operas. Although there are refinements and variations in the species, the most rudimentary definition of them is that given by Dr Burney: 'By dramatic opera, Dryden, and writers of his time, mean a drama that is declaimed or spoken, and in which songs and symphonies are introduced; differing from real operas, where there is no speaking, and where the narrative part and dialogue is set to recitative.'[2] Purcell did of course write one genuine opera, *Dido and Aeneas*, but the rest were plays ennobled, 'wrought up to a higher pitch' in Dryden's phrase, by the combination with music. Opera, far from being a purely musical form, was rather a dramatic form in which music served as an articulating element. Before all else it was a work for the stage, and for the same large popular audience who came to ordinary plays. The exclusive opera-goer did not come into being in London until the establishment of the Italian opera a decade after Purcell's death.

It might appear unnecessarily obvious to insist that the dramatic operas were above all stage pieces. What operas are not? Yet there is a strong modern prevalence, unintentionally abetted by recordings, for looking upon every element of opera except the music itself as irrelevant. Ironically this has become particularly apparent in our attitude towards Wagner. Although he is the inventor of a unique music drama which sought to combine poetry, music, and scenic appearances in an autonomous and unified work of art, more than any other modern composer he is presented in concert form. This situation would have enraged him, for of course Bayreuth was built for the express purpose that his

---

[1] A chronological list would include, among others, Thomas Morley, Thomas Campion, Thomas Ravenscroft, Charles Butler, John Playford, Christopher Simpson, and Matthew Locke.

[2] *A General History of Music*, ed. Frank Mercer, vol. ii, p. 648: London, 1935.

operas might be properly staged. The theatrical experience necessary for a genuine appraisal of Wagnerian opera is still more essential for the operas of the baroque period. In Wagner, after all, the music is strongly, even belligerently, in the dominating position of the music drama, but in seventeenth-century opera this is usually far from being true. Even the poetry, the originating inspiration which called up the passions more fully realized in the music, could not be called predominant. One could hear words and music at a concert. An elaborate stage piece designed to thrill a large paying audience had to employ more spectacular appeals as well. Ideally the production combined the arts of poetry and melody with those of the visual arts—of painting, architecture, costume, and the dance. The great designers were not mere scene-painters or decorators; they were architects and artists like Inigo Jones, Torelli, and Bibbiena, creative geniuses who found in the monumental conceptions of the baroque spectacle almost unlimited opportunities for exercising their exuberant invention. The baroque opera was almost as much a construction in architecture as in music. What the great designer, when he turned to the stage, could not execute in stone and marble, he carried out in paint and canvas. When Cesti composed *Il Pomo d'Oro* for the marriage of Emperor Leopold I at Vienna in 1666, the stage architect Ludovico Burnacini supplied twenty-five separate designs for scenes and machines, all of which were sumptuously realized. This is bolder and also more serious than mere décor.

The outsize quality of the finest of these productions reveals the baroque ideal: a splendid pomp and monumentality resulting from yoking together many varied kinds of experience, often wildly disparate, into a single entity. The sense of violence and even eruption is held in control by a masterly and masterful formal technique. Before moving on to the specific background for the Purcell opera, the masque and the heroic play, we must have before us, if only in rapid survey, the principal ingredients of baroque vision, which is the animating force behind them all. Few movements have in recent years been more widely and more imprecisely discussed. One difficulty is the term itself, which is more evocative than descriptive. It is as though a culture of superabundant energy should accept a conventional art form at the same time that it is rebelling against its restrictions; the resulting work of art creates an entirely new union within a recognizable pattern. Convention and revolt are in perfect balance.

At the basis of such a generalization, as indeed of nearly all studies of baroque, is Wölfflin's well-known distinction between the baroque ideal of movement and the earlier Renaissance ideal of rest. 'The baroque uses the same system of forms,' he says, 'but in place of the perfect, the completed, gives the restless, the becoming, in place of the limited, the conceivable, gives the limitless, the colossal. The ideal of beautiful proportion vanishes, interest concentrates not on being, but on happening.'[3] In recent years it has been found helpful to distinguish the earlier period of baroque from the later by the term mannerism, which may also be defined as the transitional period between Renaissance and baroque. We have become familiar with descriptions of contortions and surprises, of unresolved tensions and perilous balances, in many studies dealing with the art of such various but related figures as El Greco, Donne, Webster, Monteverdi, and Bernini. The distorted forms and sulphurous colours in which El Greco conceived even the most conventional religious subjects is a simple illustration. The body and the spirit are in uneasy but dramatic relationship, a dualism, a strain not decisively resolved. Tragicomedy, the favourite theatrical form of the early seventeenth century in England, is an excellent instance of mannerist psychology.[4] Both pathos and laughter are pushed to extremes with no attempt at reconciling the two or accepting the logic of either. They are simultaneously acceptable in a dualistic experience. Illogical this may be, but art can accommodate opposites in a way that logic cannot, and by that very act become dramatic. The violent contradictions in the character of Hamlet remain the classic example: his conduct to nearly everyone in the play except Horatio is appalling, if not cruel, yet the audience is convinced that he is both a noble soul in torment and a great gentleman as well. Logically this makes no sense, dramatically it is thoroughly convincing. This kind of contradiction becomes an important part of the operatic aesthetic which, as we shall see, shapes Purcell's creative powers even at the end of the century.

[3] *Principles of Art History*, trans. Hottinger, p. 10: New York, n.d.
[4] See Wylie Sypher's extensive discussion of mannerism in *Four Stages of Renaissance Style*, pp. 100ff: New York, 1955.

Veduta in prospettiva della gran Fontana dell'Acqua Vergine detta di Trevi Architettura di Nicola Salvi

PLATE I   Piranesi: *Fontana di Trevi*

Courtesy of the Victoria and Albert Museum

Courtesy of the Musée du Louvre

PLATE II Rubens: *Le général achéen Philopoemen reconnu par une vieille femme*

Following the natural course of any creative movement, the violence of mannerism gave way to something more expansive as the sense of formal arrangement became stronger in the high baroque. It is not so much the subject matter that changes as the attitude of the artist towards it. He imposes rigorous order. An eighteenth-century creation, the Fontana di Trevi in Rome (see Plate I, opposite page 6) presents a group of colossal figures—Neptune, attendant deities, charioteers, horses—fairly leaping out at the spectator with swirling, various, unexpected movements. With every figure in motion the eye is continually hurried forward to a different view, a new perspective; nothing is at rest. But towering over the group, fixing a limit to their movement and imposing a certain calm upon their excitability, is the massive façade of the building itself, a construction like a triumphal arch with tall straight columns and a central niche of geometrical regularity in which the unruly Neptune stands. The violent figures are subjected to architectural law, calm and serene, and are thereby ennobled, enlarged. The splendour of Neptune, master of the waters, is controlled by that of a greater master, the architect Salvi.

This it is, their spaciousness and sovereign authority, that gives to the greatest baroque works, in whatever medium, their uniquely satisfying quality. We are simultaneously aware of the tumultuous richness of the content and of the grandeur of conception that dares attempt so much, of the exuberant vitality of the subject matter and of the majestic control with which it is handled. The reins are never slackened. Dryden speaks for all these gigantic creators when he defines the dramatist's aim as attempting 'an absolute dominion over the minds of the spectators'. The form may be conventional—an heroic play, a Pindaric ode, a nativity scene, the façade of a cathedral—but the style permits the farthest amount of grandiose display within the simple framework. The strong imprint of the artist's personality, in other words his individual style, imposes unity of tone and order. Spiritual crisis, which is the spirit of the time, is balanced by magnificence and authority, which is the artist's style.

Examples need hardly be suggested. One has only to think of characteristic works by Tintoretto, Rubens, Poussin, or moving to other fields, Milton, Corneille, Bernini, Monteverdi. In the

Louvre there is a small painting by Rubens called 'Philopoemen'
(see Pl. II) which can instruct us in the qualities of the baroque
imagination almost at a glance. At the centre of the picture is a still
life (though far from still)—a table overflowing, groaning with
flesh, fowl, and fish. Planted firmly in the middle, it seems to
crowd everything else out of the canvas with its swirling vitality.
But on the left, in surprising contrast, are three melodramatic
figures of a man with axe raised, apparently chopping wood, and
an aged woman and man with terrified countenances trying to
restrain him. It is night and the scene would appear to be some
sort of shed or outer kitchen, an incongruous setting for the
tense, rather operatic, moment that is depicted. Who but Rubens
would have dreamed of such a combination or of such an emphasis? The dead flesh is far more prominent than the contorted
actors, and in this juxtaposition lies the drama. Yet any trace of
absurdity is at once dispelled by the unity of tone and style. The
rich reds and browns deepening into intense shadows yoke the
incongruous groups together, as do the rhythmic swirls of the still
life which are repeated in the gestures of the three figures. Thus
colour and movement transform a bizarre subject into a work of
surprising and very great beauty stamped with the extremely
individual manner of Rubens.

Or we can consider *Paradise Lost*. A conspicuous example of
seventeenth-century dualism, it is a work sternly Puritan in
philosophic and theological conception but in pictorial imagination it is richly baroque. Equally characteristic is the unification
through the medium of Milton's massive and unmistakable
style of widely varied and disparate elements: classical epic, Biblical narrative, arcadian pastoral, nature description, messianic
prophecy, and so on. The similes are at once decorative and organic; though they display a baroque preference for the ornate
and magnificent over the simple and homely, they are nearly
always dramatically operative, either by intensification or anticipation.

Such extreme contrasts woven together by the style of the
artist into an organic whole are at the very heart of a great deal
of Purcell's theatre music. To look as a preliminary example at
one of his 'mad songs', *scenas* for the female voice that take the
singer through a number of different moods, is to discover

immediately this quality. These songs, very popular in Restoration drama, are an ancestor of the famous mad scenes of nineteenth-century opera, but are difficult for a modern audience attuned to *Lucia* or *Puritani* to listen to with much satisfaction. The primary reason for this is that the operatic aria of the eighteenth and nineteenth centuries has been heavily influenced by a principle, explored with particular brilliance by Handel, of devoting each aria to the elaboration of a single emotion only. Nothing could be more characteristic of the neo-classical frame of mind. In Mozart and the composers of the early nineteenth century a cabaletta might be added in a contrasting mood in which there was ample opportunity for vocal display. Schooled as we have all been in these arias, we are apt to find Purcell's baroque technique more complex in its abrupt leaps from one mood to another.

One such song, 'Bess of Bedlam', is an extreme example of the problem, for in the space of perhaps four minutes the music moves through a dozen different moods, from the quiet melancholy of the opening where Bess describes herself wandering 'from silent shades and the Elysian groves', through a number of abrupt and increasingly violent states to the ending, where she is finally freed from her sorrow. The music, broken up into twelve sections alternating between arioso, recitative, and short snatches of song, with corresponding changes of tempo, first makes an impression of passion unassimilated, as though we were looking not at a thought but at the mind thinking. Of meditation upon passion, characteristic of the Handel or Gluck aria, there is none, though Purcell's mastery of this form may be seen in Dido's great lament or in 'The Plaint' from *The Fairy Queen*. In 'Mad Bess' ideas of motion predominate over ideas of rest, and the harmonies are consequently charged with abrupt modulations and dissonances. Yet the song is made into a satisfying whole by Purcell's technical skill. The twelve sections are controlled by key—C major is firmly reiterated at crucial points, despite frequent passages in A and C minor and occasionally in G major; there is a discernible pattern in the interruptions—the relation between the tempo and content of the recitative with the bit of song which follows it, and with minor or major mode. When her emotion reaches its climax of violence in two agitated recitatives (separated by a fragment of song), Purcell builds them up in the same way,

on major triads in the manner of a trumpet call, but in different
keys. In the first she sees her lover's flaming eyes as he flees past
her; in the second,

> I hear old Charon bawl,
> His boat he will no longer stay,
> And Furies lash their whips and call,
> 'Come, come away'.

The ending is quick and gay; her madness has released her from
sorrow except for two sudden poignant bars in the minor, 'Cold
and hungry have I grown'. But no sooner has she voiced this
complaint than she forgets it, and ends the song in a joyous
outburst:

> And Bess in her straw,
> Whilst free from the law,
> In her thoughts is as great as a king!

This triumphant passage in C major brings the song to a solid,
positive close. Purcell has achieved a synthesis of moods in a
unified composition.

It is the synthesis of the elements of music, poetry, and décor
that stimulated the imagination of the audience, a synthesis that
cannot be recaptured merely by looking at the printed page. We
need the theatre in our heads, the living impression of scenery,
production, words, and melody. Once we have achieved something of this historical recreation, the impressiveness of the
Restoration semi-opera, like that of its antecedents, the Parisian
théâtre à machines, the Venetian opera, and the Stuart masque,
begins to emerge. It must be judged by its own lights. The heroic
play is not Shakespeare *manqué*, nor is a baroque theatrical form
a romantic musical one. In plays like *The Conquest of Granada*
Dryden, as he repeatedly tells us in some half-dozen essays, was
not trying to emulate Shakespeare or Corneille but was creating
something uniquely his own. And Purcell in his major theatre
scores was not writing operas in the modern sense but rather
works formulated upon a baroque ideal that is something very
different.

To measure by Elizabethan standards an age that is not Elizabethan is idle. Can there be any sense in accrediting the Elizabethans with a vast superiority of imagination simply because their

stage was barren rather than furnished? Once the picture-frame stage came in and a roof was put over the pit, the evolution from a bare stage to a full one was inevitable, and certainly not disastrous to imaginative drama. Equally natural was that the notion of a play as the collaboration between poet and actor should give way to that of theatre as a blend of many arts. The audience acquired a taste, often a very discriminating one, for the theatre as a feast of the senses, while the creator, like a general in a great campaign, leapt to the challenge of manipulating a huge panoply of forces. That the techniques gradually became stylized is neither surprising nor especially lamentable; it is the inevitable pattern as any creative endeavour moves towards stability and formalization. No one would pretend that Restoration England was the stage on which the supreme triumphs of baroque genius were played. A multitude of conflicts, political, economic, religious, and philosophical, are all indicative of a society and a civilization that has followed upon a great creative age. As an art form the musical spectacle was bound to deteriorate in any hands less than those of genius—the design became more and more intricate (and hence hollow) as a substitute for creative imagination—but a quick comparison of Shakespeare's tragedies with those of writers like Webster and Ford (to take the best) reveals exactly the same thing.

Yet these spectacular entertainments were called operas, as were vaguely similar works in France and Italy which differed not only from the English product but from each other. No wonder contemporary definition is apt to be imprecise. Opera was in its nonage, and no one could say for certain what it was. Since the definition of one day might be obsolete the next, various things went under the name from time to time. In Italy opera had already passed through several evolutions; the original conception of the Camerata, that of a highly affective musical declamation, had given way to a simpler, less strenuous Venetian form of which the basis was *secco* recitative and aria, but this form in turn was considerably altered by choral or balletic additions in Rome and Naples. In France the opera had developed from the ballet, yet while retaining its essential relationship to the dance, it had absorbed a good deal of the Italian style from Mazarin's attempts to establish the Italian opera at Paris in the 1640's, and from Lully, who was

Italian by birth and training. By the heyday of the Restoration the English had of course assimilated something of all this via the French court, but the principal formative influence upon the opera remained the Stuart masque, which was musical only in part. Accordingly, Dryden, when speaking of opera, clearly regarded it as a literary and theatrical art, not a purely musical one. In 1678 he published his rhymed version of *Paradise Lost*, *The State of Innocence and the Fall of Man*, as an opera, which meant not the music (for it was never set) but the poem. In the opening paragraph of his preface he calls it 'an opera which was never *acted*'. Though it was to be a drama with music rather than a musical drama, it was nevertheless an opera. *Albion and Albanius*, which was sung throughout, he also called an opera, and *King Arthur*, an epic drama with music, was called on the title-page 'A Dramatick Opera'. In 1706 John Dennis, as usual laying down the law, affirmed that opera was an art form which need not be sung throughout, and that the term dramatic opera was by then generally accepted for this uniquely English species. Attacking the newly-arrived Italian opera, he distinguished the two kinds of opera and fulminated only 'against those operas which are entirely musical; for those which are dramatical may be partly defended by the example of the ancients'.[5]

Ideally the dramatic opera was a work wherein the unifying power of music was the means of combining the various elements of the spectacle. In England this ideal was realized only rarely, and almost exclusively by Purcell. In France and Italy, no matter how splendid the spectacle, even a weak composer held the position of central importance, for the music was continuous throughout the opera. As works of art the weakness that they were all prone to, whether Continental opera or English semi-opera, was in the matter of a central, organic design. It is all very well to speak of the baroque ideal, the simultaneous appeal to various arts, and in a work like *King Arthur* we can see how it was attempted and even realized, but the aesthetic effect of the typical product was liable to be diffuse and messy. The modern objection to them was summed up not surprisingly by the young Wagner in a conversation he had with Rossini in March 1860. What is

[5] *An Essay on Operas after the Italian Manner . . . with some Reflections on the Damage which they may bring to the Publick.*

most curious about this statement is its revelation that Wagner's own ideal was in some ways very close to that of the great baroque masters, but so completely had deterioration advanced that he was aware of no resemblance.

> But I am against having this music condemned to playing a servile role in some piece of light entertainment, and I am opposed to its becoming the slave of routine or being used for strictly sensuous purposes without regard to the dramatic action. It is against such a role that I have revolted and wish to react. To my thinking, an opera, because of its complex nature, is a kind of organism in which is concentrated the perfect union of all the arts that form part of it—the art of poetry, the art of music, the art of decoration, and plastique. Doesn't it debase the mission of the composer to force upon him the role of mere instrumental illustrator of some libretto or other which prescribes in advance the number of arias, duets, ensembles, in a word, of *morceaux*—which literally means things cut up into little bits—that he has to translate into so many notes? Indeed, very much like a painter who adds colours to black engravings.[6]

Wagner is speaking of opera in the early nineteenth century, but the criticism can stretch back to the Venetian operas of nearly 200 years earlier. His vision of the ideal music drama (which Rossini regarded as an impossibility) makes our frustration at the way Restoration drama used music the more acute. A good example is in Charles Davenant's rhymed tragedy *Circe*, for which Purcell in 1685 provided an inspired musical episode, a sacrificial scene at the end of the first act. The music we shall examine later, but what is of special interest here is the dialogue immediately preceding it. Circe is urging her son to reject Iphigenia, whom he loves, and take instead the princess Osmida. After her speech each of the four other personages in the scene, all under great emotional stress, comments upon his own feelings. Osmida calls for death in preference to enduring the misery of unrequited love; Ithacus, trying to put Iphigenia out of his thoughts, forgets his resolve when he looks upon her beauty; Iphigenia herself wishes she had died at Aulis; and King Thoas,

---

[6] E. Michotte took notes on the conversation which he then wrote up. His brochure, not published until 1906, Ernest Newman accepts as substantially accurate. (*Life of Richard Wagner*, vol. III, p. 21: London, 1945.)

Osmida's father, utters a summary comment as Circe prepares to invoke the infernal powers:

> My soul is with some mighty fate oppressed,
> My heart does pant and struggle in my breast.

This passage provides an ideal ensemble situation for a Mozart or Verdi opera, the characters simultaneously expressing their anguish in a musical texture of dramatic articulation. But following the Restoration operatic aesthetic wherein none of the principals sings, Purcell can do nothing with it; instead he must concentrate upon the invocation scene where the singers are priests and priestesses. The result is a scene of impressive beauty which pleased an audience convinced it was getting two for the price of one—music and drama both—but it is not dramatic in the modern operatic sense. It is, however, thoroughly characteristic of the Restoration's employment of music, the turbulence of the emotional imbroglio followed abruptly by the ceremonious calm of the incantation. This is a frame of mind which permeates Restoration heroic drama, a bizarre world in which the baroque taste for bringing together violent disparates under the regulation of a grandiose decorum found its last expression in English civilization.

II. THE HEROIC DRAMA

Except for the two Shakespearean adaptations, *The Fairy Queen* and *The Tempest*, all Purcell's operas are at their core plays built around the heroic ideal. Two are heroic romances by Fletcher (or in large part by him), *Dioclesian* and *Bonduca*, and two are Restoration heroic plays by Dryden, *The Indian Queen* (in collaboration with Sir Robert Howard) and *King Arthur*. In *Dido and Aeneas*, a very different work as it is an opera in the modern sense, the heroic figure is the heroine, yet the theme like that of all the others is the conflict between love and honour. Thus an appreciation of Purcell's achievement in his operatic scores will begin with some knowledge of that important segment of Restoration drama from which they arise, the heroic play. The Fletcherian pseudo-historical romance, with which it shares many common traits, is but an anticipation of the heroic play proper. As a type the heroic play was short-lived, except when Purcell's music gave some plays a longer life-span, and on a casual view it appears to be without complexity and not a little ridiculous. Professor Harbage has given a full and useful description which hardly mitigates such a view: 'What we have . . . in the heroic play is a story of vexed love affairs against a background of war, international and civil. The forces separating the lovers are, in the first place, physical, created by the hazards of war and the plots of the lustful, and overcome at last by the valiant prowess of the hero and the constancy of the heroine; and, in the second place, emotional, created by jealousy, the claims of honour, rivalry between friends, etc., and overcome at last by compromise, fortuitousness, and simple evaporation.'[7] One might go further and declare that it involves unreal actions in an unreal world, and is expressed in a style solemnly and consciously artificial. For most people these things form an insuperable barrier; such works they are content to leave alone. Their sole interest in these plays indeed is in asking how on earth such curiosities ever attained popularity. In short, it is easy to dismiss them.

When we turn to the criticism of Dryden, who is not only the principal creator of the heroic play but its chief explicator, we soon become uneasily aware that a cheerful dismissal of these works is frivolous. It is in similar case to throwing over Poussin or Racine, at whom some of the same criticisms can be levelled, as too cold and artificial, a judgment that no reasonably thoughtful person can make without misgivings, whatever his failure to respond to their art. Dryden is of course a master defender; no one would maintain that the plays ever quite live up to the ideals he says they embody, nor could one seriously compare their workmanship, rough and exuberant as it is, with the subtle refinements and still intensity of Racine. What one can do, however, with the help of Dryden the critic, is to begin to understand the taste for a vivid type of baroque drama from which not only our literary experience but more especially our experience in the theatre is apt to bar us.

The crux of the matter appears at once when Dryden says, 'I never heard of any other foundation of dramatic poesy than the imitation of nature.'[8] It is the oldest claim of the arts, stretching in

[7] Alfred Harbage: *Cavalier Drama*, p. 52: New York, 1936.
[8] *A Defense of an Essay of Dramatic Poesy.* This and all subsequent quotations from Dryden's critical writings are taken from the edition of W. P. Ker (Oxford, 1900).

Dryden's memory from Hamlet's advice to the players at least as far back as the Greeks. The problem is to decide just what nature and imitation meant to him, and to the contemporaries including Purcell for whom he was spokesman. Though he was notoriously inconsistent in some of his pronouncements, and also did not demur at cynically turning out occasional pieces which he 'knew . . . were bad enough to please', Dryden did not ever fluctuate in his fidelity to an idealist theory of art and nature. In the *Essay of Dramatic Poesy* (1668), in a discussion of verse drama, he maintained that the selected medium should be that which 'is nearest the nature of a *serious play*: this last is indeed the representation of nature, but 'tis nature wrought up to a higher pitch. The plot, the characters, the wit, the passions, the descriptions, are all exalted above the level of common converse, as high as the imagination of the poet can carry them, with proportion to verisimility.' This he wrote at the end of the first important decade of his career. And near its close in 1695 (the year of Purcell's death), he declared that poetry and painting 'are not only true imitations of nature, but of the best nature, of that which is wrought up to a nobler pitch'.[9] Nature is an ideal, the consecration and the poet's dream, and imitation does not mean merely copying appearances. In fact the nature that is to be imitated does not actually exist except in the imagination of the artist. What, then, is the meaning of holding the mirror up to nature? What is the purpose of a work of art?

> I am satisfied if it cause delight; for delight is the chief, if not the only, end of poesy: instruction can be admitted but in the second place, for poesy only instructs as it delights. Tis true, that to imitate well is a poet's work; but to affect the soul, and excite the passions, and, above all, to move admiration (which is the delight of serious plays), a bare imitation will not serve.[10]

Since the highest aim of art is to elevate the mind and please the senses, and to do this in a work that does not imitate the appearances of ordinary nature but of nature wrought up to a higher pitch, Dryden is constantly occupied with the means by which this aim can be realized. In what he calls a 'serious play' it is through the use of rhyme. The only argument against it—that

[9] *A Parallel of Poetry and Painting.*
[10] *A Defense of an Essay of Dramatic Poesy.*

rhyme is not so natural as prose because it is farther from conversation—does not signify, because the heroic play is aiming at
something more lofty: '. . . thoughts may be exalted, images and
actions may be raised above the life.' When writing a serious play
you could not in any event reproduce ordinary conversation,
therefore without verse 'you have lost that which you call natural,
and have not acquired the last perfection of art'. Further, 'even they
who have written worst in it, would have written worse without
it'.[11]

It is here in Dryden's relation to the rhymed couplet that one
can see most clearly his baroque quality. In the prologue to his
last rhymed play, *Aurengzebe* (1676), after confessing that he 'grows
weary of his long-loved mistress, Rhyme', he adds the revealing
comment:

> Passion's too fierce to be in fetters bound,
> And nature flies him like enchanted ground.

But this confession somewhat perversely suggests the strength of
Aurengzebe and his other rhymed plays. It is precisely in the
tension between the melodramatic plots (the fierce passions) and
the fetters (the heroic couplet) that their power lies. The greatness
of these plays is in the splendour of the language, the regularity
of the verse holding in check the extravagance of its content. In
the true baroque manner the 'fetters' lend the excitement—the
sovereign control of the tumultuous. The enclosure is necessary
to the illusion of triumphant release and power. If by 1676
Dryden really thought the couplet was restricting him, he was
mistaken, the proof being the unquestionable superiority of the
poetry in *Aurengzebe* and *The Conquest of Granada* to that in his
blank-verse tragedy, *All for Love* (1678). An earlier preface in
defence of rhyming plays, the Epistle Dedicatory to *The Rival
Ladies* (1664), gives the truer analysis of Dryden's gifts, for there he
shows his zeal for regularizing and refining poetic speech. It is
this, far beyond any question of its suitability for drama, that most
attracts Dryden to rhyme and looks forward to the poet of
Absalom and Achitophel. Besides aiding the memory and giving
pointedness to repartee, rhyme, he says, 'bounds and circum-
scribes the fancy'. When so confirmed a classicist as Dryden
speaks of binding and circumscribing the fancy he means the

[11] *Of Heroic Plays.*

kind of discipline that stimulates the imagination, that, instead of extinguishing, kindles. 'Nuns fret not at their convent's narrow room. . . .'

This kind of art confronts the modern spectator or reader with a difficult problem of dramatic illusion. The heroic ideal imposes upon the poet, as the painter, a language artificial in the extreme degree, a language never used by ordinary men. We are led into a world of deliberate contrivance in which everything is consistent, where near-hyperbole is the norm, a world which appeals not so much to the intellect as to the senses. 'The florid, elevated, and figurative way is for the passions', said Dryden;[12] hence, in a realm patently fabricated, the love of decoration, of elaborate simile and metaphor, especially in the midst of tense dramatic situations. Today we find it difficult even in ballet and opera to submit ourselves to a world completely stylized; in drama it is nearly impossible. The heroic play was admired not for realism but for colour and beauty. An audience addicted to ornamental rhetoric, which may be compared with musical coloratura, an audience whose sense of dramatic illusion was so different from our own, would see nothing incongruous in the addition of music to the play. Instead music actually extended the boundaries of illusion. In the genuine heroic play comedy is rigorously excluded, since anything jarringly out of key might send the whole façade toppling. But with music, which is dramatic in itself, much more is allowable. The introduction of a musical episode so raises the emotional temperature that a pastoral scene, say, in which there may be 'low' or even grotesque rustics, is as permissible in an heroic opera like *King Arthur* as a sacrificial scene.

In the Restoration theatre, comedy always excepted, dramatic illusion is quite different from realistic deception. The audience are spectators, never participants. Even the physical aspects of the new theatre assured this separation. The proscenium arch and a stage which retreated farther and farther behind the arch and eventually came to be separated from the spectators by an orchestra pit framed a picture remote from everyday life. When Dryden defends trumpets, drums, and other noises off stage as devices 'to raise the imagination of the audience, and to persuade them, for the time, that what they behold in the theatre is really

[12] Preface to *Religio Laici*.

performed',[13] he means not so much imitating appearances as inflaming the imagination. He is in complete accord with an earlier critic in the century who said, 'For . . . which they do, is not done to circumvent, but to represent; not to deceive others, but to make others conceive.'[14] Representation is not deception.

The passion for ancient subjects is a part of the same picture. Baroque art usually presents things not as they are but as they might ideally be—raised to a nobler pitch—and the remoteness of the past is a great aid in achieving this elevation. The stories of the classical age, apparelled in celestial light, were what appealed most strongly to the spiritual and imaginative powers. Dryden's masters were Homer and Virgil, the ultimate inspiring force of the heroic play the epic poem. The genesis of these dramas is difficult to trace because by Dryden's time the heroic ideal, a Renaissance invention inspired by the epic, had been watered by French and Italian chivalric romances as well as by Spenser and the Elizabethan drama, by Corneille, and by French critical theory.[15] Whatever view we take of their origin it is clear that they are literary in inspiration, an attempt to realize in the theatre that superhuman magnificence which was the heart of epic poetry.

Dryden himself links the heroic play to opera by tracing its origin to Davenant's *Siege of Rhodes* (1656), adding that 'the original of the music' Davenant had from the Italian opera, the heightened characters from the example of Corneille and other French poets. He goes on to say that his own heroes derive from three models, Achilles, Rinaldo, and Calpranede's Artabon, an ancestry sufficiently composite to suggest the curious progeny. And when he tells us that 'an heroic play ought to be an imitation, in little, of an heroic poem; and, consequently, that love and valour ought to be the subject of it',[16] we must feel surprised at the word 'consequently'. Chivalrous sentiment is hardly classical. Yet these statements of Dryden's do enable us to understand his own dramaturgy, as well as that of most baroque opera. Conceived less in terms of drama than of epic, the technique is in large part

[13] *Of Heroic Plays.*
[14] Sir Richard Baker: *Theatrum Triumphans*, or *A Discourse of Plays*: published in 1662 but written a generation earlier, for Baker died in 1645.
[15] See Harbage: *op. cit.*, pp. 55 ff.
[16] *Of Heroic Plays.*

narrative, and the hero takes the place of the action. The tragic passion is admiration. The conflicts, the complications, the climaxes are all designed to display the hero in different situations. This accounts for the irrationality of much of the action, the lack of cogent development, the surprising jerks between scene and scene. Like the epic it is episodic in interest and particularly inclined to the striking tableau. As in Corneille, the episodes illustrate a conflict between the forces of destiny and the unflagging endurance of the individual who is a law unto himself. This helps to explain not only the occasional unscrupulousness of the heroes and the large group of villains, all characters of indomitable will, but also the style, those cataracts of haughty invective which Dryden's splendour of diction could nearly always invigorate. Of course, even in Dryden it occasionally becomes 'abominable fustian', his own phrase for 'the practice of those writers, who, not being able to infuse a natural passion into the mind, have made it their business to ply the ears, and to stun their judges by the noise'.[17] But usually in Dryden, though one often feels a declamatory insincerity in the emotions expressed, the poetic level is high.

Against a background of such ruthless individualism the all-conquering force of love is easy to understand. Love is the elevating power, the ennobling ideal before which all else must eventually bow—valour, ambition, friendship, and sometimes even reason. Queen Isabel in *The Conquest of Granada* (Part II, 1. i) sums up the position with that succinct clarity characteristic of Dryden:

> Love's an heroic passion, which can find
> No room in any base degenerate mind:
> It kindles all the soul with honour's fire,
> To make the lover worthy his desire.

Although love is often an unreasoning and unreasonable force, the view taken of it by contemporary educated society (the audience of the heroic play in both France and England) is dictated by the reason. Nowhere can the Cartesian dualism of mind and matter be more plainly visible. In the words of one critic, 'True love between individuals is the mutual love of the good qualities of those persons; it is no unreasonable elusive emotion but

---

[17] Preface to *Troilus and Cressida*.

conscious and voluntary; a moral debt which one pays to virtue.'[18]
Hence the stress on the power of the will to achieve noble actions,
hence the imperturbable endurance of the individual.

Dryden's last rhymed play, *Aurengzebe*, is an admirable example
of the heroic drama and the baroque ideal. Although it contains
no music beyond an interpolated song, it belongs to a world
peculiarly suited to operatic treatment. Battle is always in the
background; martial music and the lofty instruments of war are
ready to be sounded. Its world is that of the ceremonial and the
sacrificial scene accompanied by ritual dances. The royal personages in their exotic setting call for excessive splendour in costume
and décor. In fact the whole experience of the play is that of a
remote world, sensuous and highly coloured, whose vividness
and reality would be enhanced by music. The action is extravagant
and of a piece with the heightened setting. It centres on the
attempts of the emperor to wrest from his son Aurengzebe the
captive queen Indamora, to whom he is betrothed. In the ensuing
action the emperor's step-son Morat is also enflamed by Indamora
and, casting his own wife aside, becomes an implacable rival of
both father and brother. A further set of complications revolves
around the frustrated lust of the empress Nourmahal for her step-
son Aurengzebe. All this produces internecine strife and much
changing of sides. One immediately recognizes here elements of
several Verdi operas, in particular *Nabucco*, *Aida*, and *Don Carlos*.
Everything is in extremity, whether heroic or villainous, yet it is
always magnificent extremity, for the imagery in which the heroic
finds expression is lofty.

> Methinks all pleasure is in greatness found.
> Kings, like heaven's eye, should spread their beams around,
> Pleased to be seen, while glory's race they run:
> Rest is not for the chariot of the sun.
>
> (III. i)

In the very limitations of these characters lies their grandeur.

> I know my fortune in extremes does lie;
> The sons of Indostan must reign, or die.
>
> (II. i)

---

[18] C. V. Deane: *Dramatic Theory and the Rhymed Heroic Play*, p. 31: London,
1931.

The contrast between hero and villain, each extreme in himself, is violent. When his father offers him conditions upon which he must renounce Indamora, Aurengzebe replies:

> To after-ages let me stand a shame,
> When I exchange for crowns my love or fame!
> (II. i)

Morat is his exact opposite.

> 'Tis not with me as with a private man.
> Such may be swayed by honour or by love;
> But monarchs only by their interest move.
> (III. i)

Aurengzebe is more consistently admirable, less murky, less volcanic than his more famous predecessor, Almanzor in *The Conquest of Granada*, and is consequently more typical of the underlying gravity of Dryden's genius.[19]

The verse too is somewhat more restrained than in the earlier plays, but the typical baroque tension between opposites, set forth in grandiloquent imagery, is here in abundance, as well as violent wrenches and juxtapositions in plot and sentiment. The evil queen Nourmahal speaks of her love for Aurengzebe in a characteristic baroque figure appropriate to a larger-than-lifesize personage.

> As love the noblest passion we account,
> So to the highest object it should mount.
> It shows you brave when mean desires you shun;
> An eagle only can behold the sun.
> (IV. i)

In an unexpected turn that would be absurd in any context other than the higher pitch of the heroic play, Morat asks his rejected wife to act as his go-between in another amour. But the wife, Melesinda, outdoes him in extravagance of gesture when, though

---

[19] The operatic solitude of Almanzor—

> Disgraced, distressed, in exile and alone,
> He's greater than a monarch on his throne:
> Without a realm, a royalty he gains;
> Kings are the subjects over whom he reigns—

makes him a prototype of the Byronic hero, different from the Dryden mould. Compare Conrad in *The Corsair*:

> Lone, wild, and strange, he stood alike exempt
> From all affection and from all contempt.

rejected to the end, she mounts her husband's funeral pyre with
these words:

> Had he been kind, I could no love have shown:
> Each vulgar virtue would as much have done.
> My love was such, it needed no return;
> But could, though he supplied no fuel, burn.
> Rich in itself, like elemental fire,
> Whose pureness does no aliment require.
>
> (v. i)

As the reader will have gathered, it is impossible to detach brief
passages from any heroic play and make them seem anything but
far-fetched (at the least), so essential is the context of heightened
rhetoric and conscious unreality. What enables Dryden to sail
imperturbably through all this extravagance is that power of
technical control so characteristic of the best baroque. Not only
do the fetters of the couplet temper the tumultuous passions, and
by the very confines make them the more credibly tumultuous,
but at the base of the fabric is a moral order which inevitably
triumphs and which at some point in the play brings awareness,
even tragic detachment, to every character, good and evil alike.

> Beauty, like ice, our footing does betray;
> Who can tread sure on the smooth slippery way?
> Pleased with the passage, we slide swiftly on,
> And see the dangers which we cannot shun.
>
> (ii. i)

Dryden is full of such generalizations and explicit statements
about the conduct of life. On every page the heroic plays prophesy
the poet of *The Hind and the Panther* and *Absalom and Achitophel*.
Despite the grand protagonists, the ultimate ideal in these plays
is a tempered solemnity. If the characters give each other a great
deal of advice, causing exasperated critics to say Dryden leaves
too little unsaid, they also speak irrefutable truth. Indamora's
speech to the dying Morat is not calculated to send him to the
grave with much comfort, but it is a clear revelation of Dryden's
own point of view, and shows why the author of such extravagant
dramas was the revered master of the eighteenth century.

> How you confound desires of good and ill!
> For true reknown is still with virtue joined;
> But lust of power lets loose the unbridled mind.

Yours is a soul irregularly great,
Which, wanting temper, yet abounds with heat,
So strong, yet so unequal pulses beat;
A sun, which does, through vapours, dimly shine;
What pity 'tis you are not all divine!

(v. i)

In spite of the flamboyance of expression and the unruliness of detail, the ultimate appeal is to the mind. The still centre of gravity, or rest, holding in order the sweeping extravagance of the façade, the whirling motion of sound and actions—these are what make *Aurengzebe* baroque.

III. THE MASQUE

When masque-like episodes of music and dance are combined with the heroic play, or variations of it like the Fletcherian romance, we have the Restoration dramatic opera. The masque is without any doubt the strongest formative influence on Restoration opera, and reveals in full clarity the English reluctance to go all the way in uniting words and music—in other words, their reluctance to create genuine opera. The origins and numerous elaborate developments of this entertainment are far too complex to rehearse here, but the nature of its connexion with Purcell can be shown. A passion for ceremonial behaviour is at the base of many of the masterworks of the seventeenth century. The importance King James I attached to the 'triumph' and its public spectacle, epitomized in the construction of the Whitehall Banqueting House, was not so much in mere love of extravagance as in an almost sacred symbolism centring around the divine presence of the monarch. James himself spoke of the 'sweet persuasion' of public spectacles with the King 'as one set on a stage, whose smallest actions and gestures all the people gazingly do behold'. 'These outward and indifferent things will serve greatly for allurements to the people to embrace and follow virtue.'[20] In the ceremonial of the triumph, rich in scriptural and Roman prototypes, an ecclesiastical tradition of processional liturgy is merged with a secular tradition of martial display.[21] The masque, in particular

[20] 'Basilikon Doron' from *The Political Works of James I*, ed. C. H. McIlwain, pp. 43, 51: Cambridge, 1918.
[21] Here I draw in part upon Per Palme: *The Triumph of Peace, A Study of the Whitehall Banqueting House*, pp. 120ff: Stockholm, 1956.

the masque of Ben Jonson and Inigo Jones, is the form of entertainment in which this ceremonial found its perfect expression.
A texture of songs, dances, and dialogues organized into a frail
allegorical drama, it appealed to the court taste because it not only
gave almost limitless scope to the designer of scenery, machines,
and costumes, but also allowed the courtiers themselves to enter
towards the end of the spectacle as dancers.

The masque ideally is a gigantic allegory celebrating the
triumph of the goddess Peace or Concord, symbolized by the
Royal Presence at whose very feet the masquers ended their dance
and ritual ceremony. The grotesquerie of the antimasque, full of
witches, monsters, and satyrs representing a world of darkness
and evil—the wickedness of the opposition both at home and
abroad—was acted usually by a professional troupe employing
the technique of satire and comedy. They served principally to set
off the triumph of Beauty and Peace, brought about by some form
of *deus ex machina* and expressed in the grand manner of heroic
poetry. This stately simplicity permitted the nobles themselves to
enter into the closing ritual before the royal dais. The aim was
exalted: the figures passing before our eyes in majestic procession
are Wisdom, Virtue, Truth, or Eternity, who soar above their
shadowy opposites; thus a microcosm of the universe, the great
globe itself and all which it inherit, takes visible form as we are
elevated and instructed by the noble verse of Ben Jonson. In this
rapt frame of mind we finally lift our gaze to the King himself, the
god upon earth. 'Through these entertainments,' says Professor
Nicoll, 'lavishly ornate in their embellishments, a monarch
displayed to an admiring world his mighty magnanimity. Meanness
and avarice by this action he thrust aside, and demonstrated to all
the liberality which was a sign of his princely nature.'[22]

> . . . His state
> Is kingly: thousands at his bidding speed,
> And post o'er land and ocean without rest.

This of course was the court masque. The professional theatre
could indulge in no such splendour, yet every student of Jacobean
drama will recognize this taste for a spectacle of exalted sentiments
permeating the very dramatic fabric of the period. The 'nobler
pitch' does not have to wait for Dryden to proclaim it. Despite

[22] *Stuart Masques and the Renaissance Stage*, p. 28: London, 1937.

the undoubted appeal of mere bedazzlement, always as much as could possibly be afforded, to call this simply vaudeville would show a gross insensitivity to its tone. One need look no further than the hymeneal masque in *The Tempest* which, however superior the quality of the poetry, is in spirit typical of them all. Prospero's famous valediction to the revels has been likened to a roll-call of the scenic beauties of the masque—Shakespeare seeing, as it were, through the eyes of Inigo Jones—the solemn temples and gorgeous palaces, the cloud-capped towers, the moving globe, the turnings and vanishings. If it is a world of dreams, the dreams are still those that animate a part of our very real existence. The masque vision becomes a part of the poet's vision. We find Milton in the early Nativity Hymn writing that 'Peace came softly sliding down through the turning sphere', a picture straight from the masque, where the allegorical figure of Peace, 'crowned with olive green', would descend in her machine from the clouds.

Since it is not wholly dramatic in principle but is rather decorative and ceremonial, the masque is much closer to the French ballet-opera than to anything Italian. The aim of the Florentine composers was to intensify the expression of drama, to make it more dramatic, hence more realistic, by declaiming it to music. Though, as I have said, the austerity of the monodic recitative eventually gave way to arias, duets, and choruses, the Italian conception was never towards the simple lyrical songs and pretty individual movements of the English and the French.[23] Despite differences of musical style and theatrical convention, however, their common and simultaneous intent is the important thing: Italians, French, and English were writing theatre music frank and unashamed, music inspired by drama and linked with dramatic action, music which weaned the composer from his hitherto almost exclusive attachment to the church.

The decorative function of music in the masque and the clear separation of music and dialogue carry over to the Restoration opera. A particularly revealing example of the kind of link that joins masque and opera is afforded in the Restoration *Macbeth*,

[23] For a treatment of the musical side of the masque, with examples from what little music has survived, see E. J. Dent: *Foundations of English Opera*: Cambridge, 1928; Sir Hubert Parry: *Oxford History of Music*, vol. III: Oxford, 1903; and Manfred E. Bukofzer: *Music in the Baroque Era*: New York, 1947.

revived by Davenant in the sixties with considerable music and dancing for the witches—it was one of Pepys' favourite plays 'for variety'—and turned into an opera in 1672 for the new Dorset Garden theatre, with scenes and machines, and with a new score in part by Matthew Locke. The long musical tradition of the play had begun with the grotesque antimasque of witches in Ben Jonson's *Masque of Queens* (1609), which not only suggested the Hecate scenes in Middleton's play *The Witch* (1610), but also supplied the dances and even the costumes which were in turn transferred bodily into a court performance of *Macbeth* later that same year.[24] To make room for Hecate and the music, Shakespeare's original text had to undergo cuts which have never been restored, since it is the musical version which got printed in the 1623 Folio. (There are no *Macbeth* quartos.) It is almost certain that this music was written by Robert Johnson, a leading composer of court masques who set Ben Jonson's *Gipsies Metamorphosed* and was the original composer of Ariel's songs in *The Tempest* and probably of the music to the wedding masque in Act IV.[25] Johnson's old score was no doubt the basis of Davenant's witch scenes, which in time acquired more and more music.[26] Here the line from masque to opera is direct.

Sir William Davenant is, of course, the most important link between the Caroline and Restoration theatrical worlds. His position is a peculiar one, for though his gifts were no more than second-rate, his contributions to the theatre are incalculable. As the last important playwright and producer before the closing of the theatres and the first and most influential after they re-opened nearly twenty years later, he was essential to the continuity of English drama. Charles I had granted him a licence in 1639 to build a theatre of his own in which, besides plays, he could 'exercise music, musical presentments, scenes, dancing, or any other the like'. By this time he had already written three masques,

[24] W. J. Lawrence: 'The Mystery of Macbeth': *Shakespeare's Workshop*, pp. 24 ff: 1928.

[25] See J. P. Cutts: 'The Original Music to Middleton's Witch': *Shakespeare Quarterly*, vol. VII (Spring, 1956), pp. 203–9.

[26] The complex history of this music and the more famous eighteenth century score long known as Locke's but probably by Leveridge is treated in my article, 'The Music to Macbeth', *Musical Quarterly*, vol. XLVII (January, 1961), pp. 22–40.

The Temple of Love (1635), *The Triumphs of the Prince d'Amour* (1636), and *Britannia Triumphans* (1638), and perhaps had already begun work with Inigo Jones upon the last masque to be presented before the Civil War, the sumptuous *Salmacida Spolia*. The rapidly deteriorating political situation frustrated the building of the new theatre, but Mr Dennis Arundell has argued most persuasively that Davenant was planning to give public performances ('a possible gold-mine') of dramatic masques, or at least of something nearly related to them, tricked out with every available splendour to attract the vast theatre audience who had never seen a court masque. If his scheme had been realized, England would have been the first country outside Italy to see public opera.[27] In May of 1656 he presented an 'Entertainment at Rutland House by Declamations and Music: after the manner of the Ancients', little more than a costumed debate on the merits of 'public entertainment by Moral Representations' interspersed with choral and instrumental music. Its importance is as a feeler towards the more ambitious undertaking of the autumn, the first English opera, *The Siege of Rhodes*. Dryden claimed that this famous work, of which all the music is lost, is really the first heroic play; though it is carried out in its entirety by means of songs, recitatives, and dances, this was only Davenant's subterfuge to get round the banning of spoken plays. But, as Mr Arundell has observed, such an idea does not fit either the implications of his early patent or of his writings, especially the preface to *Gondibert* and the prologue to *The First Day's Entertainment*, which show that this is exactly the kind of thing Davenant had been eager to try for at least seventeen years. *The Siege of Rhodes* may indeed have been redone as a play after the Restoration, but it was conceived as an opera, and Evelyn states that the new enlarged version, which he saw in 1662, was in recitative music.[28] The décor of the original production, as elaborate as the long narrow room at Rutland House would permit, had to rely upon costumes and John Webb's painted scenery, for there was no possibility of machines.

During the years of the war Davenant had lived mainly in Paris, where he was in contact with Henrietta Maria and her son, the future Charles II. He shared their enthusiasm for the Italian

[27] *The Critic at the Opera*, p. 42: London, 1957.
[28] *Ibid.*, pp. 51, 75.

opera, which enjoyed a brief existence under the support of
Cardinal Mazarin, and the more widely popular *tragédies à machines*
at the Théâtre du Marais. These were heroic plays interspersed
with much music and ballet and leaning heavily upon elaborate
machinery employed in such a manner as to form a huge crescendo
at the finale. The best known of them is Corneille's *Andromède*,
produced in 1650, commissioned by Mazarin in order that the
splendid scenery designed by Torelli for the now defunct Italian
opera might be used over again. *Andromède* is an attempt at combining the features of the *ballet de cour* with the turbulence of
melodrama, the alliance facilitated by machines even more
extravagant than those used in England by Inigo Jones. To an
impressionable man of the theatre like Davenant this kind of
extravaganza was very exciting, and influenced his introduction
of machines upon the commercial stage after the Restoration.
Andromède could be considered a model for the most ambitious
and successful of all Davenant's subsequent productions, *The
Tempest*, and for nearly all the later dramatic operas in England.

One other work from France is connected even more closely
with the Restoration opera, for it was adapted outright for the
English stage. The original is *Psyche*, a collaboration of Molière
and Lully called a *comédie-ballet* (a genre most widely known
through *Le Bourgeois Gentilhomme*), but in form not very different
from *Andromède*. In 1671 Charles II had sent the actor Betterton to
Paris to study French operatic production. So impressed had
Betterton been with the production of *Psyche* that upon his return
to England he persuaded Shadwell to make an English adaptation
for the new theatre at Dorset Garden. With vocal music by
Matthew Locke (printed in 1675) and the dances and instrumental
music by Draghi (which have not survived), this semi-opera
appeared probably in 1674.[29] A comparison of the French original
with Shadwell's version reveals how dependent the English are
upon the traditions of the masque even when they are supposedly
following other models.[30] The plot consists of the intrigues

[29] There is still confusion over the date. Everyone agrees that the prompter
Downes' date of February 1673 is wrong, but so, it would seem, is Nicoll's
of 1675, since Duffet's parody *Psyche Debauch'd* appeared at the rival Theatre
Royal in 1674.

[30] Both Dent (*op. cit.*, ch. 6) and Arundell (*op. cit.*, ch. 10) give detailed
accounts of *Psyche*, but not from this point of view.

against Psyche which are instigated by her sisters and by Venus, estranging her from Cupid until Act V when Jupiter himself descends from the clouds to unite the lovers. In the French work each act ends with a musical intermezzo, dances and songs by various deities and their followers, which is separate from the act though of course connected with it. The words Lully set in these intermezzi are not by Molière at all but by Quinault. The full panoply of music and machines is reserved for a massive finale.

In Shadwell the music is brought in at any point during the act where it might be effectively employed, the result being a work in which music seems pervasive, at once more unified and far less stylized than the French. The musical episodes are of many kinds, most of them akin to some variety of masque. The very first musical scene, for example, is pure pastoral masque, a type that goes back at least as far as Ben Jonson's *Masque of Oberon* in 1611. After Pan has sung Psyche's praises, the stage directions call for a 'short symphony of rustic music, representing the cries and notes of birds. Then an entry danced by four sylvans and four dryads.' After an echo chorus the singers mingle with the dancers and Psyche exclaims, 'Oh happy solitude! Oh sweet retreat!' The opening of the third act (as well as that of the fifth) is beholden to the antimasque with Vulcan and the Cyclops singing at their forge in Cupid's golden palace, following up with a Bacchanalian dance. Before the most genuinely operatic movement of the work, where Psyche preparing to throw herself in the river is dissuaded by the river god and his nymphs, occurs an elaborate episode in which Cupid commands a song in praise of love, ten statues leap from their pedestals and dance, cupids rise, strew the stage with flowers, and fly away. Shadwell's finale, as grandiose as Moliere's, employs a divided stage with Jupiter's palace resting on the clouds above, and most of the other principals, including Apollo and the musicians, on the stage below. After Jupiter descends in a machine with Cupid on one side and Psyche on the other, massed choruses sing in his praise and the grand concluding dance ends, in proper masque form, at the feet of the monarch of the gods.

Locke, nothing if not self-assured, published his score under the title 'The English Opera' and prefaces it with a bellicose but extremely interesting discourse on the term opera as it was

understood in England in 1675. It is a word borrowed from the
Italians and to be distinguished from comedy, which is extempore.
Operas, 'after much consideration, industry and pains for splendid
scenes and machines to illustrate the grand design, with art are
composed in such kinds of music as the subject requires: and
accordingly performed.' After boasting of the various kinds of
music he has supplied, he goes on: 'And therefore it may justly
wear the title, though all the tragedy be not in music: for the
author prudently considered, that though Italy was, and is, the
great Academy of the world for that science and way of entertainment, England is not, and therefore mixed it with interlocutions,
as more proper to our genius.' Shadwell also supplied a preface of
his own when he printed the text of the play, and makes it quite
as clear as Locke does that the most important aspect of *Psyche*
is not the drama, as literary historians would have it, but 'variety
of music, curious dancing, splendid scenes and machines'. Later
we shall see how much Purcell and his collaborating playwrights
must have been influenced by *Psyche*, especially in *King Arthur* and
The Fairy Queen.

Not many new court masques were written during the Restoration. By all odds the most lavish and well-documented of them is
Crowne's *Calisto*, performed at Whitehall during the winter of
1674-5.[31] This does not mean that the taste for masque-like
entertainments was waning but that King Charles, very prudently
for his purse, usually went to the public theatres for his spectacle.
Their content changes to some extent, as they answer to new needs,
for now that the actual courtiers themselves no longer took part,
the whole thing could be strictly professional with more emphasis
upon mood and dramatic cogency, less upon tribute to royal personages. Miniature masques continued to appear in plays. The most
famous before Purcell are probably Locke's 'Masque of Orpheus' in
Elkanah Settle's *Empress of Morocco* (1674) and a masque by Grabu
in Shadwell's adaptation of *Timon of Athens* (1678), later to be set
by Purcell. The Orpheus masque, no mere incidental diversion, is
an essential part of the drama, precipitating the catastrophe at the
moment of greatest tension. John Banister wrote music for
Stapylton's *Slighted Maid* (1663) containing no less than three

[31] For a detailed account of *Calisto* see Eleanore Boswell: *The Restoration
Court Masque*: Cambridge, 1932.

masques dovetailed into the action of the play, and for *Circe* (1677), which, as we have seen, was to have a new score by Purcell eight years later. The taste persisted into the next century. The masque 'Peleus and Thetis' accompanied Lansdowne's *Jew of Venice* in 1701. At least three times during the same decade *Dido and Aeneas* was broken up into a series of masque-like scenes to interlard the acts of plays, and various other works by Purcell often served the same function.[32]

The continuing taste for the masque down through the end of the century shows the extent to which the baroque spirit was ingrained. In the midst of a world which founded the Royal Society, the world where Hobbes and Bunyan were writing, there persisted another world which delighted in formal artifice and elaborately ornate though sedately controlled beauty. Its appeal lay not merely in the lavish spectacle which is popular at almost any time and place but in something more deeply felt—its total remoteness from the world of realism. This is also, of course, the world of the heroic drama.

IV. THE ENGLISH COMPROMISE

It is the deliberate artificiality, the exuberant unreality of the heroic play that make the introduction of musical scenes at the least permissible and in certain instances supremely appropriate. They help to achieve that 'absolute dominion over the minds of the spectators' not because they increase the illusion of realism, an atmosphere totally foreign to the genre, but because they inflame the imagination, or, in the words of a prominent contemporary, Lord Lansdowne, 'touch every sense and please every palate'.[33] The operas did not come into being as the result of any artistic theory, which is never the English way, but through a combination of forces part accident and part compromise. The scenes and machines of the Stuart court masque, in addition to more splendid refinements upon them imported from the Continent, were now the property of the public stage, and every effort

[32] E. W. White: 'Early Theatrical Performances of Purcell's Operas': *Theatre Notebook*, vol. XIII, no. 2 (Winter, 1958–9), pp. 43 ff.

[33] Lansdowne's Preface to *The British Enchanters* (published 1710). For similar contemporary testimonials see Ferrand Spence's critique of *Albion and Albanius* appended to his translation of St Evremond's *Miscellanea* (1686) and John Dennis's *Essay on the Operas after the Italian Manner* (1706).

was made to utilize them. Musical scenes in the masque tradition suggested the most obvious lead, but at the same time the public, pleased as they were with music, wanted to see in the same performance their favourite actors and actresses in rich, showy parts. What resulted was neither pure opera nor pure drama but something between the two, a typically English product.

The through-composed opera, opera in which everything is sung, rubbed against a deep-lying Anglo-Saxon instinct. Peter Motteux had said in the first number of *The Gentleman's Journal* (January 1692) that 'experience hath taught us that our English genius will not relish that perpetual singing' and suggested the reason by adding, 'Our English gentlemen, when their ear is satisfied, are desirous to have their minds pleased, and music and dancing industriously intermixed with comedy and tragedy.' Some voices, to be sure, were raised in dissent. Roger North, writing after the establishment of the Italian opera early in the next century, remembered the semi-opera without pleasure:

> . . . there is a fatal objection to all these ambigue entertainments: they break unity, and distract the audience. Some come for the play and hate the music, others come only for the music, and the drama is penance to them, and scarce any are well reconciled to both. Mr Betterton (whose talent was speaking and not singing) was pleased to say, that two good dishes were better than one, which is a fond mistake, for few care to see two at a time of equal choice. At last these were forced to yield and give place to their betters the complete operas.[34]

But the opinion of Betterton, whose talent was indeed speaking rather than singing but who was also a notably successful producer, was the prevailing one. The public wanted both music and drama, but separately. Dryden himself, apologizing for some of the verses in *Albion and Albanius*, explained that in those passages he was pleasing the hearing rather than gratifying the understanding. He wished to do both. In short, music, appealing to the senses rather than the sense, could not be the language of an English hero; the singers could sing, but he at least must speak. Though the national drama for Italy might be the drama of music, in England it could never be anything but the drama of poetry. Yet the judicious interpolation of music was always welcome.

[34] *Roger North on Music*, ed. John Wilson, p. 307: London, 1959.

It was certainly the great strength of English dramatic poetry that precluded a genuine operatic movement comparable to that of the Italians. Had there been an Italian Shakespeare or a group of dramatists as vigorous as even the lesser Elizabethans, the Florentine Camerata could scarcely have imagined that they were reviving ancient tragedy with their musical declamation, nor would they have felt any need to make the attempt. In England, music, though clearly loved by the audience, is to be taken in a completely different sense from speech. Hence a musical play will be a compromise, a semi-opera, which has been justly called a practical expedient peculiar to the English rather than a formally devised artistic creation.

That the English should have hit on such a compromise is not surprising, for compromise comes naturally to them. The mingling of tragedy and comedy, offensive to the French as to the ancients, is engrained in English drama. For a while Dryden, under neo-classical influence, refrained from the mixture, but by the time of the *Essay of Dramatic Poesy* (1668) he is justifying it in the Elizabethans, and with *The Spanish Friar* (1681) he himself writes a tragi-comedy. He defends this blending, not as Dr Johnson was to do because it is like life, but 'for the pleasure of variety'. 'I dare venture to prophesy, that few tragedies except those in verse shall succeed in this age, if they are not lightened with a course of mirth. For the feast is too dull and solemn without the fiddles.'[35] This is, of course, exactly the point of view that produced the semi-opera, 'for the pleasure of variety'. The inclination of the English for compromise which sets them off so distinctly from the Continent can be seen in many different kinds of work all through their history. From at least as far back as *Troilus and Criseyde* English literature, for instance, is prone to tragi-comedy. The Beaumont and Fletcher romance which actually gave us the term is a mingle of Shakespearean comedy and Jacobean thriller, and so is a play like *Cymbeline*. The Victorian novel is an enormous monument to tragi-comedy. Actually a successful compromising spirit is constantly cropping up in all the arts. Gainsborough, desiring to be a landscape painter but forced

[35] Dedication to *The Spanish Friar*. It should not be concealed that near the end of his life, in *A Parallel between Painting and Poetry*, Dryden reversed this decision, calling it an 'unnatural mingle'.

to make his living at portraiture, perfected the landscape-portrait. In Sir Joshua Reynolds' portraits appears a compromise between the Platonic ideal and the domestic 'speaking likeness'. Reynolds believed that most people have an innate nobility, but that it takes the painter to discover it, an idea frequently elaborated by Browning. The eighteenth century also produced the Handelian oratorio, a compromise between opera and church choral music, and the Methodist hymn, a unique combination of grandeur and homeliness. And ever looming in the background is that supreme example of compromise, the Church of England.

None of these achievements is conceivable in France. Mixtures the French distrust, for they are dilutions of purity. There is no mistaking the note of condescension that creeps into French critical discussions of English culture. That stern separation of tragedy and comedy in the seventeenth-century theatre appeals as strongly to the Parisian audience today as it did then. Returning recently from Paris, a critic of the present French scene observed:

> The French classical theatre, in its two leading categories of tragedy and comedy, shows two different worlds: the ante-chamber in a Greek palace (Racine) and the living-room of a prosperous bourgeois family (Molière). The Greek hero, Orestes, or Hippolytus, who speaks in the Alexandrines of Racine, is far more the national hero than any figure drawn from French history. The Greek hero, with the prestige of antiquity behind him, and the distance he represents from any French allusion, can be consumed on the stage, in full view of the spectators, and reach a point of pure intellectuality and analysis, which is for the French who attend such plays a joy in the achievement of lucidity.[36]

Each theatrical genre, whether *tragédie, comédie, spectacle, cabaret à chanson,* or musical comedy, has its particular style and tradition which the French public is concerned to see upheld and perpetuated. In contrast even the best English drama has always been careless of constructive principles. It is richer and fuller than the French. Not being segmented into comedy, tragedy, or *comédie-ballet,* it could easily absorb disparates; the amalgam comes naturally. A nation that produced *Phèdre* and *Bérénice* would never tolerate a work like *King Arthur,* which in England was received

[36] Wallace Fowlie: 'Return to Paris': *Yale Review,* vol. xliv (June 1957), p. 590.

joyously at its first appearance and was periodically revived for nearly two hundred years.

In opera Lully never strayed from the highly stylized genre of *opéra-ballet* or from a musical technique made up of arioso interspersed with very short airs for singer or dancer. The formula of the Italian baroque opera, first the Florentine monodic declamation, later *secco* recitative and aria, was equally rigid. On the other hand the English composers throughout the century, and especially at the time of Purcell, partook almost as a matter of course of both French and Italian styles. Motteux, describing *The Fairy Queen*, spoke of Purcell as joining 'to the delicacy and beauty of the Italian way, the graces and gaiety of the French', a distinction Purcell himself drew attention to in his preface to *Dioclesian* where he says he has studied the Italian style, music's 'best master', as well as the French air 'to give it somewhat more of gaiety and fashion'. As always, the English show an affinity for absorbing Continental influences while producing something peculiarly their own.

We are faced, then, in the dramatic opera with a type of work inevitably untidy and episodic. Moving on a dual level of speech and song, it will lack the unity of both drama and genuine opera. But it is a form that, bursting conventional boundaries, was capable of drawing in many varieties of experience, and was consequently close to the heart of the baroque notion of entertainment. Mr Kerman, a critic whose standard for opera is both very high and very restricted, has remarked that skilful contrivance, showy exits and entrances, striking tableaux, and *coups de théâtre* are not the soul of drama and not the basis of any opera worthy of the name.[37] They *are*, however, the soul of the Restoration heroic play, and of Beaumont and Fletcher (who were then revived almost as often as Shakespeare), and they are certainly the heart and soul of nearly all opera. Meyerbeer has been described as a master of effects without cause, but Handel, ploughing through the fiendish contrivances of his incredible Italian operatic librettos, could from the dramatic point of view be similarly described, as could the composers of most baroque opera. They write stop-and-go opera, an elaborate series of tableaux or dramatic moments revealing a wide palette of emotions but, like

[37] Joseph Kerman: *Opera as Drama*, p. 7: Alfred A. Knopf, New York, 1956.

the heroic play, lacking cogent dramatic continuum. More often than not the recitatives, not raised to the level of arioso, are mere patchwork to hold together the arias. The reforms of Gluck, further developed by Mozart, were directed towards giving musical coherence and continuity to opera. The lack of this kind of coherence, essentially a lack of dramatic articulation, is what the modern student finds most disappointing in both the drama and the opera of the seventeenth and early eighteenth centuries. (The plays of Racine are notable exceptions, and of course I am nowhere speaking of comedy.) We have been led on to demand more than merely 'the pleasure of variety'.

Purcell is a particularly complex figure in that he achieved the modern or Gluckian ideals of opera in *Dido and Aeneas*, as we shall now see, and this singular accomplishment causes us to think, quite mistakenly, that he could not possibly have been satisfied with all his other theatre scores where he follows the contemporary pattern, even though they were written subsequently to *Dido*. If he could write one opera which wholly satisfies our own aesthetic, is it not obvious that he must have felt frustrated at the rest of his output which satisfies an older type, based on the masque, which is not ours? Stated thus it is easy to detect our intransigence and provincialism; it is like assuming that of course God speaks English. This is not to say that *Dido and Aeneas* is not a more satisfying work of art than, say, *Dioclesian*, but once we understand the principles involved we may discover a wealth of unsuspected pleasure in the outmoded dramatic operas. In every case Purcell's music endows the work with a sense of style and order so that it achieves a certain level of art. But to generalize is a difficult matter, for each work is different and must accordingly be studied in its turn.

CHAPTER II

Dido and Aeneas

I

IT IS IRONIC that the dramatic masterpiece of England's supreme dramatic composer should have been written not for the professional theatre but for a young ladies' school. Yet the circumstance was a fortunate one, for Purcell, in being able to disregard some of the crippling conventions of the commercial stage where music was used mainly as a decorative accessory, was inspired to compose a genuine opera in which there is no spoken dialogue, an intense and autonomous work of art upon which time has made no inroads whatsoever. Although *Dido and Aeneas* (1689), like many another work of English genius, reveals its composer as highly susceptible to various influences both native and foreign, it is a creation unlike any before it, and it maintains a sovereign superiority over any English opera to appear since.

The nearest thing to a predecessor is Dr John Blow's *Venus and Adonis* (about 1682), which is described as a 'masque for the entertainment of the King' but in essentials is a miniature opera. In several individual numbers we shall see that Purcell was plainly influenced by Blow, but the conception of *Dido* as a whole moves far beyond the earlier work, charming as it is. After a pastoral prologue in which Cupid, shepherds, and shepherdesses sing to one another, Blow provides three episodes: a scene between the lovers ending with Adonis' departure for the hunt, an interlude for Venus, Cupid, and little cupids, and finally a very moving close in which the wounded Adonis dies and is mourned by Venus and the deities. Dramatically the chief weakness of the work is its lack of real conflict (Adonis does not want to go to the hunt, Venus thinks he ought to go, they argue), and musically, its indefiniteness of melody and tonality. Except for the short dance movements, French in inspiration, the whole of the little work proceeds in arioso. Blow wrote it for one of Charles II's more versatile mistresses, Mary Davies, who sang Venus, and their daughter, Lady Mary Tudor, who was the very young Cupid. It would have had only a private performance—the utter vagueness as to its date is one indication—but Purcell, Dr Blow's pupil and his successor as organist at Westminster Abbey, would certainly have known the music well.

Apart from *Venus and Adonis*, the only English operas had been *The Siege of Rhodes* (1656), which so far as we can tell in the absence of any surviving music was an heroic play faintly disguised by chanted dialogue and musical numbers, and the expensive failure *Albion and Albanius* (1685), in which Dryden had foolishly (and uncharacteristically) chosen as his collaborator a pallid French-man named Louis Grabu, whose talent for setting English verse to music left almost everything to be desired. The obvious choice, as Dryden was later to recognize, was Purcell, then twenty-six and the composer of some excellent theatre music, though none of it on a large scale. What Purcell thought of the slight by Dryden is not recorded (we require no record of what he thought of Monsieur Grabu); since he seems from the little evidence we have of his personal character to have been the most modest of men, he probably did not at that time envisage himself as colla-borator with the great poet. In any event, when Josias Priest, the head of the girls' school in Chelsea, approached him about a chamber opera he must have welcomed the opportunity to try something more ambitious than the incidental songs and dances of his earlier theatre work, and perhaps welcomed too the chance of showing Dryden how much higher he could soar than Grabu. Priest was a dancing master who had done work in the theatre with Betterton and would presumably expect the new work to allow his young ladies plenty of opportunities for dancing. Seventeen dances are called for in the libretto.

The limitations imposed upon Purcell by so modest an occasion were actually a form of emancipation. One trouble with the Restoration theatre was the weight of too much liberty, but here Purcell's narrow room dictated a work in miniature. It could not accommodate much spectacle, nor could the orchestra or chorus be large. Except for what voices they could afford to hire—Aeneas for one, and possibly Dido and Belinda and several men for the chorus—the singers would all be schoolgirls. And the endurance of the girls, to say nothing of the parents who came to watch, could not run much over an hour. Out of these restrictions came a chamber opera which displayed great freedom of form both in conception and execution, which showed Purcell the full possibilities of dramatic music, and which obviously had a marked influence upon everything he composed for the professional theatre thereafter. Furthermore, it is the one opera before Gluck which succeeds triumphantly by the very standards of that master, the pioneer of modern opera, who was not born until twenty years after Purcell died. Gluck could hardly have known *Dido and Aeneas*, for apart from its insertion as a masque in Gildon's arrangement of *Measure for Measure* in 1700 (a dubious relief to Isabella in the midst of her strenuous activities), and as an afterpiece for two other performances in 1704,[1] the opera was not performed publicly during the eighteenth century, nor was it available in printed form. The first (incomplete) edition of the score, published by the Musical Antiquarian Society, did not appear until 1841.[2] The oblivion into which it sank and the consequent fact that it was unknown to later composers constitute one of the great tragedies in the history of music.

The libretto was written by the then laureate, Nahum Tate, whose genius for the theatre may be surmised by his adaptation of *King Lear* with a happy ending, a love affair between Cordelia and Edgar (who at one point refers to her, not without reason, as 'the dear wreck'), and without the Fool. This version did hold the stage well into the nineteenth century, if that is any credit to Tate. The idea for *Dido* he took from his own tragedy *Brutus of Alba* (1678), where we discover not only the principal characters under

---

[1] On 29 January and 8 April. See Eric W. White: 'New Light on *Dido and Aeneas*': *Henry Purcell, 1659–1695: Essays on his Music*, ed. Imogen Holst, pp. 14–34: Oxford, 1959.

[2] The two authoritative manuscripts, now at Tenbury and Tokyo respectively, seem to have been copied at different times and in different hands from the same earlier manuscript (late seventeenth or early eighteenth century) of which no traces have been discovered. For details consult Mr White's article, *op. cit.*, and Imogen Holst's appendix, 'A note on the Nanki Collection of Purcell's Works', in the same volume.

other names but the witches as well. This play has been thought to be the forerunner of *Albion and Albanius* also, since Brutus deserts the Queen in order to found a kingdom in England; but *Dido* is not a mere adaptation or a condensation of the earlier play, and there are almost no verbal connexions. Despite the quality of his other works, Tate turned out a serviceable libretto; the story is simple, the action swift and sufficiently intense. Pedestrian verse, a speciality of Tate's, is not a serious limitation in a libretto, as we shall see later on.

Tate's book begins with a short pastoral prologue, perhaps suggested by Blow—Venus, Phoebus, nereids, and shepherds appear—in which Purcell apparently took little interest and never set. After that the story stays close to Virgil. Aeneas, fleeing from Troy, has been driven by a storm to Carthage where he has fallen in love with the widowed queen Dido. As the opera begins, the love-sick Dido is perplexed and anguished, but is gradually persuaded by her sister Belinda (Virgil's Anna), by a chorus of companions, and finally by Aeneas himself to yield to love. In the second act they celebrate with a hunting party but are interrupted by a storm which sends them hastening back to town. It is curious that Tate, perhaps in deference to the young ladies of the school, does not allow the lovers the solace of Virgil's cave, but hurries Dido out with Belinda. Aeneas, left alone, is confronted by a malignant spirit disguised as Mercury who commands him to desert Dido and seek the Latian shore. The spirit comes from the witches, who are merely the Restoration's peculiar equivalent of the gods or destiny. The denouement is rapid. Though Aeneas wavers when he sees Dido frantic, she scornfully sends him away and prepares to die. Her farewell to earth she takes in a glorious lament, and she is mourned in a gentle ethereal chorus as the curtains close.[3]

The stark simplification of the story is highly significant. Purcell and Tate evidently believed that the plot should be cut down to its barest bones, a decision very uncharacteristic of the seventeenth century. The modest conditions of the performance

---

[3] The libretto does not make clear the exact manner of death, whether of a broken heart or by suicide. There is no mention of Virgil's funeral pyre. In the memorable Mermaid Theatre production of 1951–53, Mme Flagstad as Dido stabbed herself and died on her throne.

obviously influenced this plan, but more important is something Purcell came to realize which exhibits his genius in the most revealing light, and which had vast implications for his subsequent work. This is simply that the intensity of tragic art is attained through spartan concentration, through the stripping away of all flamboyant and episodic intrigue, in fact, through bald austerity. The recognition of what may seem a self-evident truth has always been enormously difficult to the composer of serious opera, and of course even more difficult has been the practical fulfilment of the ideal.

Purcell may possibly have come upon it by accident, nor is *Dido* by any means a flawless work, but the fact remains that he has created the first modern tragic opera. To enjoy it fully demands no acquaintance with an older style, as do the operas of Monteverdi. Seventy-five years later Gluck, working in close collaboration with his librettist Calzabigi, quite deliberately endeavoured to free his work of all episode, to concentrate on the kind of simple yet highly-charged emotional situation that we find in *Dido*. To this kind of simplicity the greatest tragic operas, like *Norma* or *Otello* or *Tristan*, always cling unshakeably. It is the interminable and elaborately stylized Italian operas of the seventeenth and eighteenth centuries, seen at their least tedious in Handel and Alessandro Scarlatti, and the blood and thunder school of the nineteenth, epitomized by Meyerbeer, which felt the need of incessant thrills to keep up the pitch. An opera like *Dido* exposes their meretricious effects; if the intensity of feeling, and of course the composer's technical proficiency, be great enough, the music itself will take complete charge. Almost nothing in the way of stage action happens in *Dido* or in *Orfeo* or in *Tristan*. Handel one would not wish to exclude from this first rank, but the melting beauty of many of the arias does not save his operas from stupefying monotony, the inevitable result of librettos that must somehow provide thirty or forty large-scale solo numbers; his masterpieces are the starker oratorios built around the chorus. Mozart, whose finest operatic works are transcendent refinements upon the *opera buffa* tradition, is in different case altogether. *La Clemenza di Tito* and to some extent *Idomeneo*, tragedies in the old *opera seria* tradition, are as total entities static and moribund.

Having decided upon a severely reduced scale of action, and

one not without its perils, for Aeneas becomes all but a blank, Purcell then had to meet the task of organizing his opera. Dido begins anguished and ends dead, yet some way must be found of attuning all of the work to tragedy and at the same time avoiding three acts of inspissated gloom. Purcell had both the French and Italian model to draw upon, and in the usual English manner effected a happy compromise between the two. *Dido* is built around the choral and ballet plan of Lullian opera where the dance serves as a link between the narrative portions and the scenes of spectacle, but to this he adds arias which are clearly differentiated from the recitative after the manner of Venetian and Neapolitan opera where dance and chorus were negligible. Both models, however, proceed on two levels which are never very well amalgamated: Lully unfolds his plot in ambling, slightly melodious, and more than slightly monotonous declamation occasionally interspersed with very short airs, but this level is periodically interrupted for irrelevant scenes of dance and scenic splendour (*le merveilleux*) which make great use of machines and transformation effects; the Italians split their drama into rapid *secco* recitative for all the business of the intrigue, reserving the aria for the elaboration of the emotions and for providing opportunities for bravura display from the singer, who always swept off the stage at the end of the aria, which also ended the scene. Drama is quite inconceivable in such a predictable pattern, and it was against this bifurcation that Gluck aimed his reform. He orchestrated his recitatives, giving the impression of a musical continuum, and welded whole scenes together by recurring stanzas for chorus and principals.[4] But although he rejected the gratuitous spectacle of 'scenes and machines', anyone familiar with the Paris version of *Orfeo* will recall the inspired use of ballet and chorus. The important thing is not that he eschewed many of the materials of the older opera but that he transcended the double standard, weaving all the strands into a coherent and intense unit, thereby establishing the model of the modern opera.

Dido, as I hope presently to show, is an uncanny anticipation of the Gluck ideal three-quarters of a century before *Orfeo* (1762). Probably working from no theory but guided by a remarkable

---

[4] I draw here and elsewhere in this chapter from Tovey's essay on Gluck in *The Main Stream of Music*: New York, 1949.

dramatic taste and instinct, Purcell solved most of the difficulties of the two levels. It is to the chorus that he turns for his strongest unifying factor, and here we detect at once the strong influence of the English masque of which the chorus had been the musical centre. It has been noted that they perform a role in *Dido* analagous to that of the chorus of Greek tragedy, entering into the action as participants and commenting upon it as observers. They end each scene[5] and make possible the sublime apotheosis of the opera. Even stronger links with the masque are the dances which weave in and out of the work. Though they often reflect the piquant rhythms of Lully, unlike the French model they are always dramatically relevant and significant. In the midst of these ensembles and intimately connected with them Dido herself is firmly planted as the centre of the first and last acts, while the middle portion of the opera emphasizes Aeneas and the witches. The chorus is integrated even more strongly by having as its leader the other principal character, Belinda, who is the traditional confidante of neo-classical tragedy, and the heroine's sister as well.

From an exclusively musical point of view Purcell strengthens the formal unity of the work by constructing as a kind of polar centre to each act an imposing aria on a ground bass. Furthermore, he maintains throughout the opera a carefully considered plan of key relationships which give significance to a succession of short separate movements and heighten the impression of the musical whole.

The foregoing remarks will suggest, even before we look at the music, a certain stately simplicity in Purcell's dramaturgy which is indeed characteristic of most baroque opera. A recent critic has summarized the position by saying, 'The baroque musical continuity was formed by a process of unfolding rather than by dramatic development, but it was possible to arrange a grand and particularly intense sort of drama by the placing of such musical blocks.'[6] This is not to say that their plots, like *Dido*'s, were simple, for they were fairly bursting with inane complications; rather he is speaking of the musical conception of each scene. These devices are very important to Purcell, for since the time of

---

[5] What looks like an exception, the end of Act II, is only partially so, for the libretto contains a closing chorus which Purcell either did not set or for which the music has been lost.

[6] Joseph Kerman: *Opera as Drama*, p. 77.

Mozart operatic composers have depended heavily upon two resources that were unavailable to him, the vocal ensemble and the enormous resources of the modern orchestra. The ensemble, in which a number of characters express their varying emotions simultaneously, is an outgrowth of the sonata form developed by Haydn and Mozart, the form upon which our modern symphonic style is based. In nearly all Mozart operas the emotional climaxes are concentrated not upon a solo aria or duet (except for the chorus the limit of Purcell's artillery), but upon the mingled voices, *molto agitato*, of all the principals. A striking example of how different is the effect of the two methods can be seen by comparing with Purcell the episode in Berlioz's *Trojans* where Dido and Aeneas reach the point of declaring their love. Purcell is confined to a number of very short movements of increasing intensity: Belinda urges, then the chorus, then Aeneas, then Belinda and chorus again, and so on. At the climax Dido herself says nothing—'Fate forbids what you pursue', well before the end of the scene, is her last line—and we are left to gather that she yields only from the words of the final chorus, and in performance of course from her own miming. But Berlioz, after a series of lesser episodes, moves into a massive quintet in which each character most dramatically expresses what is at stake for himself as well as for the others. The concerns of Dido, Aeneas, and Anna (Purcell's Belinda) may be imagined, but those of Dido's minister of state for the future of Carthage reveal something of the scale of Berlioz's subject in comparison with Purcell's. Not he nor even Gluck could possibly have written an opera called *The Trojans*, but their resources were admirably suited to a work on Dido and Aeneas. The quintet and the following septet are the climax of the act; after the choice has there been faced and the decision reached, the other principals fade from the scene, leaving the lovers to an ecstatic duet whose mood is not torrid passion but rather serene lyricism. The vocal ensemble is the supreme instrument of dramatic development in opera before the *Ring*, and the reader will at once recall outstanding examples in *Fidelio*, *Rigoletto*, *Lohengrin*, *Aida*, and so on, as well as in Mozart. It is ironic that the beginnings of Italian opera with the experiments of the Camerata in Florence around 1600 came about largely through their dissatisfaction with polyphonic vocal music which hopelessly obscured the singers' words. Two centuries later Mozart perfected the operatic ensemble and the wheel had come full circle.

The other limitation in Purcell's dramaturgy Gluck was able to overcome by the developments of the intervening three-quarters of a century. In the dedicatory letter to *Alceste* he remarks that the combinations of instruments should be controlled by the passion of the situation. When one notes that Purcell's orchestration is merely for two violins, viola, bass, and continuo, the tale is told. The libretto twice mentions 'gitters' for dance movements, but the score does not provide for them. In his later operas his palette is larger—trumpets, oboes, an occasional bassoon—and his range of orchestral colour within these instruments is amazing. But it is not until the abolition of the continuo, the system by which the filling out of the harmonic background was given over to the harpsichordist, that the dramatic employment of the orchestra could really begin. One need only think of the short-cuts and compressions that Wagner or Strauss can effect by a mere phrase or theme in the orchestra, the functions of reminiscence or foreboding that are performed, effects that the poetical dramatist cannot convey by words, to see how the modern orchestra functions as a character in the drama in a manner undreamed of even by Gluck or Mozart, let alone Purcell.

Yet with all these limitations imposed by his time and place, it must be repeated that Purcell has composed the first modern opera, a music drama completely coherent and self-sufficient, which means that the dramatic articulation is provided entirely by the music. Unlike its greatest operatic predecessor, Monteverdi's *Orfeo*, *Dido and Aeneas* is written in an idiom entirely familiar to everyone. With the possible exception of the part played by the witches, there is not the slightest need for apologies or for any explanations of an extra-musical nature.

2

When we turn to the music itself it soon becomes evident that Purcell has triumphantly surmounted the scourge of the later seventeenth-century opera, the rigid division of the work into a speech level for narration and dialogue (the Italian *secco* recitative, the French musical declamation) and a more imaginative musical level for the development of emotion or for the Lullian spectacle. This does not mean of course that it in any way approaches the continuous opera of the post-Wagnerian period, where we have the illusion of a symphonic continuum, but that it is continuous in the sense that all the parts are bound closely together, one flowing almost imperceptibly into another because of certain preparations and other technical devices. Purcell's method of welding the recitative into the musical whole we see the minute Belinda starts to sing. After the overture in the familiar French manner, a grave introduction of thick chordal texture and frequent chromaticism, followed by a semi-fugal quick movement, Belinda begins a spritely little air that can hardly be called a song (it lasts about thirty seconds) urging Dido to 'shake the cloud from off your brow'. She repeats this line twice at the end, but in the middle, to the lines

> Empire growing, pleasures flowing,
> Fortune smiles and so should you,

she announces the rhythm that the chorus takes up in their brief exhortation,

> Banish sorrow, banish care,
> Grief should n'er approach the fair.

If the rhythmic scheme of Belinda's song be designated (somewhat freely) as 'abaa', then the chorus begins on 'b' after she has finished. Though they do not repeat any of her melody, the tune is similar, the harmonies and key identical, so that the little movement is as compact as can be even though Belinda does not sing after the chorus has entered. This is typical of the way in which Purcell handles the chorus throughout the opera; they nearly always function as an extension of something expressed by one of the principals, or occasionally as a marked contrast to it.

This latter role they play here at the outset, for their cheery advice shows them to be completely out of touch with the deep anguish of Dido whose opening lament is, apart from the great ending, the most thrilling music in the score. Out of five lines of unremarkable verse Purcell creates a simple but complete characterization.

> Ah! Belinda, I am pressed
> With torment not to be confessed;
> Peace and I are strangers grown;
> I languish till my grief is known,
> Yet would not have it guessed.

His task was to develop from these words a solid musical block that not only would fix Dido vividly in the imagination with a purity and intensity undiluted by any other consideration, but which also would serve as the musical and dramatic focus of the whole scene, a centre of gravity from which all else should take its bearings. In a work of such small dimensions, the opening impression is crucial.

His way of meeting the problem is characteristic: to lay a solid formal foundation to the movement he resorts to one of the favourite weapons of his technical armoury, a striking ostinato bass figure, a complete four-bar phrase with strong tonic cadence. Not only does it hold the composition together and allow the melodic line a freedom which mere chordal accompaniment would never permit, but the relentless unchanging phrase is of vital dramatic significance in that the queen's eloquent grief seems trapped by an unyielding jailer. Towards the middle of the aria the motive is transferred to the dominant key, and for a moment some escape seems possible, but after appearing twice it returns to the inevitable tonic. Two other strokes of Purcell's technical brilliance are illustrated in this ground bass. First, the division between the recitative (the libretto's first two lines) and the aria ('Peace and I') is almost indistinguishable—indeed the aria begins as a quotation from the ground—so that the achievement is a sense of unity quite beyond the passionate affective and unrhythmical recitatives of the early Florentines, and equally beyond the florid recitative-aria school of the Venetians; yet at the same time Purcell's recitative captures the passion of the first, while his melodiousness equals that of the arias of the second. Next, the melodic line is made independent of the bass in that the cadences of the two lines almost never occur in the same place. This means that the melodic line is continually surprising us: the first statement of 'Peace and I are strangers grown' covers four bars, though not coinciding with the four-bar ground, but its second statement is stretched over five bars, and so on. The

Dido: Ah, ah,____ ah, Be - lin - da,

I am __ pressed with __ tor - ment...

The large notes correspond to the original text; the small notes are from Dent's vocal score.

(Oxford University Press)

Peace __ and I ⟩ are stran - gers grown, Peace __ and

I are stran - gers, stran - gers grown

same is true of the recitative: the first statement takes seven bars, the second nine. Purcell's harmonic skill is directed towards several effective evasions of cadence so that there is not an instant of monotony anywhere.

All these things would of course signify little were the melody not a memorable one, or were it not suitable to Dido, but it is both. From the first phrase, soft sighs with appoggiatura on 'Ah', it eloquently conveys languishment, yet to call it sad and sweet (which it is) would be misleading, for the frequent dissonances which alter the expected diatonic progressions suggest an underlying vein of iron, particularly in conjunction with the relentless ground, and with the rhythmic delays and irregularities which in turn are made possible by the stability of the ground. The baroque technique could not be more clearly displayed. Dido is always a great queen, never a Lydia Languish. When towards the end of the opera the chorus comments, 'Great minds against themselves conspire', we feel that it is exactly appropriate, and that not Tate but Purcell has made it so. In spite of the baroque dissonance treatment, particularly in the combined use of major and minor thirds, the C minor tonality is strong, and Dido begins without pause on the same note the chorus had ended on. Not only is a continuum achieved, but the greatest possible contrast as well. All this is clearly the creation of a master at dramatic characterization, the entire episode a fine example of the application of technical virtuosity to dramatic ends. The aria instead of holding up the action is a dramatic climax. The queen stands for all time hewn from an imperishable musical block.

The rest of the act proceeds through further discussion between Belinda and the hesitant Dido, frequent commentary by the chorus, the added persuasions of Aeneas, and finally a 'Triumphing Dance'. Belinda's darting mind sets a variety of musical moods, usually taken up and expanded by the chorus, while Dido remains the ardent but apprehensive figure of her great song. The most interesting passage is that beginning with Dido's question, 'Whence could so much virtue spring?' It shows more clearly than any other place in the opera the influence of the Italian chamber cantata, which had been brought to a high peak of expressiveness by Carissimi, a favourite composer of Charles II.

These very ornamental works are given to florid elaboration on especially affective words, what often is criticized in Purcell as his over-illustrative or pictorial style. For example, on the word 'storm' Dido rapidly climbs the C major scale and leaps up to a high dominant cadence, and as rapidly descends, though with dotted rhythms, on the word 'valour'. In the next line, 'How soft in peace, and yet how fierce in arms', she twice falls upon 'soft' in languishing appoggiatura, having shifted to the minor, and then bursts into a coloratura roulade in the major upon 'fierce'. After a gentler passage from Belinda, Dido returns to her own hesitancy and to the original C minor tonality with a drawn-out ascending scale in broken rhythm which brings the movement to a tremulous and expectant close. Immediately it is answered in the bright C major duet and chorus, 'Fear no danger to ensue'.

The passage admittedly is in a highly rhapsodic style that in a lesser composer would teeter into absurdity, but Purcell gets away with it by his customary care with formal design. The accompaniment, though starting on a long tonic pedal, soon becomes more definite rhythmically, and is always in strictly measured time, arioso rather than free declamation. In addition, carefully articulated harmonic and melodic design allow him a maximum of freedom on the 'pictorial' words without any loss of flowing continuity of line. The baroque tension between extreme expressiveness and massive formal control is here beautifully illustrated. Dido's tender concern for the dangers Aeneas has passed adds another hue to her character, a concern expressed (as usual) not so much by the words themselves, which appeal only to the intellect, but by their musical treatment, which appeals to the emotions. The tenderness, a mood less austere than her opening, is dramatic in yet another way: it is prophetic of her eventual yielding and is therefore a not unfitting preparation for the happy 'Fear no danger' chorus. Further variety he creates in setting the straightforward 'Fear no danger' in the note-against-note style very common in Lully, and the next chorus, 'Cupid only throws the dart', in a contrapuntal style of airy delicacy appropriate to our notions of that miniature deity. Belinda's brisk little aria, 'Pursue thy conquest, love', heralds the climax in its accompaniment by full orchestra, all the other arias save the great finale being accompanied by continuo alone. With the hunting chorus and triumphing dance, a chaconne on a freely treated ground, the scene closes in a solid, confident C major.

Every stage work to be genuinely dramatic requires a strong element of conflict. The lack of it, as I have said, prevents Blow's *Venus and Adonis* from achieving significant stature. The conflict in *Dido* becomes evident in the next scene,[7] the witches' cave, where from out of the murky gloom suggested by the solemn instrumental prelude the Sorceress slowly emerges and begins her spectral invocation. In her very different way she is almost as impressive a figure as Dido herself, standing out lone and formidable against the cackling 'ho, ho, ho's' of her sisters. Her recitative is of a different quality from any in the opening scene, being in Purcell's rare 'horror key' of F minor, and in free declamatory style above an unchanging rhythmical figure in the accompaniment which is quite independent of the voice. The seventeenth century was not used to the kind of atmospheric effect that we have come to expect in supernatural episodes since *Der Freischütz*, yet something of it is suggested in this eerie opening. The instant the chorus of witches sings, however, it is dispelled, for they sound like jovial merrymakers returning from a harvest home. Their opening sally, 'Harm's our delight', followed by 'Ho, ho, ho' moves through three major keys (B-flat, C, and F) and are conspicuously unmysterious. They are the sole example in the opera of a Restoration cliché from which we have become alienated, but they were brought on to sing and dance in many operas, most prominently in *Macbeth*, and were adored by Pepys and everyone else. Our objection to them is, of course, mainly on the grounds of realism, and I suppose it will not avail to point out that it is doing evil which makes them gay and merry. A more serious objection is musical; before the end of the opera their choruses have become slightly monotonous, which proves that they did not kindle Purcell's imagination to the extent of handling them with any variety. These strictures do not apply to the splendid Sorceress for whom the composer can ornament even such unmitigated Tate as:

> The Trojan Prince, you know, is bound
> By Fate to seek Italian ground.

The trick is in minimizing the disastrous 'you know' by charging straight through on the same note to 'bound', after which there is

[7] In the score I. ii, in the libretto II. i.

a pause, followed by a more interesting melodic and rhythmical line.

The other aspect of the witches disturbing to a modern audience, who demand at least some approximation to psychological realism, is the utter lack of motivation of their hatred for Dido. Tate's explanation, if it can be so called, is worse than none:

> The Queen of Carthage, whom we hate,
> As we do all in prosperous state.

If we can but remember that they are the Restoration substitute for the ubiquitous classical deities of seventeenth-century Italian and French opera, to go no further back, their role should not trouble us. No one dreams of asking Gluck why Alcestis must lose Admetus. We accept 'fate' or 'destiny'. And in an opera motivation is nowhere if the music is dramatically compelling. Moreover the theme of the opera, that of love versus duty, is the cornerstone of the heroic play, and it is obvious that Purcell's audience accepted the witches as a convenient means of announcing to Aeneas the claims of duty.

After the witches have resolved upon destruction, Purcell gives us a fine moment of scene-painting as the Sorceress in imagination sees Aeneas and the Queen on their hunting expedition. Having no horns at his disposal, he writes a figure of repeated triplets for strings up and down the D major triad. The scene is ended in perfect symmetry with the first by a chorus and a dance, the difference being that here they both make use of echo effects, frequent in Lully's supernatural episodes. With a small group of musicians, both vocal and instrumental, behind the scenes, the effect is striking. The chorus 'In our deep vaulted cell' had been anticipated by Locke in *Psyche* as well as in several French operas. Apart from its haunting beauty—the sudden shift to minor with the E-flat on 'dreadful' is ravishing[8]—it is of dramatic importance, since the witches for the first time attain dignity and breadth. After a rollicking contrapuntal duet for two witches, 'But ere we this perform', the pure homophonic style of this chorus is like a draught of the clearest water. The libretto inappropriately calls for a dance of drunken sailors before this chorus, but Purcell has

---

[8] Compare the analagous shift to a minor third on 'cool' in 'To the hills and the vales' from the first scene.

ignored it altogether, waiting until the end of the act for a dance. This, the 'Echo Dance of Furies', is in Lully's style, though more contrapuntally treated. Dent comments: 'The amusing thing about the echoes is that they never reproduce the exact harmony of the original phrases; this ingenious device gives them a delightfully fantastic character, as if the human witches on the stage were answered by spirit dancers who strangely distort their movements.'[9] The tonality of the scene has been wider than that of the first, which was all in C minor and major, but it too begins in the minor (this time F) and ends in the corresponding major, firmly stabilizing its musical coherence and unity.

The first act has established the predominating positive forces of the opera, the passion of the lovers and the evil that will separate them. The second act begins, most appropriately in the light of structural balance, with a period of serenity, almost diversion, before the evil strikes. This short interlude of the hunting party is a charming reminder of the continuing English taste for the masque, because until just before the end it is really little more than that. We are taken to a grove which Belinda and then the chorus greet in 'Thanks to these lonesome vales', a movement suggested by the prologue of Blow's *Venus and Adonis*, where Cupid and the shepherds sing 'In these sweet groves'. The musical centre of the act is an attendant's wistful air on a freely moving ground, 'Oft she visits this loved mountain', describing the fate of Actaeon. Purcell's advance over Blow and his sensitivity to a unifying mood come out strongly here, for even in the midst of a joyous occasion he subtly suggests the sense of sadness which is the prevailing mood of the opera. Unlike Blow, he has the power of incorporating any kind of material into a coherent whole. The welding of this scene into the rest of the opera had already been implied by the sound of the chase in the witches' scene, and that fanfare in turn is echoed now by Aeneas' call, 'Behold upon my bended spear a monster's head stands bleeding', running up and down triads of D major. Still another unifying device is in Dido's single utterance,

> The skies are clouded. Hark! how thunder
> Rends the mountain oaks asunder!

[9] *Foundations of English Opera*, p. 193.

which is evidently symbolic of the fate that lies before her, especially as her roulade upon the word 'thunder' is in exactly the manner of her last impassioned line to Aeneas in Act III before she sends him away for ever. This kind of seaming is in principle Wagnerian, rarely found in opera before Purcell and until the *Ring* very rarely after him.

There is now a great hustle to get out of the storm. Belinda's little fanfare song, 'Haste, haste to town', can only be called quaint, and is one of the few instances where Purcell is unaccommodating to the singer; one simply cannot articulate 'haste haste' with the lightning rapidity he calls for. I prefer to lay the blame on Tate—surely his shoulders have borne enough to bear yet more—since no composer, however original, could provide anything for 'haste haste' but haste. Purcell apparently thought it a good idea, for he has added several repetitions of the word. As usual the chorus soon relieves Belinda, and the quasi-contrapuntal treatment lends a most effective compulsive drive.

Thus Aeneas is left alone to receive the bitter decree of the gods and, in an emotional recitative, to accept his burden. We note again the lack of motivation—it is merely 'great Jove's command'—and what seems to me considerable awkwardness in having the witches, whom we accept as the substitute for the gods, resort to a false Mercury to deliver Jove's command. No rationalization can really make the two very unlike instruments simultaneously acceptable. Aeneas' anguished recitative over a chordal bass is the counterpart of Dido's arioso at the beginning of the opera—its dissonances are even more emphatic—but it is far less interesting, partly because it lacks the compelling integration of the ground bass, and partly because it is not filled out with an aria in which the emotion can be contemplated and elaborated. One regrets the miniature scale of the opera here as perhaps at no other point. Aeneas actually begins his recitative in the same bar with the spirit's last word, yet we are to believe that he has passed through a lifetime of anguish between the beats of three and four! Either at this point (before 'Jove's command shall be obeyed') or two lines farther on (before 'But ah, what language can I try, My injured Queen to pacify') we should like an orchestral meditation to envelop and project the hero's torment, some Purcellian equivalent of the great pillar of Wagnerian dramaturgy. As it stands, this is certainly the weakest moment in the opera. The impossible swiftness of the action makes Aeneas little more than a nonentity. Opera often is as needful of space as of concentration. Professor Dent expresses the dismay natural to a student of Mozart's operas that the recitative (in A minor) does not end in the same key with which the act began. Purcell's intention may not have been realized, for the one copy of the libretto known to survive (now in the Library of the Royal College of Music) ends with a witches' chorus, 'Then since our charms have sped', which he might have intended to set in D minor. But no arrangement of key relationships can ever supply the need here, which is one of time and space, not of internal detail.[10]

The last act begins with a dramatic surprise, the rollicking song and dances of drunken sailors on the wharf, understrappers of the Trojan contingent. The drama is that of ironic juxtaposition and shows the contrasts which static musical forms can produce when they are thus aligned. The exhilarating swing of Purcell's setting for

> Take a boozy short leave of your nymphs on the shore,
> And silence their mourning with vows of returning,
> Though never intending to visit them more,

with a jaunty Scotch snap for the repetitions of 'No, never' requires no comment.[11] The conception as a whole beautifully balances the opening of the previous act where the tender melancholy of the attendant's song sobered the joyousness of the hunt. Here the callous revels sharpen the pathos of the rapidly approaching denouement. It is interesting to compare Berlioz's languishingly romantic treatment of the same episode. In the still moonlight

[10] It is worth noting that when Gildon arranged the opera as a masque for his 1700 *Measure for Measure*, a brief duet was added here for two friends of Aeneas who sing of the struggle between Empire and Fame, and are then joined by Aeneas himself and the chorus. The music for this episode as well as for the prologue, which in the masque is shifted to the end, has never been found. Mr White, who has discussed this masque in detail in his article 'New Light on *Dido and Aeneas*' (see note p. 40), thinks Daniel Purcell the most likely composer. Modern performances often attempt to fill the gaps in the score with other appropriate music by Purcell as a step towards the fuller realization of his plan.

[11] The libretto reads 'Take a Bouze short leave', which may indicate a variant spelling of 'boozy', or that Purcell himself changed the word when he came to write the song.

a solitary sailor sings with piercing yearning of his homeland, one of the supreme nostalgic utterances of music. Purcell's way may be better, for many listeners are more touched by Berlioz's lonely seaman than by his queen. The sailors' callousness, or at any rate their complete unawareness of the imminent tragedy, is heightened by the bright major tonality, an impression continued by the witches who now enter to speed the parting guests with a gleeful *mal voyage*. Minor tonality would take away the sharp edge of cruelty from

> Destruction's our delight,
> Delight our greatest sorrow;
> Elissa bleeds tonight,
> And Carthage flames tomorrow.

Although they may not conform with our notion of witches, there can be no doubt that they are dramatically conceived. Characteristically, Purcell blends the homophonic chorus of Lully with a contrapuntal technique reminiscent of the Renaissance madrigalists. The witches' dance is in three unequal short movements, obviously designed for specific theatrical actions—Purcell's rhythms suggest stage gesture more vividly than almost any other composer's—and manifestly influenced by Locke's experiments with the grotesque in the dances from *Cupid and Death* (1653). The sailors may have joined in the dance, for the libretto here contains the odd stage direction, 'Jack of the Lanthorn leads the Spaniards (i.e. sailors) out of their way among the Inchanteresses'.

We now approach the great catastrophe of *Dido and Aeneas*, a memorable sequence in G minor composed of dialogues first between Dido and Belinda, then Dido and Aeneas, followed by her closing lament which is flanked by two solemn choruses. The final exchange between the lovers, Dido proudly recriminative, Aeneas vacillating between two courses, has been criticized as conventional, but it is surely highly theatrical. They are the cousins of many pairs of lovers in heroic plays. The chief fault is its precipitateness: there is not quite enough time to savour any of the passions, since the duet is over almost before it has begun. It remains a superb outline. Purcell twice makes telling use of a device later to become a staple of Mozart's operatic armoury, a threefold repetition of the same words on the same notes (on 'earth and heaven' and 'by all that's good') but each time set to a different and more expressive harmony. The last angry protest she hurls at Aeneas recalls her cry in the storm in Act II. The instant he has departed she crumbles and turns towards the great shade which brings her both release and, as Purcell handles it, immortality.

Everyone who has ever written a line about Purcell has had something to say of 'When I am laid in earth'. It is perhaps the sole example of his genius to have received sufficient analysis. The technical miracle lies of course in the way that the unyielding chromatic ground, a descending tetrachord with strong tonic cadence, pursues its solemn inevitable path without hampering the lyrical freedom of an overwhelmingly expressive melody which makes use of every device—suspensions, appoggiatura, discords, climax, surprise—by which Purcell shaped powerful affective experience.[12] It is preceded by a brief recitative beginning 'Thy hand, Belinda', upon which criticism could exhaust itself, a preparation unique in its tragic glooms and in its economy and its sharpening of the listener's sense of anticipation. Together they attain a marmoreal dignity and repose—we never forget that Dido is a great queen—but more, the heroic image is spiritualized, the baroque excess purified, an achievement Dryden and his fellow playwrights could but gaze upon in vain wistfulness.

Less frequently noted have been the two choruses which protectively encircle the great solo. In the manner of the Greek chorus they supply that detachment which lends significance to tragedy. A recent critic has spoken eloquently of the first, 'Great minds against themselves conspire':

> It provides a release of tension; a sudden new vantage point, an outside point of balance from which to gauge Dido's grief; a delicate transition from the stabbing dialogue of the quarrel to the lyric pace demanded by the conclusion; a tonal preparation for the ending G minor; and a great passage of time, a lifetime of decision for Dido. The luminous B-flat chords at the start turn to G minor and to quiet repetitions of a poignant figure in the ending phrase. From the flippancy of Act I and the vaguely motivated melancholy of Act II, the chorus comes finally to gravity and awareness.[13]

[12] The ground is not original, nor is the idea of asymmetrical structure of the melody—both Bukofzer and Westrup quote a similar lament in Cavalli's *Egisto* (1642)—a fact in no way minimizing Purcell's achievement.

[13] Kerman: *op. cit.*, p. 57.

Of the close of the opera he continues:

> The lament does not end, but flows into the wonderful final
> chorus, the most elaborately extended in the opera. To a solemn
> choral dance, 'Cupids appear in the clouds o'er her tomb'; Cupids,
> though, 'with drooping wings'; Dido's agony softens and deepens
> out towards the audience through the mourning community on
> the stage. All through the opera Dido and the courtiers advance
> and converge, and at the end the courtiers, grown worthy of
> Dido's government, can take the stage after her death with full
> consciousness of the tragedy.[14]

It is tragic that such a work, an anticipation of nearly all that
Gluck was to accomplish in the reform of opera, should, because
of its diminutive scale and circumstances of production, and because of the rigidly fixed notion of English opera, remain virtually
unknown, neither rejoicing the world nor kindling inspiration in
other composers.

3

Apart from an occasional insult, I have purposely said nothing
of Tate's libretto, for it opens up the formidable problem of the
relation of music to words, a crucial consideration in all Purcell's
vocal music, and one which must be grappled with not merely
en passant in connexion with certain great passages from *Dido* but
separately and in some detail. A look at Tate's lines immediately
confronts us with the dilemma of how an operatic masterpiece
can come from a banal text, or how a libretto which poetically is
nowhere can yet serve as an excellent framework for music. Two
obvious facts need not detain us: first, that the composer must be
a genius; and secondly, that with a really brilliant libretto, like
Boito's *Otello* or Hofmannsthal's *Rosenkavalier*, the genius can
create a still more satisfying operatic experience.

One masterly achievement can be claimed positively for Tate's
libretto, the variety and the skilful grouping of its moods and
feelings. That these feelings are merely stated—'Peace and I are
strangers grown'—that there is no poetic realization or explora-
tion of them in the manner of a great dramatist or novelist is of no

---

[14] *Ibid.* In the light of these perceptive criticisms it is odd that Mr Kerman
should call the recitatives 'impersonal, courtly, and bombastic'.

importance whatsoever. This will be the composer's province; brevity and simple statement, as we shall see, are the most fertile ground for musical ideas. Even a cursory reading of the opening scene, sixty-one short lines in the libretto, reveals that Tate has at any rate suggested a dozen variations of mood, some of them slight, as between Belinda's first line, 'Shake the clouds from off your brow,' and the ensuing

> Empire growing, pleasures flowing,
> Fortune smiles and so should you,

but always arranged in natural progression. True, no one who has not heard Purcell's setting is likely to dream of how much can be made of the suggestions, as in the delicate melancholy of 'Shake the clouds' moving into the broad expansiveness of 'Empire growing'. The rhyming of 'brow' and 'allow' with 'you' will indicate that the niceties, the elegant refinements of the art, are not Tate's speciality. There are indeed a few lines memorable for one reason,

> To the musical groves
> And the cool shady fountains,

or another,

> Our plot is took,
> The Queen's forsook;

but the usual level is of pedestrian competence and no more. The maddening disparities of metre in what are designed as neat songs, as in the opening of the hunting party scene,

> Thanks to these lonesome vales,
> These desert hills and dales,
> So fair the game, so rich the sport,
> Diana's self might to these woods resort,

are a challenge to Purcell's ingenuity. He obviously enjoyed yoking such irregularity into even four-bar groups as much as he did the converse of stretching regular verses over unsymmetrical groupings. This is one of the secrets of his constantly fascinating texture and movement, which was quite innocently (one imagines) abetted by Nahum Tate. But the nostalgic note in the song about Actaeon from the hunting scene and the unthinking carelessness of the sailors later on are unusual ideas and dramatic ones. They suggest the predominant importance in a libretto of situation and character over poetry. The dramatic articulation will be provided by the music. An example, more famous than any in *Dido and Aeneas*, is at the conclusion of *The Marriage of Figaro* when the Count asks and receives pardon from his wife. Although the words could scarcely be more conventional, more trivial even, this moment to many persons is the most moving in all opera. The dramatist is not Da Ponte but Mozart.

Yet the converse is equally if not so frequently true, that is, the case where the most obvious and rhetorical musical construction, something that a composer might hesitate to resort to in an instrumental work, takes on enormous excitement in conjunction with a stage situation. In no less a work than *Don Giovanni* we find a good example in the spinning out of a chromatic tetrachord, both descending and ascending, in the Commendatore's fatal duel with the Don. Weber, on the very least estimate an uncanny theatrical genius, has repeatedly done the same kind of thing, as in Agatha's prayer from *Der Freischütz* or, better, in Rezia's great aria from *Oberon*, 'Ocean thou mighty monster'. The heroine, deserted on a barren island, hurls out her fear and defiance at the furious waves as the orchestra plays arpeggios up and down common chords. The calm which follows is conveyed by massive chords gently rising from level to level a note or two at a time. Presently, when she sees the boat that will save her, Weber expresses her excitement in rapid arpeggio passages again, which recall the beginning of the aria. The composition as a whole suggests the simplest ternary form, though by no means a strict example of it, and is musically obvious and not exactly from the top drawer. Yet as an expression of the dramatic situation, and when sung by an Amazon who can cope successfully with its towering vocal demands, its effect is overwhelming. In such a place a more sophisticated effort would not come off.

Plainly, neither the libretto nor the score can remain separate or separable. While it is true that some of the finest episodes in opera would remain great music if the situations they illustrated were totally to disappear—one thinks immediately of Gluck and Wagner—most operatic masterpieces by the interaction of music and poetry produce a new form that is unlike either and can be greater than both. Our problem is to see how this can happen.

Of first importance in studying the relation of words to music is to remember that words speak primarily to the intellect, they mean definite things and always mean them, while the medium of music is completely abstract. The chromatic ground in Dido's great lament has an abstract musical meaning—the relation of certain tones, their qualities and lengths, to each other and to the way they affect the human ear—but they have nothing to do with the death of queens, of the deep-delved earth, or remembrance, or indeed with anything except their musical relationship. The fact that this particular ground had been used by other composers before Purcell for quite different situations is one proof. Words for the most part have representational meanings, as certain failures of Gertrude Stein and Joyce testify, while music, though it can on occasion be 'descriptive', is non-representational. The difference between objective and non-objective painting is similar. Now this fact gives, or should give, the composer an enormous amount of freedom in his setting of words, because it should be clear to him that music cannot give the same effect as words but will instead bring something quite new and different to the words. The singing voice is prone to prolong vowels—what Tovey calls its natural tendency to refrain from articulation—and through most consonants, except those which hum and buzz, it cannot sing at all.[15] As a consequence the shape of a musical line is likely to be very different from that of a poetic line. Over and over again Purcell feels the need of repeating words which in the text occur but once: 'Come, come ye sons of art, come, come away', 'When I am laid, am laid in earth', and so on. And this, of course, says nothing about the note values he will assign to particular words which may have nothing at all to do with the manner in which they are spoken. Some musicians would insist, very rightly, that the majority of what we think of as vocal melodies are really instrumental melodies to which the words have somehow or other been fitted. When a composer of less than the first rank constructs a vocal line which tries to identify musical pitches with ordinary speech inflections, as in the case of Menotti, the result is often lamentable.

If anything is clear about the relationship of words to music it is simply that what is singable is not necessarily poetry, and what

[15] 'Words and Music: Some Obiter Dicta', *op. cit.*, p. 203.

is even mellifluous poetry is not necessarily singable. Most critics of *Dido* have noted the metrically lopsided character of

> When I am laid in earth, may my wrongs create
> No trouble in thy breast.
> Remember me, but ah! forget my fate.

And yet, as one of them has explained, it is excellent poetry for music because it 'suggests in simple terms the image of a woman desolated by an emotion which the words themselves cannot completely convey, an emotion so overpowering that only with the aid of music can it be given full expression. Moreover, the passage has a maximum of the appropriate dark vowel sounds and liquid consonants, with few sibilants. The important words (laid, earth, wrongs, trouble, remember, fate) are not only well adapted for singing but also are full of emotional suggestion. The very imperfections, the incompleteness, almost formlessness, of the passage considered purely as poetry are its greatest merit as a text for music, since they leave so much for the composer to add.'[16]

Unless this should suggest that the poet is nothing, the composer all, we must remember that the genesis of all songs and operas is in the words. Composers do not start with melodies and then hunt about for words to fit to them. But as a usual thing the more strongly he is inspired by the poem the stronger is the musician's imaginative invention. Schönberg once said that the first line invariably gave him the whole song, and Schubert before setting a text nearly always decided what was to be the chief feature of the song—the galloping horse in *Der Erlkönig*, the rippling water in *Auf dem Wasser zu singen*, the rattling of the coach in *Am Schwager Kronos*—and everything else had to follow from that. This complicated blend of dependence upon a text together with wide independence of it explains why Schubert, like Purcell, was as contented in setting a poem that is meretricious (or worse) as one by Goethe or Heine. His seizing upon some salient feature of the text on which to build the whole song (also characteristic of Purcell, as his love of the ground bass might imply) explains why a poem of complex density is unsuitable to Schubert's method if not to musical treatment altogether. When our intellects are

---

[16] D. Grout: *A Short History of Opera*, p. 7: New York, 1947. It has escaped notice that in the first line of the aria Purcell has added the word 'may', which is lacking in the libretto.

grappling with difficult poetry the emotional appeal of music is distracting. The greatest Shakespearean text to be set successfully to music, in Verdi's *Otello*, has been enormously simplified, not merely in the complications of the drama as a whole, which is not the point here, but in the poetic detail of individual speeches. That Othello is much the simplest of Shakespeare's tragic protagonists is certainly significant; he never thinks of more than one thing at a time. It is hard to imagine Verdi doing anything with Hamlet. In the same connexion Debussy's preference of poetic prose to poetry may be mentioned, for although a musical line must inevitably destroy subtle poetic rhythms, music not only does not destroy verbal imagery but can powerfully enhance it.[17] The prose texts are in nearly every respect simpler than the poems which Debussy set.

Although the power of a text to stimulate the composer's imagination is far more crucial than any refinements of poetic detail, it is of course not merely the germinal inspiration that makes the choice of text important. The beauties of the greatest vocal music are not in musical line alone but are owing to the sound of the words united with music. By prolonging the vowels, music can enhance the beauty and elevate the significance of a trivial text, but words thick and awkward in themselves will damage even seraphic melody, as everyone knows from hearing certain German lieder, or hearing Italian opera in English translation. In general, however, an operatic libretto is of its greatest importance in what it provides in character and situation rather than in the quality of its language. The dramatic articulation will come from the composer, who must have the freedom to follow musical ideas which a great poem is liable to stultify or at least intimidate. Purcell worked better with Tate than with Dryden or Shakespeare. And Wagner, his own librettist, could create an operatic marvel in the first act of *Die Walküre* despite such lines as,

> Friedmund darf ich nicht heissen;
> Frohwalt möcht' ich wohl sein:
> doch Wehwalt muss ich mich nennen.

It is the situation created through the words, then, and not the actual quality of the words that stirs us, and that can lend great

[17] See Kerman's discussion of *Pelléas et Mélisande*, *op. cit.*, ch. 6, 'Opera as Sung Play'.

excitement to fairly obvious and conventional music. We have noted an example from *Don Giovanni*, but it is even more apparent in the tomb scene from *Lucia*, the closing pages of *La Forza del Destino*, the finale of *Faust*, and dozens of other places from excellent theatre vehicles which no one would claim as the supreme musical masterpieces.

These observations will have suggested some of the reasons that great vocal music so often comes from mediocre verse. It remains to examine Purcell's particular gift for the setting of words. He is strongly in the English tradition, which may seem at first to be begging the question, since the earlier seventeenth-century composers in England were much influenced by the Florentine ideal of dramatic declamation from which opera evolved. The difference is in the application of the principle. In Italy, largely through the prominence of brilliant professional singers, the Camerata's ideal of 'just note and accent', pleasing to amateurs whose interest was more literary than musical, gradually gave way before an increasingly florid style in the affective intensification of the word. Its melodic lines and harmonies were wildly affective, its sense of rhythm insignificant and undeveloped. The more orderly and conservative instincts of the English, as well, one suspects, as their supremacy in the madrigal style, led the early monodists like Nicholas Lanier and Henry Lawes to adopt a more deferential treatment towards both the poetry and the time signature. The aim of the musician was to enhance the poetry, which in practice meant that he became more the servant than the partner of the poet. It is small wonder that Milton, who said he could stand and wait but who actually would not have relished taking a back seat to anyone, praised Lawes' *Comus* songs in a famous sonnet:

> Harry, whose tuneful and well measured song
> First taught our English music how to span
> Words with just note and accent. . . .

Not realizing the essential difference between the line of speech and song, Lawes painstakingly worked at giving his settings plausible speech accentuation and rhythm, but this he achieved at the expense of interesting melody and harmony. With the incisive marking of the rhyme and lingering enjoyment of the associations which each word suggests, the tension between the regularity of the poetic metre and the discontinuous cadential falls of the music makes, as Bukofzer notes,[18] a peculiar rhythmic vitality in these songs from the masques. Unhappily it also means that a sense of symmetry, of a musical whole, is virtually unattainable. Later composers like Christopher Gibbons, Banister, and especially Locke were more advanced in this respect than Lawes, but none had Purcell's awareness that the declamatory principle with its weakness for over-punctuating the words was as much in danger of strangling music as of liberating it. It is the trough into which Hugo Wolf so often drops when his unfailing sensitivity to a poetic text does not evoke an equal musical response, the result being a song that is choppy and finicky or else comatose.

Although raised in this baroque tradition of dramatic declamation, and coming especially under the influence of Locke with his fondness for cross relationships and violent pictorialism, Purcell does not often allow poetic forms to upset his sense of musical structure. His greater knowledge of French and Italian music, his greater sophistication, but principally his greater talent led him to considerable modification of the English style of recitative in the direction of musical self-sufficiency. To this nearly every recitative in *Dido* testifies. From the very nature of recitative, which Tovey defines as the art of the rise and fall of spoken language stylized in musical notes, it is clear that each language must develop its own particular type or style. In English easily the most natural is Purcell's.

In the handling of songs and arias Purcell's adjusting of words to music is perhaps even more notable than in his recitatives. By adjusting piquant and individual rhythms to a strict metrical scheme, and by a careful regard for tonality, he is able to give the voice very wide freedom in florid and affective passages. The dangers of over-illustrating pictorial effects are minimized by these technical reins, which he usually held confidently, and by his infallible sense of a musical whole. He works not in bars and phrases but in complete musical forms. Witness his delight in balancing unequal groups of bars, as in Dido's opening lament, or of dividing a rhythm of, say, eight bars into sections of five and three instead of the expected four and four, and other devices which reveal his constant concern for rhythmic, melodic, and

[18] *Op. cit.*, p. 185.

harmonic entities. His subtle variations of accent, particularly in triple metres, his beginning of phrases on the off-beat, his use of rests and so on, we shall consider as we come to particular songs. As a result of these formal and technical skills, his sensitivity to the inflections of English verse and to the emotional content of the words is not less but greater than that of Lawes.

In moving on to specific examples of his skill at word-setting one can profitably compare Purcell with other composers. The general insensitivity of all of us in these matters is proved by the unquestioning composure with which we drone out the line in 'Abide with me', 'When other hel-*pers* fail, and comforts flee', a setting which displays the sensitivity of a hippopotamus, though indeed the opening sally on '*A*-bide' is hardly more felicitous. In 'helpers' not only is the weak second syllable allotted the same note value as the strong first syllable, but it is approached by a leap from the tonic to the dominant, of all steps the most brazenly self-advertising. The important word, the verb 'fail', is given one-quarter of the time value of 'helpers'. This example I have of course chosen for its simplicity. A comparable lapse at a higher level of genius may be found in *Messiah*, where Handel, in a passage often criticized, writes, 'He shall feed his flock like a shep-*herd*'. The strong syllable of 'shepherd' falls on the harmonically weaker part of the music, while the miserable 'herd' is on the strong dominant cadence. The superiority of Purcell's treatment in the song 'Nymphs and shepherds' requires no comment to anyone who has heard the first line. Michael Tippett, a very skilful composer of vocal music, has observed that 'however much Purcell may vocalize on the strong vowel of the trochee, he never ends a weak vowel on the strong musical beat, but lets the weak vowel always fall on the other side. . . . The musical phrase ends in such a way that the word can be spoken at the very end in its natural rhythm.'[19] It is no denigration of Handel's genius to say that his oratorios contain many examples of his insensitivity to the language. Though he lived in London for fifty years, his English was not that of Addison or Dr Johnson. In this connexion it was no help that he adapted many of his English settings from songs in his earlier Italian operas.

The most striking indication of Purcell's happy word setting

[19] *Eight Concerts of Henry Purcell's Music*: London, 1951.

may be suggested by a contrast that doubtless finally convinced Dryden to employ him as a collaborator. I refer to the settings of Grabu in *Albion and Albanius*. The reception of the opera must have shaken even Dryden's self-confidence. Grabu's feeling for the English accent may be fairly sampled from the opening line of Thamesis' air in Act II:

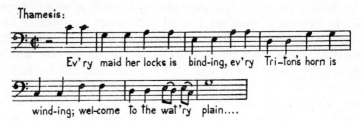

Grabu nourished a tender feeling for all '-ing' endings, to which he invariably allotted the same time value as the stem of the word, even in trisyllables like 'designing', 'combining', and so forth. Professor Dent prints a truly ridiculous drinking song beginning 'Now heigh for a Commonwealth', which may be compared with some of Purcell's to be considered later, or with 'Come away, fellow sailors' in *Dido*.

Even when the words are given appropriate accentuation, there remains a larger problem of fitting the musical phrase to the sense. An illustration I choose for its familiarity is in the ballad 'Believe me if all those endearing young charms', where the phrase, 'Like a fairy gift fading away', ends on a tonic cadence, as complete a stop as can be devised, though the sense is still in abeyance. Compare this with the long opening line in 'When I am laid in earth', where the last word is placed on the leading note creating a cadence pregnant with expectation. And notice in the same connexion that Belinda's recitatives often end on a half-cadence, appropriate to her function as a link between one episode and another, while Dido's usually have a full tonic close.

This kind of genius at textual setting we shall have many occasions of observing in due course. It is fully realized in *Dido*, which remains from the modern point of view Purcell's masterpiece, even though it is his first large theatre score. Owing to the Restoration's peculiar operatic aesthetic, in which the occasions for music usually lay outside the drama, Purcell's talents were thereafter lavished upon semi-opera. From the contemporary point of view these later scores were far more exciting than *Dido*, for they were entwined with grandiose visual conceptions, but owing to a complete change in our own operatic aesthetic the splendours of these works have dropped from sight. Accustomed to regard them as little more than tuneful decoration to preposterous plays, neither scholars of music nor scholars of the theatre have paid much attention to them. It is my hope in the course of this study to approach them as nearly as possible through Restoration eyes, thus suggesting something of the riches that we have been denying ourselves.

CHAPTER III

King Arthur

I

AMONG THAT FIRST AUDIENCE of *Dido and Aeneas*, made up largely of the parents and near relations of the young ladies at Mr Priest's academy, it is tempting to include Thomas Betterton. The foremost actor of the age, he had since the death of Davenant assumed an increasingly important part in the management of the Duke's Company and several times had worked with Priest. He was also an acquaintance of Purcell's, who on this occasion was doubtless directing the performance from the continuo. Betterton was at this time contemplating the production of a spectacular opera, always a risky financial venture, but which, if it took, would more than repay the expense and trouble. Nothing if not self-confident, he was himself writing the play, an adaptation from Fletcher. He then commissioned Purcell to write the music, the composer's first major score for the professional stage, and Josias Priest to create the dances. It is a plausible conjecture that Betterton was so impressed by *Dido*, which he could have seen only upon this occasion, that he engaged Purcell on the spot. In any event their collaboration, *The Prophetess*, or the *History of Dioclesian* (usually known as *Dioclesian*), appeared before the end of 1690 and enjoyed a quite unusual success. This work, which we shall consider in a later chapter, effectually changed the course of Purcell's career, for from this time forward his principal work was for the stage.

Dryden at last capitulated. *Dido* he probably did not know, but if he had been unimpressed by Purcell's earlier scattered and small-scale contributions to the theatre, he definitely changed his

mind after *Dioclesian*.[1] He at once engaged Purcell to write
incidental music (an overture and three songs) for *Amphitryon*,
and within the year had begun collaboration with him on one of
the most ambitious works not only of both their careers but of the
entire period. This is the dramatic opera, *King Arthur, or the
British Worthy*. In his dedicatory letter Dryden went so far as to
declare:

> There is nothing better, than what I intended, but the music;
> which has since arrived to a greater perfection in England than
> ever formerly; especially passing through the artful hands of
> Mr Purcell, who has composed it with so great a genius, that he
> has nothing to fear but an ignorant, ill-judging audience.

The immediate success of the opera went far to console Dryden
after his egregiously misplaced judgment in selecting Grabu to
compose *Albion and Albanius* six years earlier.

His original intention was that the two operas should be a part
of one large work glorifying the origins of British monarchy and
ending with a showy tribute to that nonpareil of the type, King
Charles II. Unfortunately that monarch took simultaneous leave
of the tribute and the earth even as *Albion* was in rehearsal,
necessitating some feverish changes, particularly in the last act
where Albion (Charles) is gathered up by Apollo and 'an abundance of Angels and Cherubims' to shine throughout eternity
in a higher sphere. Left to mourn below are Albanius (James II),
Augusta (London), Acacia (Innocence), and Fame (Fame), an
arrangement sufficient to indicate both the nature and quality of
Albion and Albanius. Disaster pursued the unlucky poet, for the
opening performances coincided exactly with Monmouth's
rebellion, and all labours accordingly ceased. Despite the sentiments and allegorical framework of the opera, Dryden's verse
is at the very least competent, but it could not survive the treatment it got from Grabu. In addition to selecting an inept composer, Dryden's folly extended to the monster inflation: what he
had intended as a one-act prologue of conventional praise to the
monarch (following the venerable French model), he blew up to a

---

[1] It is possible that Dryden had a hand in this work. See R. G. Ham:
'Dryden's Dedication for The Music of the Prophetesse': *PMLA*, vol. L
(1935), p. 1065; and R. P. McCutcheon: 'Dryden's Prologue to The Prophetess': *MLN*, vol. XXXIX (1924), p. 123.

three-act opera of singular inanity. The opera which was originally to have followed the prologue was *King Arthur* and was designed after a plan he describes in the preface to *Albion*:

> A tragedy mixed with opera; or a drama written in blank verse, adorned with scenes, machines, songs and dances: so that the fable of it is all spoken and acted by the best of the comedians; the other part of the entertainment to be performed by the same singers and dancers, who are introduced in this present opera. It cannot properly be called a play, because the action of it is supposed to be conducted sometimes by supernatural means, or magic; nor an opera because the story of it is not sung.

(When *King Arthur* was finally published Dryden settled upon the label 'dramatic opera' for the title-page.) This is very different from *Albion and Albanius*, which was sung from beginning to end. Contemporary reports leave not the slightest doubt that the failure of that opera was a double one, both artistic and financial, and Dryden seems to have abandoned all hope of proceeding with his sequel. Then in 1690 *Dioclesian* appeared and his hopes were rekindled.

In returning to his libretto he tells us that it had to be so extensively revised that it became almost a different work. One conspicuous reason for the revision was to slant its complimentary tone towards a very different monarch from Charles, King William III. Thus Arthur is above all else a soldier king, and the resounding final chorus of the opera begins with an unmistakable reference:

> Our natives not alone appear
> To court his martial prize;
> But foreign kings adopted here,
> Their crowns at home despise.

But more revisions were demanded by Purcell, as Dryden tells us in lines that show him fretting under the restrictions of a medium so arbitrary as music. (His willingness to mitigate his usual sovereign independence is a great compliment to the composer, thirty years his junior.) They also show his quite unusual perception of the differences between a melodic and a poetical line: 'But the numbers of poetry and vocal music are sometimes so contrary that in many places I have been obliged to cramp my verses, and make them rugged to the reader, that they may be harmonious to the hearer.' Dryden was worried that the English language is weak in feminine rhymes and is therefore less singable than the Italian. He consequently loads the lyrics in *King Arthur* with so many double rhymes (roughly fifty per cent) that a person ignorant of both languages might suppose them about alike in this one respect. His pains were really unnecessary, for Purcell had not had the slightest trouble in setting Tate's libretto for *Dido*, where the rhymes are almost exclusively masculine and eminently singable.

What enabled Dryden to bear the constraints of collaboration with equanimity if not actual enthusiasm was ambition. Both he and Purcell entertained the highest hopes that in *King Arthur* they might create that apogee of patriotism linked with the arts, a British National Opera. In combining a feast of the senses with the deepest patriotic emotions, such a work would indeed be not for an age but for all time. It was worth a Herculean effort. The English passion for erecting a national legend around a great hero was ancient and persistent, going back at least to Geoffrey of Monmouth and on through Layomon and Malory to Spenser and even Milton,[2] not to speak of the voluminous Robin Hood literature; but it would come as a surprise to find an author so unromantic as Dryden caught up in the same enthusiasm for any other reason than sheer ambition. Still, this is a motive no less worthy than patriotism, particularly if the consciousness of a formidable challenge releases the genius of two of the greatest artists of the age.

Thus the scheme was taken up, was persisted in, and by May of 1691 was triumphantly realized. Although the original libretto does not exist, there can be no doubt that Dryden's recasting of it was influenced by *Dioclesian*. The two big operatic scenes there Purcell had built up around a Druid sacrificial ceremony and, at the end of the piece, an extensive Arcadian masque. In *King Arthur* we find not only a similar sacrificial scene but two full-scale masques as well as a third in miniature. In addition there are two other musical scenes involving spells and magic plus a good deal of instrumental music scattered through the whole. The other principal shaping influence upon the text, as we shall see later, was Dryden's own operatic version of *The Tempest*, perpetrated a

[2] *Paradise Lost*, IX, 25 ff.

generation earlier with the help first of Davenant and later of Shadwell.

Compared with the stark simplicity of *Dido and Aeneas*, the plot of *King Arthur* is a bewildering maze of intrigue. It is firmly rooted in the tradition of the heroic play, never an austere form, and, as a libretto, reminds us of the ingeniously complex Handel and Scarlatti operas with which Gluck was so impatient in the next century. This does not mean that it is badly laid out or is blunderingly handled, for the opposite is in fact true, but its relation to credibility is wholly coincidental. The reader need be troubled with only those details which illuminate the music and the dramaturgy. The central conflict is a fairly conventional rivalry between the British king Arthur and the Saxon king Oswald for the hand of Emmeline, who is the blind daughter of the Duke of Cornwall. Apparently blindness was wished upon the heroine purely for the theatrical effect of a scene later on where her sight is magically restored. Her beauty is nevertheless provocative enough to have plunged the two kingdoms into war, and as the opera opens they are preparing for their tenth battle. At the end of the first act the Saxons have been driven back to Kent (Oswald's kingdom), leaving the forces of good triumphant—'Victoria! Victoria! the bold Britons cry'—and with this prophetic strain the opera would presumably be over were not magic now invoked to embroil us in complications for four more acts. Oswald, a decent enough sort, is aided by an evil magician Osmond (their twin names are as exasperating as Edgar and Edmund in *King Lear*) and his earthly spirit Grimbald. Assisting Arthur are the great Merlin and a spirit of air, Philidel, clearly suggested by Prospero and Ariel. In the second act they successfully lead the Britons out of the marshes and bogs into which the disguised Grimbald has enticed them, but they come to Emmeline's pavilion too late to save the sightless heroine from being kidnapped by the Saxons.

In Act III we have reached an impasse, for though Merlin's magic is strong enough to restore Emmeline's sight—the airy Philidel gets through to her with a magical essence—he cannot yet break Osmond's spells which keep her prisoner in an enchanted wood. But now Osmond himself, inflamed by her charms, chains his king Oswald in a dungeon and makes his intentions known to Emmeline in one of Dryden's most forthright lines: 'My name is Osmond and my business Love.' (The poet added to his ferociousness by giving him 'penthouse eyebrows'.) When she replies that she is frozen with horror, he puts on a display of magic to show her the power of love in warming back to life the inhabitants of a region of ice and snow. This is the famous Frost Scene, the first of the extended masques in *King Arthur*.

In Act IV Arthur in the magic wood is tempted by wanton visions and sensuous music in a scene suggested by the enchanted grove of Armida from Tasso's *Jerusalem Delivered*. When he strikes a tree to break the spell the hero hears a cry from Emmeline, who appears to be trapped in the trunk, but as he rushes to embrace her Philidel's magic wand reveals that it is Grimbald in disguise. Arthur cuts his way through the woods and reaches the Saxon castle. In the last act Oswald, having been released from his chains by the evil magician, challenges Arthur to single combat but is defeated in the ensuing fight. King Arthur magnanimously frees his enemy, embraces Emmeline, and is hailed by Merlin as a Christian Worthy, first lord of a great empire to be. After predicting that the Britons and Saxons will be joined together into one nation, Merlin waves his wand and calls forth the spectacular concluding masque, 'A Vision of Britain, the Queen of Islands',

> Fairest isle, all isles excelling,
> Seat of pleasure, and of love.

This summary gives only a hint of the plot's intricacies. Its components of magic, military heroics, sacrificial scenes, and pastoral interludes are suitable for musical treatment, while the final masque is designed to bind them all together and launch the mighty galleon upon the waters of immortality. It is patriotic extravaganza, and its appeal is wildly irrational, but no more so than much romantic opera—witness *The Flying Dutchman* or *The Ring of the Niebelungen*. Actually *King Arthur* has been called a prototype of *The Ring* with its background of barbaric legend, its enchanted forests, and its episodes wherein duellists are pawns in the hands of visible supernatural powers, the hero is accosted by river sirens, and the Frost Genius arises slowly from the earth like Erda.[3]

[3] Dent: *Foundations of English Opera*, p. 209.

Dryden's skill at putting all these elements together in a strong progressive movement reveals his cunning instinct for the theatre. Yet in any opera the libretto provides only the skeleton; the dramatic articulation must come from the music. The greatest achievement of *King Arthur* is that Purcell, working against the heavy odds of the English operatic tradition that all occasions for music should lie outside the plot, was able to provide this articulation, for from first to last all that matters in *King Arthur* is what is regulated by the music. Dryden does all that he can, working within this frustrating tradition of the semi-opera, to keep the musical and dramatic scenes in the closest possible contact—for example, the supernatural is introduced chiefly for its musical possibilities—and the result is so successful that the two levels of speech and song are no more disturbing to the spectator than in a musical comedy, or than the levels of *secco* recitative and aria in Italian opera. What must have keenly distressed Purcell was that with only one of the leading characters a singer, the airy spirit Philidel, the great power of dramatic characterization he had revealed in *Dido* must go for absolutely nothing. Nevertheless, his deployment of musical masses is beautifully arranged with his usual sense of variety and climax.

Purcell's power of mitigating what to the modern taste is perhaps the worst banality in Dryden's libretto is an extreme example but a revealing one. It is from the Pavilion Scene of Act II, just before the shepherds and shepherdesses appear to entertain Emmeline. She is talking to her confidante, Matilda, in that vein of semi-innocence which Dryden's Miranda had already thoroughly explored.

> MAT: Great Arthur is a royal conqueror now
>   And well deserves your love.
> EM: But now I fear
>   He'll be too great to love poor silly me.
>   I mean to die: but there's a greater doubt,
>   Since I ne'er saw him here,
>   How shall I meet him in another world?
> MAT: I have heard something, how two bodies meet,
>   But how souls join, I know not.
> EM: I should find him,
>   For surely I have seen him in my sleep,
>   And then, methought, he put his mouth to mine

And ate a thousand kisses on my lips;
Sure by his kissing I could find him out
Among a thousand angels in the sky.
MAT: But what a kind of man do you suppose him?
EM: He must be made of the most precious things,
And I believe his mouth and eyes and cheeks
And nose, and all his face, are made of gold.
MAT: Heaven bless us, madam, what a face you make him!
If it be yellow, he must have the jaundice,
And that's a bad disease.

I can win no recruits for this passage by pointing out the seventeenth century's delight in such surprising incongruities as the conceit about jaundice, but their delight is at least a fact. The important thing about Emmeline, however, is her beauty, her helplessness, her innocence, and it is to these that Purcell gives dramatic realization by having the shepherds pay tribute to her in music of the most enchanting delicacy. After hearing and seeing this (a dance accompanies the singing), we cannot feel indifferent to Emmeline. The flatness of an outmoded poetic idiom is thus absorbed in a timeless musical one. This kind of thing he does over and over again, as an examination of the score will reveal. Unhappily, when a scene contains no music, any banality is left high and dry, like sea-weed on the shore, beyond rescue. Had Emmeline been able to sing, in other words had Purcell been able to write a genuine opera like *Dido* instead of merely aggrandized incidental music, there would have been no dead wood, or very little. As it is, the music is frequent enough and on an important enough scale to make of *King Arthur* an almost perpetual delight.

2

Purcell's original score appears to have been lost or destroyed possibly in his own lifetime. Of the early seventeenth-century manuscripts that still exist and an even earlier one dated 1698–9, none is complete. One maddening aspect of the period is the casual attitude taken towards theatre music. While hundreds of worthless plays were printed and sold in pamphlet form at the door, the musical score, which would become the property of the house, would lie around until it wore out, or was lost, or destroyed in a fire, or it might be discarded altogether if new music were commissioned for a revival. At any rate it seldom got printed except occasionally in snippets in some sort of miscellaneous collection called 'Ayres for the Theatre'. Purcell himself had raised a subscription to publish his *Dioclesian* score, a judicious form of advertising, as it may have captured Dryden; but such a procedure was unusual. By a collation of every available manuscript the Purcell Society has gathered together most of the important music of *King Arthur* except that accompanying the restoration of Emmeline's sight in Act III which apparently is lost irretrievably.[4]

What first impresses one in this score is Purcell's much larger musical battery than in *Dido and Aeneas*. The orchestra now includes trumpets, oboes, and flutes, while the choral writing is on a grander and more complex scale. In a piece with spoken dialogue there is of course little recitative, and perhaps in consequence the songs and arias are often longer than in *Dido*. There is also much more concern with spectacle and splendour and massive effects, for it was put on at Dorset Garden with its extended resources. Despite the lavishness of the production, it made money for the company.[5]

The dramatic irrelevancy of overtures in Purcell's day is evidenced by the fact that both the First Music and what is labelled the overture had been used before, the former in a welcome song for James II back in 1687, the latter in Queen Mary's birthday ode of only the year before. Nevertheless, this overture, composed of bright antiphonal fanfares between strings and trumpets, sounds the martial note at once and is an appropriate opening. On the other hand, the Second Music, the only original number of the introduction, is merely the conventional two-part Lullian overture.

King Arthur is, apart from *Dido*, the lone example in Purcell of a work conceived from the beginning as an opera. How much the composer actually suggested to Dryden is impossible to say, but the construction of the libretto is never less than interesting in

---

[4] The problems of editing the score of *King Arthur* are discussed by J. A. Fuller-Maitland in *Studies in Music*, pp. 185–98: New York, 1901.

[5] John Downes: *Roscius Anglicanus*, p. 42: London, 1708.

what it shows of their ideas on how drama and music should be combined. For once we can leave theory and examine its fruits. The first act, though musically not the richest, reveals the lay-out most clearly. Dryden devotes the greater part of the act to exposition of the two conflicts, military and romantic, building it up to end in what modern producers call a big production number. To bring the soldiers into the musical part of the drama is all that he can manage here; the love interests can wait till the next act. We are in King Oswald's rebel camp at 'A Place of Heathen Worship', probably a sacred grove, where before large pedestalled statues of Woden, Thor, and Freya six Saxon soldiers stand ready to give themselves as human sacrifices. Two priests invoke the deities in turn, the chorus repeating the final phrase after each call. Priests and chorus next pay tribute to the voluntary victims, 'Brave souls, to be renowned in story', who are led out, and then they respond in a spirited chorus to the priestess's invitation to a Bacchic celebration. As all this takes up only about thirty very short lines in the libretto, it is plain to see that although Dryden has provided a framework, the real material of the scene will be Purcell's. It is a good example of his skill at managing a continuous dramatic scene. In a situation that normally inspires little variety of musical treatment—think of the dozens of sacrificial scenes in Italian opera which even a seraphic air like 'Casta Diva' cannot render very variable—he avoids monotony at every point, and, what is more unusual, proceeds to a climax very unlike what the beginning would suggest.

The first musical number is of a type that he had done before, in *Circe* and elsewhere. The bass priest, who sings twice, is given a sonorous and stately line in contrast to the tenor, who has a showy roulade running down ten degrees of the scale on the word 'thundering'. Here Purcell's penchant for pictorial representation, as often elsewhere, serves a formal end by separating both in mood and style the two statements of the basso. Furthermore each of the three statements with its choral response is put in a different key (F major, D minor, B-flat major), after which the orchestra modulates back to the original F major, thus giving us in a complete musical form the sense of a little journey and a return. The next episode, 'To Woden thanks we render', is different, a duet between the tenor and a third priest, an alto, to which the chorus replies in simple imitation contrasting with the strictly homophonic opening chorus. A third type of choral treatment appears in the most impressive number of the scene, the monumental 'Brave souls'. After the introduction, a short soprano recitative from the first priestess who for no very sensible reason sings a roulade on 'shall', this chorus at once assumes a Handelian character; its fugal treatment, piling up of choir upon choir, and its grave sonority go far beyond the simple imitations of the preceding chorus. At the words 'Die and reap the fruit of glory' the broad F major harmonies suddenly give way in a typically baroque treatment to the tonic minor with clashing dissonances on augmented fifths in the seventh bar. Six stately bars from the orchestra cover the exit of the sacrificial victims before a second priestess, a mezzo, abruptly disperses every trace of gloom by sounding the call to revelry in an Italianate aria of swinging rhythm which is in part taken up by the chorus. With the infectious triple metre and the written-out slide on the strong beat, the whole movement, which was surely accompanied by some sort of dance, suggests a jolly drinking song. This looks like singularly unseemly activity for a group of priests in a sacred grove, and thus it appears on first reading over the scene, until one realizes that the chorus would be not priests but soldiers, a type sufficiently volatile to pass in a moment from religious ecstasy to Dionysian revelry. The priestess herself, I fear, cannot be defended.

Apart from the obvious stage effect of contrast, the real dramatic significance of this rollicking finale to the sacrifice does not appear until the closing moments of the act. It is here that the Britons sweep in upon the revelling Saxons, a battle is heard behind the scenes, and the full orchestra with trumpets blaring bursts forth with twenty bars of the song of triumph, 'Come, if you dare', which is then taken up by a British Warrior and the full chorus. In simple four-part harmony, it is a stern and rousing challenge to the Bacchic chorus. There is not a hint of dancing or merry-making, but rather the popular heroics of the brave soldier winning his spurs in battle. The Britons are thus elevated above the Saxons, and Purcell turns what at first seemed to be a conventional drinking song into an important movement of the drama. 'Come, if you dare' was from the first one of the most popular things in Purcell—for this moment at least the British National Opera seemed a reality. Along with its four-square simplicity, it has a beguiling swing that is typical of Purcell's special way of setting words:

And pi-ty man-kind that will pe-rish for gold

At first glance it would appear a *gaucherie* to give the final syllable of both 'pity' and 'perish' the longer note value, but read the line aloud and notice where the pauses or at least the falling cadences occur. It is a perfect example of adapting a speech rhythm to a musical line.

If I have devoted what may seem an inordinate amount of attention to this scene it is in order to save time later on, for it illustrates in a fairly simple manner Purcell's management of a continuous dramatic scene. The devices seem obvious enough when catalogued—dividing the solo passages among contrasting voices; treating the chorus differently in each of its five appearances, and placing the most complex of the choruses not at the end, where there is exciting stage action, but in the middle at the climax of the relatively static sacrifice; starting at a low point of tension and by variations of mood and pace leading up to the highest point; withholding the full resources of the orchestra until the last episode; maintaining a fairly strict control of tonality (in this case stricter than usual, for everything is predominantly F major until the bright burst into C major at 'Come, if you dare'). But it is quite another matter to realize all these intentions in a coherent entity which is fresh with rhythmic and melodic inspiration, and which in addition is in perfect consonance with the spirit of the libretto as a whole.

The forces of good have emerged victorious at the end of the first act. The unfolding of the magic and supernaturalism Dryden saves for the second where, with the abduction of the heroine, the forces of evil are in the ascendant. The act is built around two musical scenes which are in contrast to each other as well as to the scene we just examined. Both are to some extent inspired by *The Tempest*, the first, involving Philidel and Grimbald, the spirits of air and earth, being actually full of verbal resemblances. There is also an echo of *Paradise Lost* in lines that indicate how ludicrously Dryden could change Milton:

> PHIL: The last seduced, the least deformed of hell.
> GRIM: I had a voice in heaven, ere sulphurous streams
> Had damped it to a hoarseness.

The act opens with two instrumental passages apparently to accompany the stage directions which are not in Dryden's text but appear in some of the manuscript scores, 'Philidel on the battlefield laments the slaughter' and 'Merlin descends in a chariot drawn by dragons'. Admittedly the first air could accompany almost anything vaguely melancholy and the second would do for any entry, with or without dragons, but they indicate the balletic conception of the opera. As soon as Philidel begins to sing, however, her character is defined. Purcell conveys a sense of the supernatural with some delicately airy mood music. A graceful melody with falling cadences evolved from a broken scale in G minor to the words, 'Hither this way, this way bend', alternates with a melodious whine of oboes and violins in the accompaniment, all subtly suggestive of wandering as Philidel attempts to lead the Britons out of the marsh. Mime, perhaps even a near-dance, obviously plays a part in the scene, for Philidel is answered antiphonally by a chorus who are seeking to follow her. The Caliban of the piece, Grimbald, tries to divert them from their path with a suavely lilting song, 'Let not a moon-born elf mislead ye' in A major. Since he is disguised as a shepherd, the innocent-sounding song appropriately suggests the most benevolent of spirits, yet the sense of unsettled wandering is maintained by the cadence on an oft-repeated 'Hurry, hurry, hurry on'. Philidel's attendant spirits return with a reprise of 'Hither this way', warning Arthur against 'that malicious fiend', rounding off this first movement of the scene in a manner that is structurally neat and dramatically apt.

Musically the second part is even more interesting, for Philidel's success at leading the Britons out of the mire is celebrated in a quintet and chorus that begins like a canon and presently breaks off for a short duet in thirds for sopranos before returning to the chorus. The melodic line is based on an evenly descending scale betokening easy assurance in contrast to the broken scale which

gave 'Hither this way' its wandering, unsettled feeling. The scene ends with an inspired idea; to the words,

> We brethren of air,
> You heroes will bear
> To the kind and the fair that attend ye . . .

Purcell writes a short chorus, first given out by an unaccompanied trio, of the purest lyricism. In solid, strict homophony, which sets it off from the earlier choruses, it is also rarefied, light as down. It is his way of joining the heroic to the world of magic. Patriotism is given a spiritual significance, while the supernaturalism becomes more than a mere exotic curiosity. Thus ends a scene which has been controlled entirely by the music. Between the musical numbers are a few lines of spoken dialogue which, as Dent observes, emphasize the supernatural character of the spirit choruses without breaking up the musical unity of the scene.

A revealing insight into Purcell's instinct for stage movement, his habit of thinking in terms of actual performance, is afforded if we compare this little scene with the additions made by Arne for Garrick's sumptuous revival of *King Arthur* in 1770. All Purcell's music presumably was retained, but there were 'grander' additions. Arne writes a long recitative for Philidel, 'Alas the horrors of this bloody field', followed by a full-scale aria, 'O Peace descend', which might have been rejected from *Messiah*. In triple time with ornate oboe obbligato, it is pleasant to hear but much too grandiose for the aerial Philidel, and of course hopelessly alien in spirit to 'Hither this way' which followed hard upon. That it completely stopped the action and vital impulse of the scene while the soprano stood, an immobile stone, before the footlights goes without saying.

The second scene begins with the curious dialogue we have already examined between Emmeline and Matilda, who are in a pavilion awaiting Arthur's return. Laying out his libretto, Dryden, after introducing the supernatural to musical accompaniment in the first scene, decides that it is now time to bring the heroine into the music. Though she is not a singer, she can be made the centre of a musical scene as Arcadian figures do homage to her beauty. The music of the shepherds, resembling a fragment of a pastoral masque, we need not pause over beyond noting that Purcell has shown his usual sense of discriminating variety in treating three songs of similar sentiment. The duet, 'Shepherd, shepherd, leave decoying', the only place in the score where flutes are indicated, is a ravishing example of his Arcadian style. It is set to one of Dryden's most daintily sophisticated lyrics, now piously bowdlerized in all available scores. The original begins:

> Shepherd, shepherd, leave decoying,
> Pipes are sweet as summer's day,
> But a little after toying
> Women have the shot to pay.

The utter innocence of the music makes more dramatic Emmeline's abduction at its close.

Dramatically the end of Act II is exactly opposite to that of the first act where the forces of good were successful. The action has now reached an impasse, and the third act is a period of waiting. The heroine must be kept in cold storage, as it were, and we are given (not inappropriately) the Frost Scene. This is the most celebrated musical episode in *King Arthur*. Though it is in itself dramatically conceived, which is another way of saying that Purcell has given it dramatic life, the fact that it is detachable from the opera as a whole calls Dryden's dramaturgy into question. The reason such a scene can exist in the very middle of the work, usually the turning point of a play (witness Shakespeare's nearly invariable practice), is simply that in *King Arthur* the middle of the play rather than later on is the point of rest during which the opposing factors are gathering their strength. Although the opening of this action is the dramatically irrelevant scene in which the heroine's sight is restored by magic, such an episode affords rich opportunities for music. The vision of spirits in the shape of men and women who are presented to Emmeline's wondering sight—one recalls Miranda's 'O brave new world'—doubtless stimulated both the choral and balletic imagination of Purcell. That the loss of the music is damaging to the opera as a whole is made the more emphatic when we look at the characterless sweetness of what Arne has supplied to fill up this gap in Garrick's production.

The Frost Scene may be even less needful to the plot, but that is not necessarily fatal in opera. Actually the startling degree of its irrelevancy is its very fascination to the baroque taste. Osmond has merely to say of Love, 'I'll show his force in countries caked with ice', and strike the ground with his wand, and the scene changes to 'a Prospect of Winter in Frozen Countries' in which the scenic designer might display his ingenuity. When Cupid descends in a machine, the show is on indeed. Everyone has noted the thrilling business of the Cold Genius rising from the frozen spaces to a tremolando accompaniment that had been used already by Lully and several Italian composers, and the way the shiver is carried into the notation of the voice parts and is further enhanced by the weird dissonances of the Spirit's great aria. But equally impressive is Purcell's structural power in building up a scene of eight musical numbers, cleverly diversified, culminating in a joyous choral climax that carries all before it.

The opening recitative for Cupid (a soprano) moves freely above a long tonic pedal in C major moving on to the subdominant and purposely kept quite simple, prolonging our sense of expectation for the eerie appearance of the Cold Genius. Here is the one movement of the original performance of *King Arthur* that we are lucky enough to recapture through the eyes of an on-the-spot spectator. Since Pepys had stopped keeping his diary in 1669 long before Purcell was composing, and the other meagre records of the Restoration stage are in the main drearily statistical, a veil necessarily lies between us and all these operas which all our efforts at imaginative reconstruction cannot remove. Roger North, who was in the Dorset Garden audience for one of the early performances, lifts this veil for just an instant:

> I remember in Purcell's excellent opera of *King Arthur* when Mrs Butler, in the person of Cupid, was to call up Genius, she had the liberty to turn her face to the scene, and her back to the theatre. She was in no concern for her face, but sang a recitative of calling towards the place where Genius was to rise, and performed it admirably, even beyond anything I ever heard upon the English stage. And I could ascribe it to nothing so much as the liberty she had of concealing her face, which she could not endure should be so contorted as is necessary to sound well, before her gallants, or at least her envious sex. There was so much of admirable music in that opera, that it's no wonder it's lost; for the English have no care of what's good, and therefore deserve it not.[6]

The Cold Genius emerges stiffly from out of the earth to the famous tremolando passage in C minor, his aria being built on slowly rising semitones, the basis of all the transitory modulations. The excruciating effect of the slow chromatic climbing of the octave ends with a rest of two bars before he begins a descent to an F minor cadence, Purcell's 'horror key', which quite

---

[6] *Roger North on Music*, ed. John Wilson, p. 217: London, 1959. The reference to the loss of the music may possibly refer to the original score, but it is far more likely that North has confused it with the score of *The Fairy Queen* which was lost after Purcell's death and not subsequently performed. *King Arthur*, whole or nearly whole, continued straight through the eighteenth century. See below, p. 93.

unexpectedly turns to a melting F major in a manner characteristic of Schubert. The last movement of the piece is a climb to high E-flat before sinking gradually to the tonic ten notes below. It need hardly be pointed out that the aria is not a simple matter of moving up and down the scale; the uneven duration of notes and the occasional breaks in the scale are replete with subtle variety. Although this is the most exciting single number, the rest of the scene proceeds in ingenious contrasts both of mood and form. Cupid's answer, for example, is in miniature rondo form, the second theme ending on the expected dominant cadence but the third ending in D minor (the tonic is C major); while the next aria for the Spirit is a broad melodic declamation in C major, the vocal range being the same as before (C to high E) but the triadic leaps and the major harmonies redolent of strength and vigour far removed from the creeping semitones of his earlier song. (He is beginning to thaw.) And so on through the scene. Cupid holds it together—every second song is hers, and each in a slightly different style, Purcell using delicate pictorialism as a means of characterization—and guides the picturesque 'shivering dance' and chorus, as well as the jubilant finale, ''Tis love that hath warmed us', for full chorus and strings.

The scene is like a masque, and, though from one point of view dramatically dispensable, it is thoroughly congruent with the strictly formal nature of the heroic drama. Not only does the most frequent subject, love versus honour, become little more than a formal convention, but the aggrandizement of the protagonists and their passions and the deliberate avoidance of anything approaching realism make of the genre a thing apart from life, a vehicle of sheer entertainment. In contrast to the Elizabethan age, there was nothing heroic about the Restoration, but, as Professor Nicoll once observed, it was not so cynical as to throw over entirely the inculcation of heroism. Yet to present heroism in plays of real life 'would have raised too sharp a distinction between what was and what might have been, and accordingly in the heroic tragedy heroism is cast out of the world altogether and carried to an Eastern or an antique realm of exaggerated emotions, mythical and hopelessly ideal. The heroic play is like a Tale of a Land of Nowhere. We are interested in that land, but we do not hope ever to enter therein. The persons who move and speak there are not our equals, nor do they even draw the same breath as we do.'[7] This goes far towards explaining one of the cornerstones of baroque taste, a love for the abstractions of allegorical figures, whether in the living form of the masque or in the plastic embodiments of Poussin and Bernini. To find two elaborate (though quite different) masques embedded in such an undertaking as the British National Opera is not to be wondered at.

The last two acts of the opera return to the central conflict between the forces of good and evil. Dryden, a past master at theatrical contrivance, has cleverly divided it into a double conflict; in Act IV Arthur's struggle is with himself, in Act V with external forces symbolized by the rival king. It is music that enables him to dramatize the internal conflict. Of the entire work this scene (IV. ii) is the most operatic in conception. In an episode of temptation and of trial we are reminded of Sir Guyon in the Bower of Bliss and, as Arthur in pantomime struggles through the enchanted forest to the accompaniment of music, of Pamina and Tamino going through the ordeal of fire and water. Dryden has provided opportunities for considerable theatrical spectacle in addition to a good deal of music, at least two numbers of which have not been preserved. He calls for 'soft music' at the lines,

> Hark! Music, and the warbling notes of birds;
> Hell entertains me, like some welcome guest . . .

and soon after there follows the first song of the siren, 'O pass not on' (the music is missing). The second song, 'Two daughters of this aged stream', is one of the highlights of the score. There is no better example of music's chastening power over an erotic text. The nymphs, naked in their bath, invite King Arthur to step in for a romp, not really a ludicrous notion if we can forget the marmoreal hero of Malory and Tennyson. The crucial point is that the girls' obvious wantonness would have no appeal for the nonpareil Dryden has made of his hero, and it is therefore up to Purcell to suggest the temptation by the refinement and delicacy of music. He does so in a limpid contrapuntal duet in G minor for two sopranos, with fragile continuo accompaniment that will not obscure the timbre and interweaving patterns of the voices.

---

[7] *A History of English Drama*, vol. 1, p. 88: London, 1952.

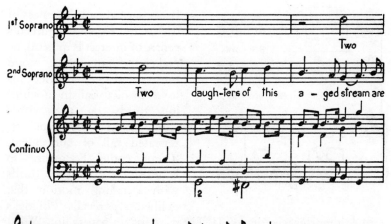

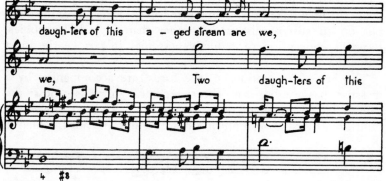

Because of the obviousness of the stage situation Purcell's centre of interest is musical; he makes no attempt at mood music, and even restricts his love for pictorialism to winding thirds on the words 'circle round'. The sirens' oft-repeated call of enticement, 'Come, come', he realizes in languishing minor thirds with a falling motion that deliberately recalls Philidel's airy 'Hither this way' in Act II. The most inflammatory line, 'What danger from a naked foe?' is made the affective climax of the piece but on an austere dissonance rather than in lush harmonies. Purcell's conception of seductiveness may in fact be the most seductive of all.

The hero's temptations in the forest are accompanied by a massive passacaglia, for sheer technical impressiveness the primary achievement of the score. It is a very long movement built on a four-bar ground of a descending tetrachord, which is

at one point inverted and in two other places broken, with a rest on the second beat of each bar. Laid out in solos, duets, trios, and choruses, and set for oboes and strings, it is a brilliant mosaic of differing yet very similar melodies: each one is in large part an outline of the tonic and dominant triads of G minor. Dryden directs that it is to be danced throughout, showing that the scene is conceived in terms of a spacious ballet with vocal accompaniment (a form elaborated in modern times by Stravinsky in *Les Noces*). No other place in the work enforces so strongly the necessity of seeing *King Arthur* staged, not merely of hearing a concert performance. Wholly a creation of the theatre, it must have the resources of the theatre if it is to achieve anything approaching an adequate realization. The spectacular transformation scene of the destruction of the forest, which ends the act, means absolutely nothing as we read the single line of the stage direction. Everyone knows that masques must be seen as well as heard, and there are two in *King Arthur*, but when we realize that in the second and fourth acts not merely the decoration but the very action itself is made possible only through music and mime, then the futility of the 'Grand Purcell Concert', with soloists and chorus in evening attire, is obvious. A concert anthology of *King Arthur* is no more feasible than an evening called 'Gems from *Otello*'.

For the last act we have no music until the masque after the play has ended, but it would seem likely that the duel between the rival kings was fought to musical accompaniment. The elaborate stage directions give it the air of ballet, its stern formality emphasized by having the real directive forces, Merlin and Osmond, plainly visible, like Wotan and Brunnhilde in the second act of *Die Walküre*. The ritualistic quality asserts itself in full force in the masque where Merlin in a series of tableaux foretells the future greatness of Britain. Everyone who has written of *King Arthur* has regarded this masque as dramatically pointless, but it does in fact exactly what it aims to do, suggesting the future of the empire in a number of differing moods or aspects, and in this way makes sense out of all the widely varying episodes of the opera. It imposes a sense of unity hitherto lacking, and what can be more dramatic than that? Though the quality is not uniform, each component of the masque has a share in this broad welding process; it will suffice to speak of only two or three.

The beginning is on the heroic scale. The back of the stage opens, disclosing 'the British Ocean in a Storm' with Aeolus appearing in a cloud machine to sing a stirring aria of invocation,

> Ye blust'ring brethren of the skies,
> Whose breath has ruffled all the wat'ry plain,
> Retire, and let Britannia rise
> In triumph o'er the main.

It is easy to sense the effect of Purcell's treatment with the agitated accompaniment beginning on rapid semiquavers, gradually slowing to quavers, to crotchets, and to minims as the winds retire at the broad sweeping C major invocation of the god, which covers nearly two octaves in majestic leaps. The procedure is like that of Weber in 'Ocean, thou mighty monster', its power in no way diminished by its obviousness. The second half of the aria,

> Serene and calm and void of fear,
> The Queen of Islands must appear . . .

changes to a triple metre in C minor, and one can imagine the island slowly rising to celestial harmonies under a long sustained note at every repetition of 'calm'. The gentle lapping of the waves is suggested by a persistent rhythmic figure of the accompaniment, ♪ ♪♫ to shifting harmonies. What Purcell does in this song is to combine the patriotic-martial bluster with a sweetness, even a spirituality, which may be considered the principal aim of the whole opera. These are the two prime qualities which any work that can be called national must have, and they are not easily combined.

Before returning to the patriotic note for the final curtain, the masque in its middle portions touches upon other veins. The chief of these, the pastoral, Dryden and Purcell have revealed in a surprisingly wide and varied scope. In 'Your hay it is mowed', a consciously naive imitation of a folk air with a swinging refrain on 'Merrily roar out harvest home', they depict the world of the jolly farmer, the simplest life close to the land; in the most famous song of the opera, 'Fairest isle, all isles excelling', they touch a higher sphere, an idyllic Arcadianism yet with no hint of preciousness; finally, in a miniature drama of five short numbers between a shepherd and his sweetheart, we experience the passion that humanizes the pastoral. The compass of moods and styles in this little dialogue is remarkable. The soprano's opening recitative suggests a paler Dido with swooning appoggiatura bespeaking the pangs of a girl in love but fearing to yield. The shepherd's answer in a lilting triple metre with a wide range of nearly two octaves is blandly confident, yet there is a tenderness in the G minor harmonies which is anything but cocky. Her reply, 'Love has a thousand ways to please', gentle and beguiling, sobers him completely, and his answering recitative shows his hearty confidence shaken. Thus we are led to the restrained joy of the final duet which changes to the major key, though with an occasional surprising minor third, evenly divided between note-for-note and antiphonal setting.

'Fairest Isle' is too familiar to require comment, but something must be said of the ending, which there is reason to believe may be spurious. It verges on the grandiose as Honour (a soprano) sings the glories of St George, who presumably becomes identified with King Arthur, and the Order of the Garter. She carols forth a series of calls on the tonic triad which may be thought to suit Dryden's inflated verse, and which can certainly be found elsewhere in Purcell, but are sadly disappointing for so crucial a position in the score. The opera closes with a full chorus, *maestoso*, to the sovereign. It is a hymn tune with a touch of martial pomp, and may have been a model for 'Rule Britannia'. With a thundering orchestral reprise it may just get by for the curtain, a position where subtlety counts for nothing. What it fails to accomplish is a reiteration of the note of spiritualized patriotism, the inevitable close for the British National Opera.

3

The hope that Purcell and Dryden cherished of becoming a part of the national tradition has not materialized. *King Arthur* is on the shelf. It was not always thus. The first production at Dorset Garden was assured of success not only because its idiom was contemporary but owing to the dazzling splendour of the spectacle lavished upon it and to a distinguished cast which included Betterton as Arthur, Mrs Bracegirdle as Emmeline, and Mrs Butler doubling as Philidel and Cupid. It was performed throughout the eighteenth century, significant revivals occurring in 1736, 1770 (Garrick's), 1781, and in 1784 when Kemble first played Arthur and still more music by Linley was added to that composed in 1770 by Arne. We get a notion of the kind of production it received in the eighteenth century from Gray's letter to Horace Walpole on 3 January 1736:[8]

... the Frost Scene is excessive fine; the first scene of it is only a cascade, that seems frozen; with the Genius of Winter asleep and wrapt in furs, who upon the approach of Cupid, after much

[8] *Correspondence*, ed. P. Toynbee and L. Whibley: Oxford, 1935.

quivering and shaking sings the finest song in the play: just after, the scene opens, and shows a view of arched rocks covered with ice and snow to the end of the stage: between the arches are upon pedestals of snow eight images of old men and women, that seem frozen into statues, with icicles hanging about them, and almost hid in frost, and from the end come singers, viz: Mrs Chambers, &c: and dancers all rubbing their hands and chattering with cold with fur gowns and worsted gloves in abundance; there are several more beautiful scenes. . . .

In 1803 Kemble's sister, Mrs Siddons, came on as a very mature Emmeline—by that time she could have appeared as Britannia herself—and other revivals followed in 1819 and in 1827 when the Arne music was dropped but additional Purcell numbers were lifted from *Dido and Aeneas* and *The Indian Queen*. The rage for Production, with which the nineteenth century so ponderously enveloped Shakespeare, reached a kind of apogee (at least for anything Purcellian) in 1842 when Macready put on *King Arthur* with twelve new characters, a new masque, much interpolated music from other Purcell scores, and with such a profusion of 'sparkling of the waters in the sunlight, and the glittering spray as it descends from a rocky eminence', that the audience could spare little attention from the production for the music.[9] These splendours may have intimidated future producers, for after this we hear only of an earlier adaptation called *Arthur and Emmeline*, which in 1851 George Hogarth spoke of as still 'Frequently . . . performed at different times.'[10] So far as I can discover, there has not been a single professional performance of *King Arthur* in the twentieth century.

The popularity of the opera for nearly two centuries is sufficient commentary upon its theatrical effectiveness. Since it is the only one of Purcell's works even to approach such a run, it is natural to ask why this should be so, and at the same time to consider why, despite this success, it did not become the British National Opera.

To begin with, it is for several reasons clearly separated from the usual product of the age. In most Restoration opera the music

[9] Quoted by Dennis Arundell from *The Dramatic and Musical Review*, 19 November 1842.

[10] *Annals of Opera*, vol. I, p. 116: London, 1851. This anonymous adaptation was first produced at Drury Lane in 1784.

was much less important than scenes and machines, but in *King
Arthur* it is the music which controls the entire structure. Each
act is built around one or more extensive musical episodes so that
both dramatic and musical elements are elevated beyond the
customary practice. Then the subject itself is on another plane
from that of the usual oriental potentates and barbaric slaughters.
The ending emphasizes the animating purpose of the whole, to
combine the pseudo-historical with the supernatural, the British
soldier king with something about the gods and a flavour of
religious ritual. One has only to glance at Dryden's other dramas,
Aurengzebe, say, or *The Indian Queen*, to appreciate the loftier tone
of *King Arthur*. As for the music, Purcell with his singular eclectic
powers succeeds in combining certain Italian and French elements
while creating something wholly English.

The moment seemed ripe for creating a purely English form of
musical-dramatic entertainment. Its ancestor, the masque, had
evolved a tradition in which both composers and dramatists were
well-versed. They could draw upon the great developments in
France and Italy of staging, of music, and of the dance. Nor was
it a difficult thing to combine masque-like features with the heroic
play, made up after all of a succession of great moments and heroic
postures. A scene which could work up to such a speech from
Arthur as,

> Mistake me not, I count not war a wrong:
> War is the trade of kings, that fight for empire . . .

is surely the stuff from which operas might be made. And yet,
despite the propitious moment and the eclectic nature of English
genius, an enduring operatic form was not established. *Dido and
Aeneas* remained unheard and forgotten, and though the *King
Arthurs* and the *Dioclesians* continued to be performed with great
success, no more were written after the turn of the century.

It is chiefly the Restoration's operatic aesthetic that has pre-
vented *King Arthur* from achieving its authors' ambitious hope.
The age saw opera as an essentially formless 'entertainment', a
mélange appealing to every kind of sensuous taste simultaneously
—in music, the dance, architecture ('scenes'), and sheer extravaganza (costumes and machines). It was a monumental synthesis of a
number of arts, something which the baroque taste could take
seriously. The genre is a mixture, a compromise, a dilution of

purity which would appeal to the English with their talent for compromises, their serene disregard of artistic rules in favour of muddling through to an end that has been reached by all sorts of pleasant by-paths.

The only thing wrong with all this is that we cannot take it seriously enough. In trying to appeal simultaneously to two kinds of taste that, though perhaps not mutually exclusive, are nearly so, it confuses the modern spectator. On the one hand is the effort, in *King Arthur* at any rate, towards something truly epic, the desire to make the work broadly human and deeply serious, as befits the great hero and the exalted theme; but on the other hand is an effort almost wholly frivolous—to exploit to the full the 'entertainments' connected with the genre, its deliberate artificiality, its distractive, episodic, picturesque aspects. It is hard to see how any work can partake of near-vaudeville and of an almost religious patriotism at one and the same time. A highly sophisticated taste might possibly be capable of making such an adjustment, but that kind of audience would always be limited; actually *King Arthur* was just in time to catch the most sophisticated audience in the history of the English theatre. In the 1690's the character of the theatre-going public was perceptibly changing, as the emergence of the sentimental comedy and of Jeremy Collier before the end of the decade both testify.

A comparison with the drama is illuminating. *Henry V* undoubtedly comes close to being the British National Play. It contains ingredients of very wide and elementary appeal—the soldier-king, the battles against seemingly hopeless odds, the traditional enmity with France, the many various strains of comedy from Pistol to the rollicking wooing of Kate—and all these Shakespeare manages to manipulate and juxtapose with matters of considerable dignity and nobility—the big patriotic speeches, the prayer before the battle, the pressure of national crisis underlying the high spirits, the strong sense of unity running through the variety. These things can scarcely be done in a genre so unrealistic to the English as opera; and certainly they cannot be done in the Restoration's 'dramatic opera'. *Henry V* is characterized by an aggrandized realism, whereas the Restoration opera creates a world of palpable artificiality.

Still another reservation touches *King Arthur*. The taste for grandiose heroics combined with irrelevant grandiose spectacle, a taste so eminently baroque, has not proved a permanent one. The baroque taste is not national but historical. The crucial question is that of dramatic illusion. The fact that the actors did not sing, of course, shows that illusion was not a primary consideration to the seventeenth century; the music promoted mood rather than more intimately dramatic ends. Illusion we must not expect; we accept the whole as a representation of a world that never was. This is a very different thing from operas as diverse as *Le Nozze di Figaro, Aida,* or *Der Rosenkavalier,* which are convincing because of their psychological and emotional realism. A striking example of the problem occurs in *King Arthur* at the end of Act III where Emmeline, threatened with rape, cries:

> Heaven be my guard, I have no other friend!
> Heaven ever present to thy suppliant's aid,
> Protect and pity innocence betrayed.

In such a situation Handel and all later opera composers would bring the heroine's plight to emotional life by having her sing to these very words an aria which would develop and intensify her anguish. Instead of this Purcell and Dryden have the would-be ravisher put on the masque of Cupid and the Genius of Frost. Its sole purpose is to promote the mood of supernaturalism, and thus we have the curious phenomenon of perhaps the best music of the opera being dramatically irrelevant.

We cannot accept the condition of the music and drama being on the same level, as we do in the great Italian and German operas since Gluck. In France and England the drama of poetry will never be supplanted in the public affection by the drama of music. In the prologue to *Andromède,* a prototype of the Restoration opera, Corneille makes it very clear that he could never for a moment imagine the most important part of the drama expressed in music; the principals must not sing but speak. This is exactly the English point of view and explains why the music cannot carry the play. Changes in taste play havoc with popular drama; what was thrilling to one age may be banal to the next. But the fact that it thrilled once means that beneath all the ephemera of fashion, beneath the disguise of an outmoded idiom, lies some core of truth or seriousness implicit in the situation, and it is to this truth that music can hold the key, to this that it can give vitality. The banality of *The Bride of Lammermoor* disappears in a good performance of *Lucia*, as does that of *Le Roi s'Amuse* in even a mediocre performance of *Rigoletto*. From tarnished time-worn librettos the music has created endurable works of art, but with so much of Purcell's music standing outside the principal action, this has not been possible in *King Arthur*.

In spite of the close connexions of a work like *Andromède* with Dryden and Purcell, the French were never concerned with creating a national opera. *Andromède* was strictly a spectacle, while Lully was classical and courtly, and in spite of all the fulsome compliments to the monarch there was not a hint of the patriotic or nationalistic. That is to say, nothing expressing the ideals or emotions of the nation is involved in Lully's operas; they are untouched by even the slightest shadow of democratic principle. If there is a national institution in French music it is probably Gounod's *Faust*, a work so French in character that the Germans call it *Margarethe*, but it has nothing to do with France or the French.

Even if all these conditions were changed—in other words, if the British could adopt a different frame of mind about music drama—it is possible that Purcell's style is too refined for a British National Opera. Consider the lyric most fully expressing patriotic sentiment, 'Fairest isle, all isles excelling', and compare its exquisite pastoral style with the resounding wallop of 'Land of Hope and Glory'.

If it then be asked how, with all these reservations, *King Arthur* could remain a popular work for two hundred years, one answer lies in its stage history. The additions to the music made by Arne and Linley show that it was a work capable of expansion and decoration in keeping with the age—in fact, like Shakespeare. The changing splendours of scenic production reveal the same thing. Walpole somewhat disdainfully reports that Garrick had mounted the sacrificial scene (the temple of Woden) with 'a pretty bridge, and a Gothic church with windows of painted glass'.[11] Furthermore, until well into the nineteenth century most opera and a great deal of drama were every bit as extravagantly irrational as *King Arthur*. English audiences were not worried that it lacked the consistency of an opera by Gluck or Mozart,

[11] Letter to Conway, 25 December 1770.

because of such work they knew either travesties of the originals or nothing at all. The more one studies the nineteenth-century theatre in England the clearer it becomes that the spectators were essentially a pantomime public, in large measure a product of the Industrial Revolution. The label of the particular entertainment does not make a great deal of difference. If they did not see Purcell's *King Arthur*, they saw a near relation to it which they liked even better. The nearest approach to some sort of compromise between speech and music has indeed been in pantomime, a thoroughly British national institution, where for several weeks during the Christmas season each year one can see in entertainments about Dick Whittington or St George a brand of sentimental patriotism combined with fanciful spectacle. But pantomime is for children (of whatever age). Not only is it non-serious in Dryden's sense, but hopelessly non-musical in Purcell's.

Yet when all this has been regretfully noted, one indisputable fact remains: because of Purcell's music *King Arthur* was still being performed nearly a century and a half after Dryden's other heroic plays had all but disappeared from the stage. This is principally owing to the music's capacity for keeping the artificial conventions of heroic drama within the bounds of acceptability. Music has an abstract power which moves us without any reference to 'nature'. Although the aggrandized personages of these dramas are stagey and overblown, Purcell's music, affecting the senses directly, suggests that the feelings and situations are within the experience of the audience. Though the hero does not sing, the grandiloquent music of the score as a whole casts its spell upon the drama and at every point gives strength to the elaborate façade. The baroque after all is an art given to superlatives, and its *métier* is magniloquence. The exaggerated rhetoric of Dryden's heroics often brought him dangerously close to absurdity, and not merely in the eyes of a later age but, as *The Rehearsal* testifies, in those of his own day as well. Yet joined with the splendour of Purcell's music, the magnificent façade holds up. Like so much of the baroque, however, it is a perilous balance, and it is unthinkable that such a conception could become an enduring national institution. If a British National Opera should ever appear it will be wrought of simpler and plainer stuff than *King Arthur*. Meanwhile it is to our great loss that we allow a work of such beauty to remain unperformed.

CHAPTER IV

The Fairy Queen

I

KING ARTHUR showed Purcell what he could do in a large-scale work for the theatre. Its striking commercial success inevitably brought him a commission for what was in some ways an even more ambitious undertaking; at least it is his longest score and most elaborate production. This opera, *The Fairy Queen*, produced at Dorset Garden in the spring of 1692, is a sumptuous entertainment adapted freely from *A Midsummer Night's Dream*. Josias Priest again collaborated on the dances, which were many and various, but the author of the libretto is not known for certain. Elkanah Settle is the most likely candidate.[1] Although its success was instantaneous, it made very little money for the company because of the exorbitant cost of the production. Various persons grumbled about it: the author himself in the preface to the libretto, the prompter Downes in his memoirs, and Colley Cibber fifty years later in his *Apology*.

During the next season, 1692-3, the opera was slightly revised and more music added, probably for the performance attended by Queen Mary on 16 February, but after that it apparently disappeared from the repertory. Though a few separate songs were printed in various collections, nothing could illustrate better the shocking casualness of the theatre towards its music than the fate of this score. A great popular hit, the most elaborate score of the leading composer of the age—and it was lost! Six years after

---

[1] F. C. Brown, *Elkanah Settle* (Chicago, 1910), presents the case for Settle's authorship, which is accepted by Woodward and McManaway in *A Checklist of English Plays, 1641–1700* (items 1034–36), but the attribution remains doubtful.

Purcell's death the *London Gazette* for 9–13 October 1701 advertised:

> The score of music for *The Fairy Queen*, set by the late Mr Henry Purcell, and belonging to the patentees of the Theater-Royal in Covent Garden, London, being lost by his death: Whoever brings the said score, or a copy thereof, to Mr Zachary Biggs, Treasurer of the said theater, shall have 20 guineas reward.

The next week the advertisement was repeated with the following alteration:

> Whoever first brings the said score, or a true copy thereof . . . shall have 20 guineas reward, or proportionable for any act or acts thereof.

Some of the score seems to have turned up, for one act was presented in concert form on 1 February 1703[2], but the score as a whole was thought to be lost for ever until it was most surprisingly found in the library of the Royal Academy of Music at the turn of the present century.[3] The fact that it was not revived soon after 1695, when Betterton seceded to Lincoln's Inn Fields taking most of the leading actors with him, suggests that the score had already disappeared. The Drury Lane manager, Christopher Rich, left with a second-string acting troupe and feeling that he needed all the musical splendours he could lay his hands on, lost no time in reviving a number of other operas. Even though *The Fairy Queen* itself vanished from the repertory, it is likely that the costumes, scenery, and machines were absorbed in various other productions.

The reason for the especially lavish outlay on *The Fairy Queen* lies in the peculiar nature of its musical scenes. *King Arthur* Dryden had planned from the beginning as an opera libretto with each act built around one or more considerable musical scenes which in large measure dictated the action. No such principle informs *The Fairy Queen*; most of the music is contained in quite detachable masques which are appended to the ends of the acts.

[2] See Eric W. White's article, 'Early Theatrical Performances of Purcell's Operas': *Theatre Notebook*, vol. XII, no. 2 (Winter, 1958–9), pp. 43–65.

[3] The bibliographical complications arising from various manuscript scores are fully dealt with by J. S. Shedlock in the Purcell Society's edition (1903), but they are irrelevant to the present discussion.

Often accompanied by ballet, it is full of pictorial and even humorous appeal, but in the final analysis it is mood music pure and simple. The work as a whole is unique for Purcell in that drama, opera, and ballet are here on an equal footing. We have seen that the masque in itself was not new to him—in fact it is the one essential ingredient of all his professional operas—but in *The Fairy Queen* there are four masques, and if one's definition is sufficiently flexible even five. A very flexible definition is actually all that can be given. The masque even in its Caroline heyday was never a very carefully delimited type, and by the time of Charles II the words masque, masquerade, ball, and ballet were apt to become interchangeable.[4] By Purcell's time it is best to define it as a musical interlude involving song, dance, and (if available) spectacle.

Now it is very easy when confronted with the Restoration's employment of the masque to throw in one's hand altogether and call it irrelevant decoration lugged in to prop up plays too feeble to stand unsupported; in fact this is the inevitable line taken by historians of the theatre. Music and machines introduced by Davenant to disguise plays (it is supposed) were kept on to mend them. And Colley Cibber's sarcastic comment on 'how many more people there are who can see and hear than can think and judge'—he was doubtless remembering his own thought-provoking masterpieces, *Love's Last Shift* and *The Careless Husband*—is reminiscent of Ben Jonson's exasperated protests a century earlier against Inigo Jones:

> O to make boards to speak! there is a task!
> Painting and carpentry are the soul of Masque![5]

These vastly dissimilar authors both make the mistake of applying standards of pure drama to an entertainment whose aims are quite different. To point out that Cibber is objecting to masques grafted

---

[4] Eleanore Boswell: *The Restoration Court Masque*, p. 135. Evelyn called the masque *Calisto* a comedy, then a pastoral; the Clerk of the Kitchen called it a ball, the tailors a masquerade. Its author John Crowne spoke of it as an entertainment, but the word masque appears on the title-page.

[5] *An Expostulation with Inigo Jones.* Some critics are reluctant to ascribe this poem in full to Jonson, but it is obvious evidence of a very real and personal attack.

on to plays rather than to the independent entity is largely irrelevant when one considers that these particular plays were geared
for and constructed around the masque. It has already been
pointed out that this taste for masque, acquired from the very
beginning of the century, if not earlier, played a major part in
moulding the character of seventeenth-century entertainment,
and in particular of Purcell's operas. Although it is certainly true
that magnificence and show were at all times more important to
the popular taste than the more exalted aspects developed by Ben
Jonson, yet it is Purcell's regard for the potential of dignity and
seriousness in the masque that makes *The Fairy Queen* a masterpiece.

During the Restoration the status of the masque had of course
undergone changes. For one thing the splendours had been
transferred from the court to the professional theatre, especially
after the construction of Dorset Garden in 1671, where the King
could see them without wrecking his treasury.[6] There were no
longer any such librettists as Ben Jonson, and definition had
become confused when works like *Circe*, *Albion and Albanius*, and
Venus and Adonis were called both masques and operas. Still the
most frequent practice, as in the earlier part of the century, was to
insert a short masque as a movement in a play. I find it impossible
to believe that Purcell had no hand in planning the text for the
masques in *The Fairy Queen*, for not only are they often different in
tone from the spoken dialogue, but it is through them that he is
able to impose a kind of unity out of disparateness, creating a
notable example of baroque art. There is little point in saying that
the Restoration audience did not share Jonson's ethical concept
of the masque—of course they did not—or that they were not
thrilled chiefly with the variety and sheer gaudiness of the spectacle—clearly they were—but it is obvious that the creative spirit
capable of bringing all this off was one of seriousness and integrity. If Purcell had demanded less than the highest that the
genre could give, the opera would have failed to attain anything
beyond pleasant irrelevancies, but, aware of the masque's noble
tradition, he was able to formulate from a most unpromising

[6] See below, p. 124. The sole example of a full-scale court masque under
Charles II is Crowne's *Calisto* in 1675. It cost something under £5,000 as
compared with more than £21,000 for Shirley's *Triumph of Peace* in 1634.

libretto a unified whole of rare beauty. Far too much is said about Purcell the genius of haphazard decoration, and (*Dido* aside) almost nothing of him as the genius of integral design. This is not to claim that *The Fairy Queen*, even in its musical portions, is impeccable, for he does not completely succeed with Act III, but the enormous score as a whole makes convincing an arrangement that looks on the face of it like a patchwork quilt, its masterly style bringing order to waywardness.

We can make quick work of the contribution of Elkanah Settle, if he is the anonymous librettist, for his only concern was to shorten Shakespeare's text in order to make room for the musical splendours. (In the 1692 text the length, omitting the songs, is slightly over 1,400 lines.)[7] This is managed by dropping Hippolyta and cutting most of Theseus, by reducing the wrangles of the four lovers (a happy stroke), and by moving the Pyramus and Thisbe play forward to Act III where it is treated as a rehearsal. Each of the last four acts ends with a masque-like entertainment ordered by either Titania or Oberon and devised to complement some aspect of the action immediately preceding. The revised version of the play presented the next year[8] cuts out the first scene where the lovers' quarrel is introduced and adds the musical interlude of the drunken poets. Thereafter it is identical with the first version except for the addition of two songs in later masques. Though Shakespeare's text is usually retained, the poetry is occasionally mangled, particularly in octosyllabic passages of Oberon and Puck which the librettist likes to turn into pentameter:

> I know there is a bank where wild Thyme blows,
> Where ox-lips, and the nodding violet grows,
> All over-canopied with woodbine sweet,
> Where eglantine, and where musk-roses meet.

---

[7] There is flagrant if not comical disagreement on how long the complete opera would have taken to perform. Dent has said 'over four hours', while Constant Lambert in the same publication has claimed seven hours. See *Purcell's Fairy Queen as presented by The Sadler's Wells Ballet and the Covent Garden Opera*: London, 1948.

[8] Dated 1692 (old style) and advertised on the title page as 'With alterations, additions, and several new songs'. The bibliographical complications of the two editions are discussed by Paul Dunkin: 'Issues of *The Fairy Queen*': *Library*, vol. XXVI (1946), p. 297.

The most odious transformation in the play is that inflicted upon Theseus' celebrated speech about lunatics, lovers, and poets, which makes one feel that the librettist, though curiously anonymous, is an ingrained show-off (another reason perhaps for suggesting Settle).[9] Since Purcell did not set a single line by Shakespeare, the text need detain us no further.

Restricted as he was to supplying masque-like shows at the ends of the acts, Purcell's ingenuity at mapping out large musical blocks that not only will be appropriate within themselves but will make sense in relation to each other and pull the whole opera into some semblance of a unified conception is quite staggering. In no other work are his powers of musician as dramatist taxed so severely. In each of the four masques his effort was to bring to a focus some large movement of the play, thus forging a link to what had preceded as well as establishing a point of progression towards the next movement. The conception is accordingly that of a continuum, no easy thing to do by music alone (the libretto is the frailest of props) when each masque is separated by a longish act of not very sensible spoken dialogue. For the moment we may ignore the interpolated scene of the drunken poets, which was admittedly an afterthought to Act I, and move to the ending of Act II. Purcell divides the scene into two parts: the first establishes the atmosphere of the fairy wood through various devices to be examined presently, while the second, the Masque of Night and Sleep, actually gives visual and aural embodiment to the midsummer night's dream. In Act II, at Titania's command to 'prepare a fairy masque to entertain my Love', he arranges a group of songs on the subject of love, and intersperses them with dances. Though the songs are divided between those appropriate to the clowns

[9] Lovers and lunatics have pregnant brains.
They in a moment by strong fancy see
More than cool reason ere could comprehend.
The poet, with the mad-man may be joined.
He's of imagination all made up,
And sees more devils than all hell can hold,
Can make a Venus of an Ethiop.
And as imagination rolls about,
He gives the airy fantasms of his brain,
A local habitation and a name.
And so these lovers, wand'ring in the night,
Through unfrequented ways, brim full of fear,
How easy is a bush supposed a bear!

and those suited to the lovers, with the dances given to the fairies, the impression of the whole is something of a hodge-podge, the least successful block of the score. Act IV celebrates the jubilation at the awakening of Titania and the birthday of King Oberon. Everything is pitched very bright and high, establishing the splendour of Oberon. The first half of the scene, triumphal celebration, is followed by a Masque of the Seasons, a more reflective extension of the joy: all nature, the seasons themselves, are a part of Oberon's universe, and come with their god Phoebus to praise him. The opera ends with a hymeneal masque, an epithalamion to the mortal lovers. It imbues them with a dignity almost approaching that of Titania and Oberon in the preceding act. Thus, as in Shakespeare, the play is brought to an end with a lyrical nuptial celebration which places the worrisome complications of the past hours in their proper perspective as merely a midsummer night's dream.

2

The Fairy Queen is the most difficult to discuss of all Purcell's theatre scores since, besides being much the longest, its four large musical scenes, for all their appropriateness to the world of the play, are separable from the action and from each other. It consequently demands of the student an historical sense of a kind that the music to *King Arthur*, growing out of plot situations, does not. Just as we must have some acquaintance with the musical style of a composition before we can appreciate its particular achievement, so knowing something of the masque convention is necessary for entering completely into the beauties of Purcell's opera. The masque's complete lack of dramatic motivation, so puzzling to us, was never a consideration to the more formalized ritualistic conventions of the seventeenth century. The same thing is apparent in Italy and France no less than in England. After the spectacular Venetian opera hit its stride in the 1630's, the Monteverdi model of highly passionate dramatic recitative languished, giving way to a series of glittering tableaux in works like the *Andromeda* and the *Bellerofonte* of Sacrati. Lully's operas in France, thoroughly impregnated with the ballet tradition, contain long scenes of processionals, sacrifice, pastorale, and descents of the deities, divertissements for eye and ear having little to do with the action of the opera. The modern instinct is of course to ask why these incidents happen, but it would no more have occurred to a seventeenth-century audience to question them than to ask why Orpheus must lose Eurydice. It is Purcell's distinction in *The Fairy Queen* not that he makes his masques indispensable to the action, which would be to demand the impossible, but that by sensitivity to the mood of the play he creates music which lifts the whole work from the realm of mediocre farce to that of ethereal enchantment. Again, the entire value of the work dramatically is Purcell's and his alone.

Originally he supplied no music for the first act beyond the usual orchestral preludes and overture. The casualness of these opening movements is indicated by his frequent borrowing from earlier works of his own, or by utilizing the tune of an instrumental movement for a song later on. The hornpipe here, for example, is the melody of his song 'There's not a swain in the plain' written a year later for the play *Rule a Wife and Have a Wife*. The first three items in the score are all fairly straightforward and vigorous; the delicacy of the fairy play is not suggested until the fourth, a simple rondeau, for all its brevity one of the rarest inspirations in Purcell. From the G minor-B flat major tonality there is an abrupt change to a bright D major trumpet call which opens the overture, a stirring martial movement with antiphony between trumpet and strings, to be taken up much later in the Oberon birthday masque. A fast dance movement in triple time completes the overture and the play begins. At the end of the first act Titania enters with her Indian Boy and commands her fairy choir to 'sing and entertain my dear'. A soprano and basso sing a duet beginning,

> Come, let us leave the town,
> And in some lonely place,
> Where crowds and noise were never known,
> Resolve to spend our days . . .

clearly intended to lead us into the Arcadian atmosphere of the play. The two voices weave in and out of a texture nicely balanced between antiphony and two-part harmony, with much repetition and decoration of words. As they try at the end to outdo each other with graceful spun-out rhythms on 'slide' ('Thus time shall slide away'), they suggest not only the humour but the delicate artificiality of the play. These are qualities difficult to combine with either point or taste. The score nearly always manages to do both.

Purcell's chief contribution to the act is the scene of the drunken poets which follows immediately. In this miniature comic drama, a descendant of the antimasque, the fairies lead in three drunken poets, one of them blinded. This blindfolded poet, after staggering through an opening song, 'Fi-fi-fi-fill up the bowl', is then turned about and pinched by the fairies until he confesses to being both drunk and 'scurvy', and is finally allowed to go to sleep after he promises to write a sonnet in their praise. Since he is a worthless poet this is dubious payment, but such illogicality is equally allowable in *A Midsummer Night's Dream* and in opera. It is a perfect little *dramma per musica*, a suitable musical complement to Bottom and the clowns, as well as a joke on the stuttering poet Thomas D'Urfey, and is most ingenious in the way that the ever-changing rhythms convey completely the pantomime of the scene. In making the stage directions explicit through the music, Purcell reaches the eye through the ear. The poet (a baritone) usually sings in plain triple time, but is continually being interrupted by rapid passages from the fairies in common time to 'trip it' or 'around' or 'pinch him'. The poet breaks in in triple time again, but his entries now are on the off-beat, suggesting his dizziness as he is turned round about in a game of blind man's buff. When he confesses, 'I'm drunk, drunk, as I live, boys, as I live, boys', the bass line lurches after him in close imitation, the timbre of the double-bass contributing to the comedy. (High strings would count for nothing.) The chorus of fairies alternates with two sopranos singing in close and very rapid imitation, giving a vivid impression of relentless pursuit. The movement works up to a splendid close with a short chorus of intricate polyphony to 'Drive 'em hence away', the complicated texture signifying utter rout and confusion, followed surprisingly by four bars of stillest calm, 'Let 'em sleep till break of day', which introduce a startling false relationship, music totally unlike anything in the score thus far. Only a baroque sensibility would expect a dying fall in so boisterous a comic movement, but this too

is the enchantment of the magic forest. We are now in the emotional frame to come under the spell of Titania.

Although the drunken poet scene is an amusing introduction to the freakish yet lyrical world of the play, it possibly blunts the effect of what Purcell had originally planned as his first scene, the masque at the end of Act II. This sizeable movement contains eleven separate numbers most imaginatively mapped out to woo the audience into a willing suspension of disbelief. It occurs after the Titania-Oberon quarrel, much reduced from Shakespeare and here the sole content of Act II. When Oberon storms out, Titania calls for the revels to begin, and Purcell at once sweeps us into the fairy realm. The scene he divides in two, creating appropriately complementary moods. The first six numbers, all in C major, are joyous. The swift little prelude suggests rustling of wings and introduces an exhilarating bravura air for tenor, 'Come all ye songsters of the sky', with long lines pouring out over a rushing ground. A brief instrumental movement of the nightingales follows, deliciously imitative of bird voices. The element of magic is now sounded in a double echo trio—spirit voices are heard from behind the scenes—succeeded by an echo dance offering ample opportunity for dynamic variation in the massing and volume of the trumpets. The entire chorus then takes over in 'Now join your warbling voices all'; by staggering their entries on 'warbling' Purcell has them all but gurgling with joy. Finally the skittish and mischievous side of the elves wells up in a capricious rhythm of the soprano's 'Sing while we trip it', taken up by the chorus.

Sing, sing while we trip it, trip, trip it, trip, trip it up-on the green....

Thus one side of the fairy world. But Purcell, like Shakespeare, and like Mendelssohn later, is equally concerned with something that reaches deeper: the mystery of the dream forest and its ethereal tranquillity. Titania's spoken lines:

> Sing me now to sleep,
> And let the sentinels their watches keep,

serve to call forth perhaps the supreme inspiration of the entire score, the entrance of Night with her train. This a perfect masque in miniature. The stately procession of allegorical figures—Night, Mystery, Secrecy, Sleep—suggesting that in a sense all the world is here, brings to mind Prospero's lines on the evanescence of man and his purposes. The accompaniment of music, flowing robes, slow dance, and dimly lit stage all induce serenity of spirit. What lingers in the memory from Shakespeare's very foolish play is the poignant impression that we are such stuff as dreams are made on, and our little life is rounded by a sleep. It is at this point in the score that Purcell recreates that experience.

Although there are five musical items, all in C minor, the episodes which bring about the alchemy are the songs of Night at the beginning and of Sleep at the end. Night is accompanied by the three upper strings which, entering in turn, one fragile layer of sound upon another, form a seventeen-bar introduction of incredible suavity before the languishing soprano air commences. This is built, like the introduction, upon a descending sixth, much of the seraphic repose owing to the predominantly descending melodic line. The only notable exception, a most effective contrast, is a spun-out gently rising line on 'murmuring' in which the harmony momentarily becomes major. Nothing is allowed to disturb the repose; the cellos and basses remain silent throughout, the chromaticism is not extreme, and no hint of any affective writing on words like 'noise', 'despair', or 'spite' ever creeps in. It is sublime music, sufficient in itself to elevate Titania to the Spenserian associations of her title. The two ensuing songs, those of Mystery and Secrecy, are brief and pleasant, the second being charmingly accompanied by two flutes, but they lack any special sense of characterization. Perhaps this was by design, the better to set off the haunting air of Sleep, 'Hush, no more', in which the measured silences between his muted exhortations take on dramatic significance. The song harks back to the rapt mood of Night's song, but the voices of bass soloist and chorus give it a quite different colour. The chorus, repeating Night's air in a slightly extended form with several subtle harmonic changes, gives the impression of pronouncing benediction upon a complete movement. Their words, together with the pregnant pauses in the music, suggest their actions as they slip quietly from the stage:

> Hush, no more, be silent all,
> Sweet Repose has closed her eyes,
> Soft as feathered snow does fall.
> Softly, softly steal from hence,
> No noise disturb her sleeping sense.

Mysterious dancers, 'the Followers of Night', are left to perform as Oberon squeezes the juice of the magic flower on the eyelids of the sleeping queen. The dance is in one of Purcell's more ingenious technical forms, a canon of four in two, which means that the first violin and bass are playing in strict canon, though a bar apart, simultaneously with the same relationship between second violin and viola. That the audience contained few musical connoisseurs aware of the composer's learning would in no way spoil the aptness of the dance as a graceful ending to the masque. And the masque is in this case the drama. It is not by the feeble spoken dialogue but through the music and its visual accompaniment in stage movement and dance that the fairy world is brought alive to the audience. Purcell has created the midsummer night's dream before our eyes and ears and enabled it to enter into the mind and heart. Before speaking of 'dramatic irrelevance' in connexion with these masques, one might ask what would be left were they removed.

Having said all this, I must admit now that in the music for

Act III the composer failed to achieve any kind of unity or even much sense of coherence. His problem was, of course, different from that of the previous act where he is persuading us to believe in the enchanted forest. Nor is there any large movement of the play to be brought to a focus or to a conclusion as in the two final acts. His only motivation is a direction from the voluble Titania:

> Away, my elves; prepare a fairy masque
> To entertain my love; and change this place
> To my Enchanted Lake.

When we remember that her love is Bottom wearing an ass's head, Purcell's uneasiness over what kind of entertainment to provide is understandable. In any event the action has reached a resting place, as in the Frost Scene of *King Arthur*, and the composer can really do little beyond providing something that is pretty in itself.

Fortunately the scenic aspects of the production relieved him of some responsibility, for it is at this point that the first of the beloved transformation scenes occurs. Not only do the painted shutters draw apart to reveal Titania's enchanted lake behind, but during the course of the scene two swans floating on the lake turn into fairies when they reach the bank, and, being ballerinas as well, dance to a graceful little air until they are frightened off by the Green Men (presumably savages) whose vigorous dance ensues. The savages are survivals of the grotesquerie of the antimasque, as in a milder vein are the bumpkin lovers, Corydon and Mopsa, whose duet is the most engaging number of the act. Purcell fills out the rest with songs on various aspects of love, none of them likely to appeal to Bottom. The first, 'If love's a sweet passion, why does it torment?', might be accompanied by some amusing pantomime between the Fairy Queen and her long-eared lover, its ludicrousness enhanced by the delicacy of the music, but it is more likely that this song, which Gay later took for *The Beggar's Opera*, was given as at a concert. Certainly a straight-forward kind of presentation would apply in the two bravura arias, 'Ye gentle spirits of the air' (added for the 1693 revival) and 'A thousand ways we'll find', both showing the motto beginning with repetitions of the ornate line in the best Italian fashion. We

are at a stylish recital. If Bottom is bewildered by all this refinement he can at least savour the low comedy of Corydon wooing
Mopsa (an alto disguised as a hulking shepherdess). In this music
depicting the lout's eagerness and the maid's affected modesty
Purcell suggests as much pantomime as he does with the drunken
poet earlier on. It shows again one of his most endearing traits,
and one of the most practicable for the theatre composer, a feeling
for personality and characterization. A great weakness of the
masque as a genre is its remoteness, even its lack of humanity in a
sense, for the concern is not with men but with either allegorical
personifications or heroes. It is what kills *Albion and Albanius* even
before Grabu puts in his oar. Yet Purcell in this most conventional of forms can break through with a bovine drab or a stuttering drunk. His earthier side, seen at its clearest in his numerous
catches, is a surprising and welcome addition to *The Fairy Queen*.
The chorus gives us a reprise of the last song in the set, but despite
the undeniable fact that a choral movement makes a good ending
to any group, in this case it can hardly be said to sum up anything
so disparate as the nine numbers.

With the fourth act we move on to another level altogether.
The time has come for elevation. The action itself, mainly taken
up with a reconciliation between Oberon and Titania, comes to an
end with a birthday masque on which Purcell lavishes some of his
finest music. He arranges it, as in Act II, in two parts, the first a
triumphal celebration, the second a miniature Masque of the
Seasons. The symphony which opens the festivities, replete with
kettledrums and trumpet calls, is the loudest and most sumptuous
number of the score, and employs the full resources of the
orchestra. It is in four movements, more complex than what
usually passes under the label of symphony in Purcell; for example,
besides the martial movements there is a canzone of intricate
counterpoint and a ravishing largo built on the chromatic scale
over a dominant pedal. The bright D major tonality dictated by
the trumpet establishes the joyful confidence of the celebration.
While this is going on the scene changes to a Garden of Fountains, and the stage directions call for a splendid sunrise. Over a
ground of wide leaps, the soprano, joined by the chorus, hails the
rising sun, which is linked with the birthday of Oberon. The
opening line contains an example of that unexpected phrasing

which is a delight in Purcell: the first cadence on 'sun' is not on the expected tonic, but on the mediant, the tonic being delayed another two bars:

A duet for altos, 'Let the fifes and the clarions and shrill trumpets sound', prolongs the jubilation and leads into a flourish of trumpets and drums betokening the entrance of the god Phoebus. Though he descends majestically in a machine and sings a brazenly self-advertising song, it is musically not very striking, perhaps because the A minor tonality pales before all the D major from trumpets and chorus. Another triumphal chorus with interesting alternation between common and triple time praises the great parent, 'light and comfort of us all'; if Phoebus cannot impress on his own, the chorus deputize admirably for him.

The second half of the act, the Masque of the Seasons, is the reposeful side of the celebration. It implies that Nature herself, the whole of the universe, is involved in this pageant of praise. The four seasons, richly costumed figures dear to the hearts of baroque painters and poets, participate in a ceremonial of solemn beauty designed to touch a deeper emotional chord. Here Purcell is reaching towards those more profound overtones of the masque that had interested Ben Jonson. However jaded or frivolous his auditors, however little they may have felt beyond the mere prettiness of the show, the composer himself was moved by the solemnity of a majestic tradition. He could not otherwise have achieved the nobility of the concluding pages.

Each of the four songs is preceded by a ritornello which undoubtedly accompanied a dance. The songs are given variety by differing from each other in key, form, and mood as well as in the type of voice designated. Spring's is the least original, relying heavily on dotted roulades on words like 'round' and 'tribute' that are virtually indistinguishable from many other passages in Purcell, but the two stanzas of Summer's infectious air illustrate his rhythmic variety within a very short triple-measured form.

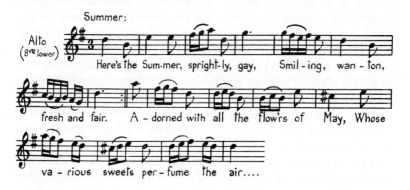

Autumn's 'See my many coloured fields' is a gently plaintive melody in long phrases of antiphony with two violins. But the masterpiece of the group is reserved for the last.

> Now Winter comes slowly, pale, meagre, and old,
> First trembling with age, and then quiv'ring with cold.

Beginning with a lonely high violin the four strings enter separately, each part built on a descending chromatic scale. Eventually the voice quietly commences with yet another chromatic descent, so that the contrapuntal texture is extraordinarily rich. Its complexity may be compared with the analogous basso song of the Frost Genius in *King Arthur* where there is only one chromatic line with the strings merely filling in the harmony. In the earlier song the vocal line at first seems unadventurous; it gradually ascends and then descends the scale, but this is in reality a telling dramatic stroke, for it gives the impression that he is too cold to move more than by inches. Here Winter's vocal line is of greater freedom, including at least one considerable leap which is made the more striking by the only major cadence in the piece. It is easy to imagine how this song, in beautiful contrast to everything that has gone before, lends weight and significance to the whole. The proof is at the end when the chorus 'Hail great parent' is repeated and is discovered to have taken on added grandeur.

And finally the last act. After the impressiveness of Act IV we may wonder what can remain to be done; the danger of anticlimax is in fact not entirely surmounted. Musically the grand concluding masque is a string of lovely separate numbers, but the smaller-scale episodes in the second and fourth acts are not only more unified from the musical point of view but are more persuasive dramatically. The principal function of the final masque is, as I have already said, to provide an epithalamion for the mortal lovers that will complement the celebration to Titania and Oberon. Its dramatic justification, in theory at any rate, is that in doing for the lovers what Act IV had done for the king and queen it rounds off the action with a balance beloved of Restoration and neo-classical audiences. In actuality it provides another theatrical spectacle, this one the showiest of all, for a public seemingly never glutted.

Purcell tackles the problem with his customary ingenuity and succeeds in pulling together a very sprawling series of lyrics. In the play the lovers had managed to get themselves straightened out, an accomplishment Theseus hails with his bemangled version of the famous speech on imagination, but he adds that he cannot believe the 'antick fables' and 'fairy toys' told by the lovers. Oberon, the contriver of it all, is sufficiently stung to put on a show.

DUKE: I hear strange music, warbling in the air.
OBERON: 'Tis fairy music, sent by me,
To cure your incredulity.
All was true the lovers told,
You shall stranger things behold. . . .

No less a personage than Juno herself, drawn in a chariot by peacocks, is the first of these strange things. Apparently she does not object to being so described for she obliges with a florid arioso, 'Thrice happy lovers', followed by a smooth triple-measured song, 'Be to one another true', mingling blessing and advice. This is mere prelude. As she disappears in her machine the scene changes to a fanciful Chinese garden, a magical realm where the rest of the opera takes place.[10] In one sense this Chinese scene is sheer extravaganza, but it is also a kind of apotheosis representing Paradise. Oberon has decreed, 'Let a new transparent world be seen,' and this is subsequently described in an alto aria sung by 'A Chinese Man'. The words make clear that it is a Garden of Eden:

Thus the gloomy world
At first began to shine,
And from the Power Divine
A glory round it hurled;
Which made it bright,
And gave it birth in light.
Then were all minds as pure,
As those ethereal streams;
In innocence secure,
Not subject to extremes.
There was no room for empty Fame,
No cause for Pride, Ambition wanted aim.

Preliminaries aside, the first part of the masque describes life in this ideal world of light and love. There is no reason on earth why it should be Chinese except the desire for yet another variety of sensuous experience; certainly in 1692 it could not have been any

[10] At this point in the 1693 revision the famous, but here completely in-appropriate, soprano aria known as 'The Plaint' was stuck in, an indication that it may already have become a popular favourite. It is a long and austere lament in D minor with violin obbligato, and bears a certain relation to Dido's farewell, for it is constructed on a descending chromatic ground and is rich in affective dissonances. Baroque taste would not resent the intrusion of so melancholy an air into the joyousness of the finale.

more authentically Chinese than *Turandot* but it is an elysium for lovers and suitable to the ending of the opera. About midway along Hymen (not exactly Chinese) is called up, and the work ends with an extended epithalamion.

One peril Purcell had to guard against was that of merely repeating himself in the music of jubilation and triumph, the prevailing moods of much of Act IV. The way he manages it is as clever as anything in the score. Oberon had been ushered in by a clarion major invocation replete with trumpets and drums. The invocation in Act V, a soprano air, is less grand, more intimate, and in a minor key. Phoebus appeared after a huge trumpet fanfare, but Hymen enters to a triple-time prelude of strings only. Phoebus, a tenor, began in florid declamation; Hymen is a basso with a more subdued (and more telling) song. The magnificent chorus 'Hail great parent' makes use of rolling counterpoint, while the hymeneal chorus which closes the opera, 'They shall be as happy as they're fair', is in triple time and mainly homophonic.

Every one of the sixteen separate musical items of the last act has some point of interest or distinction which may best be savoured by examining the score or hearing the recording. The variety of mood within the prevailing spirit of joyousness is always a wonder in Purcell. The alto's 'Thus the gloomy world' is a full-scale *da capo* aria with trumpet obbligato. Another trumpet aria, 'Hark, the ech'ing air', is a familiar showpiece for a few sopranos who can cope with its long bravura line, but it is even more attractive in the original score where it has a short choral finish, five rousing off-beat shouts of 'Hark!' (It was a mistake, however, to have it follow immediately upon another soprano air, 'Hark, how all things in one sound rejoice', because though the orchestral textures are very different, there is too much similarity in vocal timbre and in general sentiment.) A little love song for alto,

> Yes, Xansi, in your looks I find
> The charms by which my heart's betrayed,

is a familiar type of the period with gentle minor melody and dotted rhythms, but it never falls into cliché because of a persistent off-beat accompaniment which is irresistible:

The duet for sopranos heralding the god Hymen's entrance, 'Turn then thine eyes', has been revealingly analysed by Mr Holland as an example of Purcell's merging the principle of pictorial illustration (the series of triplets on 'turn') into that of abstract design (carrying on the triplets in an ascending sequence on 'flames', creating a consistency of formal pattern).[11] The impression of unity, the easy flowing of one number into another, is strengthened as usual by the tonality, here predominantly C major, the other possible key for the natural trumpet. He has returned to the key of the first important block of the original score, where (in Act II) we entered the enchanted wood.

The ending to such a large score, and, of course, to such a series of spectacles, presents the kind of challenge that has knocked many composers flat. Purcell's particular problem lay in devising a movement that would not only be impressive musically but which would also join the four great pillars of his opera, song, dance, drama, and sheer spectacle. His solution looks back in its plan and its stately splendour to the Jacobean masque. The last moments are given over to a reprise for full chorus and orchestra of the hymeneal paean,

> They shall be as happy as they're fair;
> Love shall fill all the places of care:
> And ev'ry time the sun shall display

[11] A. K. Holland: *Henry Purcell*: Penguin Books, London, 1948.

> His rising light,
> It shall be to them a new wedding day,
> And when he sets, a new nuptial night.

This follows immediately upon a spacious chaconne, the longest dance in the opera, in which presumably all the characters join, ending up in some attitude of obeisance before the throne of King Oberon, just as the masquers had done in the great days of Ben Jonson and Inigo Jones. Mortals and immortals are woven together in a pattern that joins elegant formalism with exuberant joy.

Thus the most elaborate spectacle of the closing decade of the century repeats the glories of the opening decades, as if the violent changes of the intervening years had never occurred at all. This may suggest an unruffled continuum in theatrical conditions that is not strictly accurate, but it also warns against the error too often encountered even now that the Restoration theatre represents a firm break with the past. Rather is this theatre an accumulation of all that had gone before pushed to the farthest limits and acquiring certain new directions in the process. *The Fairy Queen* combines the urbanization of a Shakespearean pastoral comedy, a familiar Restoration phenomenon, with the still remembered splendours of the Stuart masque. Without Purcell it would not have come to very much, but with him it is one of the important works of the seventeenth-century theatre. His vital importance to this kind of enterprise is a simple historical fact: some of his operas, their popularity unaffected by the advent of Italian opera, played on and on through the eighteenth century, occasionally gathering new bits and shedding old as revival followed revival,[12] but after his death in 1695 no new operas had much success, and very quickly all attempts at writing them ceased.

3

The accounts by such witnesses as Downes, Motteux, and Cibber of the success of *The Fairy Queen* make it plain that what

---

[12] At various times, for example, both *The Tempest* and *King Arthur* acquired new musical numbers from Dr Arne as well as extracts from other Purcell scores. Had the *Fairy Queen* score not been lost it would almost certainly have enjoyed a similar popularity. *Dioclesian* and *The Indian Queen* did not last as long, but continued to be played well into the eighteenth century.

swept the audience away was downright bedazzlement, the splendour of the scenes and machines in conjunction with lavish costumes and large musical effects. This kind of spectacle played such an important part in all Purcell's bigger theatre scores—we have already noted the Frost Scene and the concluding Masque of Britain from *King Arthur*—that an attempt should be made to recreate in our imaginations something of the stage picture. Actually without a considerable degree of this imaginative visualization we are cut off from a major segment of the seventeenth century theatrical experience both in England and on the Continent. Theorists were always at pains to explain the reasonable foundations upon which the great effects of baroque art were based. Its very irrationality and unexpectedness is, after all, a reason. That Sir Thomas Browne should enjoy losing himself in an *o altitudo*, in believing the inexplicable simply because it was inexplicable, seemed perfectly reasonable. To the creators of the spectacular Venetian opera, of the Parisian *théâtre des machines*, and of the Stuart masque, as well as to their audiences, the scenes and machines made perfect sense. There are so many apologists to choose from that one might suspect a puritan twinge of conscience lurking behind the joy in all this sensuous indulgence. The best documented of the spectacles are Italian, hardly surprising as Italians not only were first in the field but remained undisputed champions. When Evelyn commends an English spectacle he must add that it was much inferior to that of Venice.[13] In explaining the reasons for the visual aids to the drama, the Italian theorists insist that the appeal is to the mind and to the most elevated feelings. The machines were the technical means of introducing the supernatural into the plot; a god cannot merely walk on to the stage like an ordinary mortal. The scenes in perspective were to lead the senses away from servitude to the machines along lines suggested by the story, and to allow the imagination to play upon the intellect.[14] When Davenant produced *The Siege of Rhodes* at Rutland House in 1656, the scenery was not introduced as illusionary setting at all, but as an accompaniment to the opening mood of the play. In the first act the scene of the action shifts

[13] *Diary*, 5 May 1659.
[14] S. T. Worsthorne: *Venetian Opera in the Seventeenth Century*, p. 16: Oxford, 1954.

three times (once to Sicily), but the painted backdrop remains the same, the town of Rhodes facing the sea with a fleet of Turkish ships threatening on the horizon. It contributes to the atmosphere of a city under threat of siege, but is not a presentation of the actual surroundings of the protagonists. As Mr Southern has explained, 'It is high convention of the theatre, but is not within hailing distance of being naturalism. It is scenery in the stage sense of the decking of a stage, but not scenery in the landscape sense of a background seen behind people.'[15] A sense of this atmospheric though by no means illusionary setting is essential to understanding the effect of seventeenth-century spectacle. It is an art that petered out early in the next century, not to reappear until our own time in symbolism and expressionism, particularly as it is seen in ballet. The really ambitious productions of the eighteenth and especially the nineteenth centuries were loaded down with realistic impedimenta.

The spectacle became an end in itself, of course, and eventually, as Cibber so loudly complains, nearly wrecked the theatre. Unlike Ben Jonson, the librettist was usually content to follow the guidance of the designer. One of the Venetian opera's foremost triumphs, *Il Bellerofonte*, put on at the Teatro Novissimo in 1642, is remarkable not for the libretto by Nolfi or even for the music of Sacrati, but for the magnificent scenic designs of Jacomo Torelli, the drawings of which have survived along with a detailed explanation of how the machinery worked.[16] 'I freely confess', Nolfi says of his script, 'that in its composition I have not wished to observe other precepts than the sentiments of the inventor of the apparatus'; and further, '. . . the story, ruined from the Ancients, has been renovated by my pen in dramatic shape in the briefest of short times in order to receive the beauty of the machines and theatrical apparatus.'[17] In fine, a familiar myth was

[15] Richard Southern: *Changeable Scenery*, p. 114: London, 1952. This is easily the authoritative work on the technical problems of seventeenth- and eighteenth-century staging in England.

[16] Conte Maiolino Bisaccioni: *Apparati Scenici per lo Teatro Novissimo di Venetia nell' anno 1644 d'Inventione e Cura di Iacomo Torelli da Fano*: Venice, 1644. The most famous work on Italian staging is Nicola Sabbattini: *Practica di Fabricar Scene e Machine ne' Teatri*: Ravenna, 1638.

[17] Translated and quoted by Worsthorne, *op. cit.*, Appendix V, where also a number of Torelli's designs are reproduced.

to take on new life in the body of a highly intricate baroque design.

These designs, full of detailed perspectives stretching into far distances, are of staggering elaborateness. They also show machines for bringing on deities from behind the clouds (the commonest of all devices) and for accommodating Bellerophon mounted on a mechanical Pegasus. At the beginning of Act II he slays the dragon while flying back and forth in the air and darting from time to time to earth—singing the while. The costumes, rich as in any painting by Veronese or Titian, are also described in detail. The stage was arranged in much the manner of the later Inigo Jones masques and of the Restoration operas. On each side in diminishing perspective a series of flats (in some cases stationary mansions) representing buildings, colonnades, or trees remained immobile throughout the scene, while transformations took place either by changing the backdrop which appeared at the far point of the perspective—it was usually bisected down the middle so that it could be drawn apart to reveal another scene behind it—or by lowering machinery from the clouds. (The upper part of the back stage normally had its own apparatus, operated on grooves from above and independent of the lower half of the stage.) It must be remembered that the most ornate of the scenes, in distinction from the machines, are merely painted backgrounds which the actors and dancers performed in front of, not an environment in which they lived. Pictures had not yet merged into scenery. Thus we can understand how certain of the *Fairy Queen* scenes, which read as though they might overwhelm such engineers as Reinhardt or Ziegfeld, are actually quite manageable with a good scene-painter.

The accounts of English spectacles are very meagre beside those of the Italian and the French,[18] but Professor Nicoll, by assembling all the Inigo Jones designs of sets, costumes, and machinery which are preserved at Chatsworth, and interpreting them in the light of Serlio and Sabbattini, where all the mechanics are explained, leaves no doubt that England knew all the Italian devices, and in the court masques went a long way towards

[18] See H. Prunières: *Le Ballet de cour en France avant Benserade et Lully*: Paris, 1914.

reproducing them.[19] Jones himself once defined the masque as 'nothing else but pictures with light and motion', a nebulous enough definition but very suggestive of its appeal to the pure artist who can see time, space, and action bodied forth in flowing rhythmic patterns. It is at once airy nothing and palpable reality. The professional theatre was never able to equal the extravagances (in at least one sense) of the court masque, but in the decade of the 1630's it introduced more and more scenery after the royal pattern.[20] The greater part of this heritage passed on to the public stage at the Restoration. We have already noted the importance of Davenant, one of the last collaborators of Inigo Jones, who hired as his scenic designer for *The Siege of Rhodes* a pupil and assistant of Jones, John Webb. The line from the Caroline masque is all but unbroken.

During the first decade of the Restoration the spectacle was comparatively modest, partly because the two available theatres were not equipped with much in the way of machinery. Pepys, who adored any kind of gaudy splendour, reports very little. He loves the ballet of witches in *Macbeth*, but he says nothing about Hecate's flying machine, which she did not acquire till the next decade. The ordinary play would have no more than a few stock scenes with the simplest sets.[21] A real rouser like Dryden and Howard's *Indian Queen* (1664), later to be revived with a Purcell score, was largely a show of exotic costumes and painted scenery. It was mainly to supply this lack of machinery that Davenant's heirs built Dorset Garden in 1671 and began to put on operas. As we have seen already, it is their prompter, John Downes, who gives us the best evidence of just how elaborate and expensive these productions were. *The Fairy Queen* is one of the last.

The scenery for the spoken part of the opera is quite commonplace, 'A Wood near Athens'. It is here that the inserted interlude of the drunken poets takes place. Immediately upon their exit, 'The Indian Boy falls asleep, and to hide him from Oberon,

---

[19] *Stuart Masques and the Renaissance Stage.*

[20] See Alfred Harbage: *Cavalier Drama*: New York, 1936.

[21] In tragedy the usual scenes were grove, palace, and temple; in comedy, the room, hall, garden, and street. See Nicoll's discussion of stock scenery in *The Development of the Theatre*: London, 1927.

Titania causes the earth to open, into which he sinks'—merely a matter of a trap door. The scenic splendours do not begin until the masque at the end of Act II. After the lovers have been cleared off, Titania enters to a stage direction, actually a scenic description, which will illustrate the most familiar of all the perspective arrangements both in the Italian and French opera and in the English masque:

> The scene changes to a prospect of grottos, arbours, and delightful walks: The arbours are adorned with all variety of flowers, the grottos supported by terms, these lead to two arbours on either side of the scene, of a great length, whose prospect runs toward the two angles of the house. Between these two arbours is the great grotto, which is continued by several arches, to the farther end of the house.

It is a tripartite arrangement, a central bower flanked by two avenues in perspective. All that is lacking is the mass of clouds above the bower (upper backstage centre) which would part to reveal a deity in a machine, an effect Purcell reserves until later on. Of the four sets this is easily the simplest. In front of it the fairies dance their moonlight revels and the procession of figures who sing in the Masque of Night moves serenely by.

The next act ends with Titania commanding the stage hands to 'change this place to my Enchanted Lake'. Since changes of scenery almost invariably took place in full view of the audience, who delighted in this as an important part of the show, there is never any awkwardness about drawing off one series of side flats and replacing them with others; or, if the triangular pillars called *periaktoi* were used, they could simply be given a third of a revolution to present a new view. The advance of this set over the previous one in intricacy, and hence in dramatic excitement, is that it involves a transformation.

> The scene changes to a great wood; a long row of large trees on each side; a river in the middle; two rows of lesser trees of a different kind just on the side of the river, which meet in the middle, and make so many arches; two great dragons make a bridge over the river; their bodies form two arches, through which two swans are seen in the river at a great distance.... While a symphony's playing, the two swans come swimming on through the arches to the bank of the river, as if they would land; these turn themselves into

fairies, and dance; at the same time the bridge vanishes, and the trees that were arched, raise themselves upright.

The cardboard swans would disappear at the moment that two white-feathered ballerinas emerged from their places of conceal-ment, as in the second act of *Swan Lake*; the bridge, bifurcated in the middle, would be drawn off from the sides.

The masque celebrating King Oberon's birthday brings up the problem of special lighting effects, one area in which the modern student is apt to be scornful of earlier generations. Electricity has, of course, revolutionized stage technique, but even a casual examination of the masques or of the opera indicates that audi-ences must have derived much pleasure from the soft lights of candles and of lamps which were caught up in the glittering costumes, and whose intensity and colour could be changed very swiftly. First let us examine the description of the scene, ordered by Titania, the sovereign commander of the back-stage crew in *The Fairy Queen*.

> The scene changes to a garden of fountains. A sonata plays while the sun rises, it appears red through the mist, as it ascends it dissipates the vapours, and is seen in its full lustre; then the scene is perfectly discovered, the fountains enriched with gilding, and adorned with statues: The view is terminated by a walk of cypress trees which lead to a delightful bower. Before the trees stand rows of marble columns, which support many walks which rise by stairs to the top of the house; the stairs are adorned with figures on pedestals, and rails; and balusters on each side of 'em. Near the top, vast quantities of water break out of the hills, and fall in mighty cascades to the bottom of the scene, to feed the fountains which are on each side. In the middle of the stage is a very large fountain, where the water rises about twelve foot.

The opening of this scene was most probably managed by setting what Nicoll calls 'diaphonal glasses'—glass lamps whose globular bowls were filled with coloured liquid—in front of other lamps or torches all concealed behind the side flats. The lamps had metal reflectors behind them to intensify the glow. First seen through a transparent curtain or skrim, then, as the skrim is drawn away simultaneously with the red bottles leaving a much brighter natural light, the effect of the description is perfectly achieved. As for the scene itself, the cypress trees and statues would be painted in diminishing perspective on the side flats while the sumptuous series of stairs and fountains can only have appeared on the painted backdrop. After the triumphal chorus, 'Let the fifes and the clarions and shrill trumpets sound', a cloud machine, doubtless flaming in splendour, descends from overhead in the middle distance, momentarily blocking out the distant prospect of the waterfalls:

A machine appears, the clouds break from before it, and Phoebus appears in a chariot drawn by four horses.

The Masque of the Seasons follows with Phoebus viewing it from his machine or, more likely, alighting to join Titania and Oberon on their dais.

The final masque, the most spectacular by far, gives us not only another *deus ex machina* but also, with the Chinese scene, an important clue as to who painted the scenery. It will be remembered that after the lovers' tangles are unravelled the goddess Juno 'appears in a machine drawn by peacocks. While a symphony plays the machine moves forward, and the peacocks spread their tails, and fill the middle of the theatre.' This implies, I think, that after the clouds have drawn apart the machine is lowered to the stage and the divinity steps forward and sings while the peacocks are spreading their tails to make a colourful background for her.[22] After her song of blessing she returns to her chariot and is drawn upward and away. Oberon, for once getting in before Titania, orders that 'a new transparent world be seen', which is described in the stage directions:

While the scene is darkened, a single entry is danced; then a symphony is played: after that the scene is suddenly illuminated, and discovers a transparent prospect of a Chinese garden, the architecture, the trees, the plants, the fruit, the birds, the beasts quite different to what we have in this part of the world. It is terminated by an arch, through which is seen other arches with close arbours, and a row of trees to the end of the view. Over it is

---

[22] Juno and her peacocks had already appeared in *Albion and Albanius*, and were revived for George Powell's *Brutus of Alba*, or *Augusta's Triumph* (1696), an opera which may have utilized some of the *Fairy Queen* sets (see especially the descriptions at the opening of Acts II and III). As the title and the opening description of Augusta and Thamesis indicate, this whole unsuccessful enterprise was suggested by *Albion*.

a hanging garden, which rises by several ascents to the top of the house; it is bounded on either side with pleasant bowers, various trees, and numbers of strange birds flying in the air, on the top of a platform is a fountain, throwing up water, which falls into a large basin.

The simplest device for darkening the stage was to close a pair of shutters fairly far forward, leaving plenty of room for the dancers at the front, who would be illumined by the chandeliers in the house itself and probably by side stage lights as well. This allowed time for the Chinese garden to be put into position behind the shutters, which would then be drawn back to reveal the 'transparent prospect'. Clusters of lamps with reflectors would be attached to the backs of the rows of side flats (the colonnade of arches), providing brilliant light for the 'new transparent world'. Lights could also be placed on movable machines worked by pulleys at the sides or the top of the stage. The hanging gardens with the birds and fountains were painted on the back scene.

Although this scenery could not much have outlasted the century, and no record of the designer's identity has survived, the recent acquisition of a set of decorative panels by the Victoria and Albert Museum enables us to make an almost certain conjecture as to who he was and what his stage designs would look like. The painter is Robert Robinson, an English decorator whose speciality was the painting of rococo *chinoiserie* long before that style properly came into being. He has left a painted room[23] depicting a fantastic primitive world mixing the remote east with the even remoter west, and which Mr Edward Croft-Murray, to whom we owe the ascription to Robinson, thinks was inspired by Aphra Behn's *Oroonoko*. Mrs Behn describes 'a Continent whose vast extent was never yet known, reaching from East to West; one way as far as China, and another to Peru'.[24] The Victoria and

[23] Formerly no. 5 Botolph Lane, now in Sir John Cass's School, Duke Lane, Aldgate.

[24] In his article 'Robert Robinson, Painter of Chinoiseries' (*Country Life Annual*, 1955, pp. 174–9) Mr Croft-Murray describes the panels thus: 'A prince takes the air before his pavilion; a princess dashes by in her light stag-drawn chariot; along a waterway, skirting the turrets of a fairy city glides a party of ladies and gentlemen in their gondola, as richly caparisoned as any which ply on the Grand Canal in one of Canaletto's regattas.' This is followed with a description of the exotic flora and fauna of this imagined world.

Courtesy of Country Life Annual

PLATE III   Robert Robinson: *Imaginary Landscape*

PLATE IV   Robert Robinson: *Imaginary Landscape*

Courtesy of Country Life Annual

Albert panels show us airy pagodas, misty hills and glens with palm trees, quaint round-faced figures surrounded by exotic birds and beasts—pictures from a land remote and unreal enough to stimulate the fancy. We know that Robinson worked for the theatre as well: there exists a contract with Elkanah Settle, the probable librettist of *The Fairy Queen*, for 'severall sets of scenes and Machines for a new Opera', for 18 March 1700, probably *The Virgin Prophetess; or The Fate of Troy*, first performed at Drury Lane in 1701. In the light of these things, as well as the fact that almost nothing else of the Chinese found its way into the Restoration theatre, Robinson would seem to be our artist.[25] If the sets of the fifth act, and perhaps of the whole opera, were painted in Robinson's *style chinois*, they must indeed have ravished the sense and, together with Purcell's music, created the ideal world for a fairy queen.

[25] The best known source for the Chinese during the period is John Ogilby's translation of *An Embassy from the East-India Company of the United Provinces to the Grand Tartar Cham, Emperor of China* (London, 1669), with numerous engravings showing pagodas, yaks, palm-trees, fringed umbrellas, and people in vague, bundlesome, undistinctive costumes. It is revealing to note the names of the leading characters in Settle's play, *The Conquest of China* (1675); they are Orunda, Alcinda, Amavanga, Quitazo, and Lycungus. The cult *chinois* is of course eighteenth century and is well chronicled by B. S. Allen in *Tides in English Taste* (Cambridge, 1937).

CHAPTER V

Dioclesian & Bonduca

I

PURCELL'S major theatre scores are *Dido and Aeneas*, *King Arthur*, and *The Fairy Queen*. Since of these *Dido* was written for a school performance and *The Fairy Queen* as an ingenious Shakespearean adaptation, *King Arthur* remains the sole example in the composer's output of a work from the very beginning conceived as an opera for the professional stage and planned in terms of a large-scale libretto. He composed four other theatre scores large enough to be considered operas, in every case for a play which had proved its popularity with more than one generation of playgoers, a veritable classic of the repertory, and was now being brought forward to take on new dimensions as a 'dramatic opera'. On the face of it this merely means 'with musical additions', as we know, but in actuality Purcell's music assumes such a dominating position as to become in at least two of these productions, *Dioclesian* and *The Tempest*, the controlling element of the work.

In *Dioclesian*, particularly, everything is under the spell of music and gains significance from it. Not only is this work a great deal better than Fletcher's play *The Prophetess* on which it is based, but all its superiorities are owing to the musical additions which make of it an impressively beautiful work of stately elegance. No one would expect that turning a play into a musical could ever produce quite the kind of organic unity achieved by *Dido* and *King Arthur*. Here Purcell's task, though less complicated, was actually more difficult, because even if the amount of music and its controlling function was less than in *King Arthur*, the problems of working it into an already existing and clearly etched play were more formidable. It is simply the difference between being brought in as a partner on the ground level and being drawn in at a later stage after all the policies have become immutably fixed. Purcell apparently enjoyed the challenge such a metamorphosis involved, for after the great success of the opera he devoted himself almost exclusively to the theatre. Although he had supplied incidental songs and dances for an occasional play as early as 1680, *Dioclesian* opened up a vein he had not really mined and led immediately, as we have seen, to *King Arthur*.

The Prophetess was the most successful of Fletcher's collaborations with Philip Massinger (not Beaumont, as most commentators have it), a play as popular after the interregnum as before. The fact that it appeared in 1622[1] at the highest point in the fortunes of the court masque suggests perhaps the major influence upon the play as well as a clear link with the Restoration; for although the great Beaumont and Fletcher folio of 1647 labels it a 'tragical history', the heavy reliance upon music, spectacle, and supernaturalism aligns it fairly closely with what the Restoration regarded as an opera. *The Prophetess* is certainly swelled with action enough for several plays, but as dozens of operas including all the early Verdi well testify, this is not always incompatible with a serviceable libretto. When Betterton in 1690 turned his practical commercial eye upon it with the intention of making as much as possible of the spectacular scenes, he made no noticeable changes in the action, so perfectly did it suit his notion of a good opera. Since he added texts for various incidental songs and choruses as well as for the final masque, which is entirely sung, he found it necessary to reduce the length of some of the speeches and occasionally to purify (as he thought) the diction, but the plot remained intact.

The scene is ancient Rome, that civilization concerned exclusively, as we know from countless dramatists, with love and war. The prophetess Delphia acts as a highly talented mistress of ceremonies in both these activities, directing her powers principally upon four characters. Her niece Drusilla is engaged to marry the

---

[1] On 14 May according to the manuscript of the licenser, Sir Henry Herbert. Herbert chose it for his own benefit later in the decade, a clear indication of its success. On its stage history see G. E. Bentley: *The Jacobean and Caroline Stage*, vol. III, p. 394: Oxford, 1956.

young soldier Diocles, an apathetic lover but mighty in arms and
ambition. Delphia prophesies that he will become emperor when
he slays a great boar, a prophecy fulfilled when, in a flamboyant
scene, he exposes and then kills one Aper (the Boar), who has
secretly murdered the late emperor. In the ensuing jubilation
Diocles is proclaimed emperor, a dignity signalized by his assuming the name of Dioclesian, and is also awarded the hand of the
late emperor's sister Aurelia. So spellbound is he by her beauty
that he forgets his vows to the less glamorous Drusilla.

Act III opens with a counter action involving the other leading
character, Dioclesian's nephew Maximinian, seen thus far as
simply a bold warrior but now revealed as jealous of his uncle's
power and himself violently in love with the princess Aurelia.
He appeals for aid to the prophetess, who is of course already
angered at Dioclesian's jilting of her niece. Delphia plies her magic,
and the air is thick with intrigue and misadventures until Dioclesian, contrite, again pledges his fidelity to Drusilla. Thus does he
regain the delphic backing which enables him to triumph over the
Persians in a huge battle at the end of Act IV. Finally, all am-
bitions realized, he resigns his crown to Maximinian (who now
has won the beautiful Aurelia) and declares that he will devote his
remaining years to simplicity and retirement—and Drusilla. The
speech, interesting as an echo of Cardinal Wolsey's 'Long farewell
to all my greatness', which Fletcher (a student of *Othello*) had
written ten years earlier, gives an idea of the tone and the quality
of the poetry.

> Hitherto
> I have lived a servant to ambitious thoughts
> And fading glories: what remains of life
> I dedicate to Virtue; and, to keep
> My faith untainted, farewell, pride and pomp!
> And circumstance of glorious majesty,
> Farewell for ever.

In the last act, after the ubiquitous prophetess has thwarted an
attempt on Dioclesian's life by the still-jealous Maximinian, she
puts on an elaborate rustic masque in honour of Dioclesian and his
wife, and the opera is over.

As a 'tragical history', such a curious series of actions, far more
jumbled than this simplified précis, plainly leaves something to be
desired. As heroic-operatic romance it is thoroughly entertaining.

To fall under its spell one must accept the tenets of the Beaumont and Fletcher world, must enter willingly into that realm of romance which is built upon a withdrawal from reality. It is the world of tragi-comedy which, notwithstanding its great vogue early in the century, is really the *donnée* of all heroic drama and of Purcell's operas. They deliberately sought fairyland, and sought a mood which Miss Ellis-Fermor has described as 'lying somewhere between the light-heartedness of unshadowed comedy and the apprehension of shock and mystery which attends a tragic catastrophe'.[2] It is the ideal terrain for operatic inspiration.

In *The Prophetess* we find ourselves in a remote setting which yet vaguely and subtly suggests that the weight of history has been added to the gossamer of romance and magic. The courts of the Romans and Persians provide a pageant of exotic splendour against which the heroic actions and declamations of the principal personages seem quite natural. They are like figures in a slow ballet or in a tableau, struck in elegant and commanding postures as they pour forth their aggrandized sentiments. In this formalized world, character types are appropriately simplified. Dioclesian is the noble warrior-hero who at the end prefers peace of mind to wealth and glory. He is at no point a particularized being, but rather an ideal of what is heroic. Drusilla is the wistful love-lorn heroine, a type exquisitely elaborated in several of the most famous Beaumont and Fletcher plays, badly treated, all-forgiving, and ultimately rewarded. Aurelia is the haughty beauty who gets her come-uppance, Aper the murderous villain, Dioclesian's servant Geta a near relation of the *miles gloriosus*, and so on. They are all convenient dramatic counters, easily manipulable, superficially believable.

It is largely by virtue of these familiar types that opportunities abound for those generalized statements on universal themes which were to become so much admired by Restoration and eighteenth-century playwrights, speeches which detach themselves from the background and become set pieces. They are the natural 'aria situation' of eighteenth-century opera, and betoken a frame of mind in which the illusion of realism, whether in speech or action or pace, plays no part. Dioclesian lamenting the fickleness of the gods—was there ever an heroic play without this moment?—

[2] *Jacobean Drama*, p. 204: London, 1936.

reveals Fletcher's fondness for specific statement as well as the rhetorical effectiveness characteristic of the verse in general.

> Talk not of comfort: I have broke my faith,
> And the gods fight against me; and proud man,
> However magnified, is but as dust
> Before the raging whirlwind of their justice.
> What is it to be great, adored on earth,
> When the immortal powers that are above us
> Turn all our blessings into horrid curses,
> And laugh at our resistance?

Although this speech was written in 1622, it is unmitigated heroic both in the rhetorical language and the concept of the hero, whose pitch is clearly as high as it is wrought up. The affinities of Restoration and Jacobean drama are more remarkable than their differences.

This conception of characterization and speech, strained to its farthest in the figure of the prophetess Delphia, is congruent with a common feature of tragi-comedy, its nebulous character motivation. As his first objective the dramatist conceives of a striking situation or a colourful emotional crisis, the motivation being worked up afterwards—if possible. It is like designing the façade before drawing up the floor plan. If the whims of an omnipotent prophetess are all the motivation he can contrive, then, that will have to serve. This accounts for our impression of brilliant, detachable scenes rather than organic wholes, and helps to explain why the set rhetorical speech is so excellently adapted to this genre. The play lacks cumulative force; the sum is less than its parts.

This is the dramaturgy of most operas. Even Wagner, always claiming to be more responsible than other librettists, in the second act of *Die Walküre* turns the entire story upon the moods of a petulant goddess, but the power of his music is such that we do not mind. In a play the consequences may be more serious. A single illustration from *The Prophetess* will suffice before we turn to the music. At the opening of the third act Maximinian enters alone, a man we know as a bold soldier, a kinsman and intimate of the hero. He bursts at once into agitated speech:

> What powerful star shined at this man's nativity,
> And blessed his homely cradle with full glory?

What throngs of people press and buzz about,
And with their humming flatteries sing him Caesar!
Sing him aloud, and grow hoarse with saluting him!
How the fierce-minded soldier steals in to him,
Adores and courts his honour!

The entire speech, in fact the entire episode, has an obvious
theatrical appeal, but nothing we had seen in Maximinian has in
any way prepared for this turn. If rankling jealousy had been
tearing at him all along, why were we allowed to see no hint of it
earlier? The answer is simply that the authors could find no motivation for it. Later in the scene Delphia tells us that it is she who
through magic has inspired Maximinian's passion in order that
he may win Aurelia from Dioclesian. In a play of supernatural
effects this may pass for sufficient motivation and enable us to
enjoy the several turbulent situations that result from it. The
examples could be easily multiplied; character in these plays is
constantly sacrificed to plot and situation.

All this forces upon our minds the fact that *The Prophetess* is a
play which music will considerably enhance. From the beginning
it is conceived as a masque-like extravaganza with Delphia's
magic the pretext for spectacle. Music introduced at the appropriate moment can become symbolic of her occult powers. This
is the hint that Betterton worked on in his adaptation; all the new
lines are for songs, all the new stage directions for tableaux or
spectacle.[3] To say that the story would be unaffected if the music
and spectacle were removed (whether from Fletcher or Betterton)
is pointless, for the play thus stripped would not only have been a
failure on the stage but would not even have been conceived of
in the first place. Thus the heavier responsibility in the 1690
adaptation will obviously be not Betterton's but Purcell's. It is
only the composer who can take the stilted and sprawling (though
sporadically effective) vehicle and shape it into some sort of unity
of impression, and through his seriousness elevate it at times to a
grandeur of expression totally absent from the play. In short, the
finer qualities of *Dioclesian* are purely musical. We shall now see
how Purcell brings this about.

[3] It is almost certain that none of the original lyrics had survived, for the
usual practice in the 1647 Beaumont and Fletcher folio is to print the words
of all songs, if they are to be had. In *The Prophetess* we find merely 'Music' or
'Loud Music', 'Dance', 'Song', etc.

2

Of the five divisions of Purcell's score to *Dioclesian*, two are to some extent detachable from the play. They are the customary curtain tunes and overture, which at least suggest the mood and set the predominant tonality of the score, and more important, the elaborate masque at the end which greatly influences our final impression of the work as a whole. The three middle groups of musical pieces are vital parts of the action itself.

Although Professor Dent, the only critic to treat the opera at any length,[4] has curiously concentrated most of his attention on key relationships, he points out two important facts about the score. First, the greater part of the music is not associated with supernatural effects, with visions or incantations, the almost invariable rule in operatic plays of the Restoration, but with scenes of purely human character. This is even true of the masque where we should expect it least of all since the principals are given the names of classical gods. The other notable fact about the music is that it is performed largely by the crowd of men and women who form in effect an operatic chorus. Though the chief actors of the drama could not sing, to treat the crowd as singers gives the play a musical background and the music humanity. Betterton, concerning himself primarily with the places where music might be introduced for spectacular effect, has for these occasions strung together some lyrics of no special merit. The beauty of the result is Purcell's.

The purely musical device by which the composer achieves continuity and coherence is a familiar one, the grouping of the various numbers of each act in a pattern of key relationships and the relating of each act to the others in like manner. The principal key of *Dioclesian* is C major, a key to which the score of thirty-six numbers returns again and again, and around which related keys and other easily accessible keys (particularly the tonic minor) revolve. The predominant tonality is firmly established in the instrumental opening, for 1690 very elaborately scored with trumpets, oboes, and bassoons in addition to the usual strings and continuo.

The first operatic episode does not come until the big ceremonial scene at the end of Act II. Betterton divides the musical

[4] Dent: *Foundations of English Opera*, pp. 197–205.

portion of the scene into three parts, first, a group of two songs celebrating the hero's slaying of the murderous Aper, second, two songs accompanying the crowning of Dioclesian as emperor, and third, wholly instrumental, a dance of furies to indicate Delphia's rage when Dioclesian forsakes her niece for the queenly Aurelia. The problem before the composer was how to achieve diversity of mood as well as musical variety in the four songs, and at the same time to invest the whole movement with a sense of unity, even inevitability.

The stage picture is striking. Throughout the scene the prophetess and her niece are seated in her celestial chariot, evidently perched in the middle distance upon a machine which was concealed in folds of light material to represent clouds.[5] Below we see the bold Dioclesian tear open the curtains of a litter containing the body of the dead emperor, publicly revealing the murder to the horrified soldiers ranged around. After several heroic declamations about honour and justice, he slaughters Aper in full view of everyone, while the invisible Delphia shouts, 'Strike music from the spheres!' The stage direction requires 'A Symphony of music in the air' as the introduction to the first song. Since the music for the entire scene is to be ceremonial in nature and suggestive of praise and thanksgiving, Purcell takes great pains to distinguish different aspects of this general mood, so that at no time do we feel that he is merely repeating himself. Accordingly, the first mood is one of awestruck contemplation of the deed and the might of the deliverer. A deep-voiced priest intones the G minor arioso, 'Great Diocles the boar has killed', the full chorus replying with two prolonged 'Sing Io's'. Then, more excited, they burst into contrapuntal calls of 'Praise the thund'ring Jove', but settle again into quiet four-part harmony at the closing words,

> Pallas and Venus share,
> Since the all-charming Queen of Love
> Inspires the God of War.

The sensuous appeal of the accompanying strings underlines the stately beauty of the opening mood without introducing any bright orchestral colour. In this manner has Purcell established

[5] Cf. the line from Hecate's song in the operatic *Macbeth*, 'Sits in a foggy cloud and waits for me'. The clouds added mystery to stage 'flights' and transformation scenes.

the dignity and impressiveness that the text calls for but never really evokes in itself. The music is more than an echo of the sense: it *is* the sense.

The first song of the score, 'Charon, the peaceful shade invites', a slow air for soprano and two flutes, follows without pause. The impression is actually that of a trio, for the three melodic lines weave gently about each other in Purcell's favourite key of languishment, G minor. The lines of the text suggest sympathy for the slain tyrant, an indication that characterization is irrelevant; they are here solely to give Purcell an opportunity for a momentary tenderness which will more strikingly usher in the massive choral paean of rejoicing, 'Sound all your instruments of war'. A duet between soprano and basso alternates with the chorus while the strings are augmented by oboes and trumpets, the increased richness of sound adding to the unrestrained jubilation, very different from the solemn joy of the opening mood.

As in *King Arthur* the musical sections are separated by short passages of spoken dialogue, not unlike the Sarastro portions of *The Magic Flute*. The effect of this is to keep up the lofty and incantatory quality of the scene without ever losing contact with the play itself, which might be the result were the scene entirely sung. Maximinian proposes Diocles for emperor, and the senators and soldiers joyously concur. During the songs which follow he is invested with imperial robes and (to judge from the words) entertained with simultaneous dancing and singing. The alto solo, 'Let the soldiers rejoice', is a smooth triple-time dance movement in the simplest binary form. Its refrain is scored for trio, the alto and tenor singing mainly in thirds and answered antiphonally by the basso. The form, a fourfold repetition of the phrase, 'Rejoice with a general voice', illustrates one of the happiest and most characteristic devices of all Purcell's theatre music in its creation of emphasis without monotony. In this instance the phrase takes up five bars the first two times it is given out, then six bars, and finally eight. The augmentation is often achieved by ornaments in his favourite dotted rhythms, as here on 'rejoice', and full cadences are avoided by overlapping of phrases.

Purcell understood that repetition of words is very important in all theatre music and an absolute necessity where the chorus is involved. Everyone is familiar with the numb exhaustion that can result from sitting through a Hugo Wolf song recital, say, where one must strain to catch each word. (The custom of printing the texts in the programme speaks for itself.) It is a completely untheatrical practice, despite the fact that Wagner categorically refused to allow repetition in his librettos, and in the earlier *Ring* operas would not even permit two characters to sing simultaneously in a duet. It was unrealistic, as though the mere act of setting a text to music had not already freed him from every consideration of realism. Purcell's aesthetic is of course far more practicable, and in its many repetitions much less monotonous than most Wagnerian declamation. The music of this number is happy in mood, but different from the jubilation of the previous movement, for its suavely graceful tune and its relaxed triple rhythms suggest ease rather than exultation. And, unusual for Purcell, there are almost no suggestions of chromatic or even minor harmonies in any of it.

For the climactic movement of the music, easily the most interesting and technically the most brilliant, we should have the words before us:

> Since the toils and the hazards of war's at an end,
>   The pleasures of love should succeed 'em;
> The Fair should present what the Senators send,
>   And complete what they have decreed 'em.
>
> With dances and songs, with tambours and flutes,
>   Let the maids show their joy as they meet him;
> With cymbals and harps, with viols and lutes,
>   Let the husbands and true lovers greet him.
>
> Let the priests with processions the hero attend,
>   And statues erect to his glory;
> Let the smoke from the altars to heaven ascend,
>   All sing great Diocles' story.

It is obvious that the treasury of poetry has not here been much enriched. The first line is ungrammatical, and the third and fourth downright obscure, nor is the breezy shortening of 'them' much of an adornment. And why the husbands and true lovers are introduced in line eight remains a mystery. Worse, all three verses are in the same overemphatic anapaestics, and, apart from several pictorial possibilities, might seem to offer a composer nothing

beyond a walloping entrance or exit chorus. Yet Purcell not only
treats each of these stanzas in a manner entirely different from the
others (can the powers of imaginative discrimination reach
further?), but in the first and last stanzas he actually ignores the
poet's rhythms and creates new ones of his own that are dramatically
compulsive. As Aurelia is now to enter, the attention will be
turned from martial glory to love. The opening stanza accordingly
employs two flutes to accompany the alto arioso which is set over a
predominantly pedal bass, the suspensions creating frequent
chromaticism. The harmonies are thus richer than at any previous
place in the score—the harmonies in Purcell are always of more
significance than whether a number is grave or gay—and we have
advanced far beyond the simple non-chromatic arioso by solo
bass which opened the scene.

For the second stanza he continues with the alto and flutes
and writes a chaconne on an unchanging ground of five bars.
Here the triple metre and the melodic line follow with fair strict-
ness Betterton's anapaestic rhythm, though Purcell's familiar
pictorial representation of 'joy' by dotted rhythms gives a feeling

of spontaneity and freedom. The most fascinating feature of the movement is the disregard of the melody for the periodic returns of the chaconne bass, the technical basis of Dido's famous lament, thus setting the anapaests against another pattern and doubling (at least) the musical interest. That a dance accompanied this stanza is indicated not only by the words and by the chaconne form but also by a short ritornello after the singing has ended.

The treatment of the third stanza is quite different, a masterly example of contrapuntal structure in a quartet of voices who sing the first three lines, combined with sonorous homophony from the chorus at the end. In the quartet, layer upon layer of sound is added in the staggered entrances of the voices beginning with the basso, each higher voice entering in turn—this scene doubtless suggested by the line, 'Let the smoke from the altars to heaven ascend'—and making a rich harmonic texture because of the constant alteration of the triad. At the last line the oboes join all the voices for a majestic climax, the words trebly repeated with subtle and unexpected rhythmical variation.

Thus from Betterton's pedestrian lyrics has Purcell forged a massive musical movement combining his feeling for dramatic moments of pictorial representation and surprise with his care for larger effects and the more formal aspects of his art. In laying out the score with painstaking attention to such matters as the variation of musical forms and the alteration of voices in the various episodes, he has achieved the illusion of a happy balance between freedom and restraint, between formality and gusto. Besides bringing to life the latent possibilities of a somewhat stilted and rhetorical stage situation, he has created a self-contained musical composition of infinite variety and beauty. The more meticulously one studies Purcell's theatre scores the more astonishing appears their ability to expand, or better to recreate, the dramatist's text in purely musical terms, thereby realizing a quite different and much more powerful effect than that of bare words. His genius, in other words, is eminently operatic.

It is of course easy to see that this scene from *Dioclesian* is not quite opera. The English public were (and are) stubbornly opposed to the idea that any Englishman might express his emotions, let alone act out his destiny, in song. Although *Dioclesian* was a great hit, his countrymen's infuriating lack of imagination must have caused Purcell to despair when reading a critic like Charles Gildon who objects to its success on the grounds of good sense:

> Sometimes a song or a dance may be admitted into a play without offending our reason . . . but always with a regard to the scene; for by no means must it be made a business independent of that: In this particular our operas are highly criminal, the music in 'em is for the most part an absurd impertinence: for instance, how ridiculous is it in that scene in The Prophetess, where the great action of the drama stops and the chief officers of the army stand still with their swords drawn to hear a fellow sing, Let the soldiers rejoice—'faith in my mind 'tis as unreasonable as if a man should call for a pipe of tobacco just when the priest and his bride are waiting for him at the altar.[6]

Men like Gildon should keep out of the theatre. When we look at the extreme exaggerations of heroic plays it is inconceivable that critics, and they include Dryden, could speak of musical scenes as 'offending our reason'. What Purcell has made of *Dioclesian* has utterly eluded Gildon. Though he is the man who admired *Dido*

[6] *Comparison between the Two Stages*, 1702.

and Aeneas sufficiently to stick it as a masque into his adaptation of *Measure for Measure*, he cannot see that the stature of Diocles and the grand solemnity we associate with his presence is the creation not of Fletcher or of Betterton but of Purcell.

What made the Gildons of the world return several times to *Dioclesian* was probably the splendour of the spectacle and the intoxication they felt at its prevailing exoticism. That it would all have fallen flat without the music escaped their notice. At the ending of this very scene, for example, the prophetess angrily breaks up the rejoicing with thunder, lightning, and a monster. The stage direction reads, 'The music flourish. They who made the monster separate in an instant, and fall into a figure, ready to begin a Dance of Furies.' The darkness and turbulence is conveyed as much by the composer as by anything occurring on the stage. In the next act there is a 'Chair Dance' accompanying some comic discomposure of Geta, exactly what it is impossible to say, taking place amidst a very lavish *mise-en-scène* 'representing the entrance into the inner part of a magnificent palace', which undergoes a magical transformation later on.

The third act also contains one of Purcell's most popular songs, 'What shall I do to show how much I love her?', a good example of the way music can strengthen the dramatic cogency of a situation. In the play the mutual passion suddenly engulfing Maximinian and Aurelia is an arbitrary and unconvincing contrivance of the prophetess. The song subtly and perhaps unexpectedly manages to make that passion believable. Maximinian himself does not sing, but stands in rapt adoration of Aurelia while an unseen singer voices his love; it is the technique of the spoken thought. The audience, wooed by the song's wistful tenderness, is by the end sympathetically disposed towards both Maximinian and Aurelia; the play engenders no such feeling. The lover's half-painful languishments are suggested in the timbre of the two oboes in the prelude to this song, which is another instance of Purcell's taste in chastening a very erotic lyric.

The fourth act opens with one of those effects that can only remind one of the Radio City Music Hall, an arena from which criticism retreats abashed. Delphia, forgiving the repentant Dioclesian, tells him that had he not returned to Drusilla she had 'dreadful torments' in store for him, and Aurelia would have died.

I'll show you what a noble monument
You would have raised to the memory of this Princess.

(She waves her wand thrice. Soft music is heard. Then the curtain rises and shows a stately tomb: Aurelia lying in the midst of it, on a bed of state. Delphia stamps, and it vanishes. Behind it is seen a large cupola supported by termes on pedestals. The Prophetess waves her wand, the termes leap from their pedestals, the building falls, and the termes and cupola are turned into a Dance of Butterflies.)

Admirers of Fletcher may be pleased to know that this whole episode was thought up by Betterton. On the other hand, those who can submit to the irrational spell of this particular world will take delight in its oddly graceful beauty. It has no reasonable foundation (we must agree with Gildon) and no dramatic significance, but it is spectacular and it is theatrical.

The major part of the music in Act IV is associated with Dioclesian's triumph over the Persians. In an elaborate aria and choral movement beginning 'Sound, Fame, thy brazen trumpet sound', Purcell by the sheer martial splendour of the music makes credible and forceful one of the notorious weaknesses of much of our older drama, the battle scenes. To be told that they must be regarded as ritual or symbol makes a modern audience take them no closer to their hearts than if they were told nothing. In *Dioclesian*, as in *Aida*, the celebration of victory is so overwhelmingly resounding that there is no need to show any of the fighting. Both the virtuoso alto aria and the following chorus are interspersed with brilliant trumpet fanfares, in mounting excitement, the whole movement constituting a massive block of sound calculated to blow the roof off. The critics who call Purcell's fanfare style conventional or tedious might examine with more imagination the occasions where it is employed. Sometimes a thundering blast of tonics and dominants is all that will do. Refinements would be wasted.[7]

[7] Purcell and his contemporary composers were inspired to write much florid trumpet music by the Shore family, who by 1690 had brought the instrument to the agility and something over the tessitura of the oboe. The presence of a Shore in the orchestra pit would often tempt a composer to a display of trumpet fireworks in virtual disregard of the text of the play, though in Purcell they are usually dramatically apt. The key of D major is dictated by the nature of the instrument, the only alternative being C major. For this note I am indebted to J. S. Manifold: *The Music in English Drama from Shakespeare to Purcell*, p. 113: London, 1956.

In the last act of Fletcher's play Diocles and Drusilla, lately wed, amble into a rural bower on his farm, praise their lot—'And here in poverty dwells noble nature'—and are entertained by a dance of shepherds and shepherdesses provided by the ever-reliable Delphia. The fact that a shepherd disguised as Pan leads the men and a shepherdess (as Ceres) the maids shows its inspiration to have been the Jacobean masque. Here was an irresistible invitation to a Restoration producer, and Betterton was not reluctant to accept. In fact for just this moment he had been saving his biggest guns, a full-scale masque celebrating the triumph of love. Since it occupies half of Purcell's score and takes three-quarters of an hour to perform, we can see the necessity of shortening speeches throughout the play. Fletcher's little dance at this point could not have taken above two or three minutes, and after it is over the play resumes; Betterton gets the play over first and then cuts loose with his splendours. It is quite probable that the *Dioclesian* masque is the most sumptuous 'scene' in the Restoration theatre, though *The Fairy Queen* two years later is a formidable rival. The everyday method, illustrated by a revival of Fletcher's *Island Princess* set to music by Motteux in 1699, was merely to employ painted back-scenes and fairly simple machines.[8] In contrast, Betterton's masque must have taxed the Dorset Garden facilities to their limit, as the remarkable opening stage direction will suggest.

> While a symphony is playing, a machine descends, so large it fills all the space from the frontispiece of the stage to the further end of the house, and fixes itself by two ladders of clouds to the floor. In it are four several stages, representing the palaces of two gods and two goddesses. The first is the palace of Flora: the columns of red and white marble breaking through the clouds; the columns fluted and wreathed about with all sorts of flowerage, the pedestals and flutings enriched with gold. The second is the palace of the goddess Pomona: the columns of blue marble wound about with all kind of fruitage, and enriched with gold as the other. The third is the palace of Bacchus: the columns of green marble, wreathed and enriched with gold with clusters of grapes hanging round them. The last is the palace of the Sun: it is supported on either side by rows of termes, the lower part white marble, the upper part gold. The whole object is terminated with a glowing cloud on

[8] See A. Nicoll: 'Scenery in Restoration Theatres': *Anglia*, vol. XLIV (1920), p. 223.

which a chair of state, all of gold, the Sun breaking through the cloud, and making a glory about it; as this descends there rises from under the stage a pleasant prospect of a noble garden, consisting of fountains, and orange trees set in large vases; the middle walk leads to a palace at a great distance. At the same time enter Silvanus, Bacchus, et al. The dancers place themselves on every stage in the machine; the singers range themselves about the stage.[9]

This surpasses anything that *The Rehearsal* had dreamed of, and is quite literally beyond burlesque. It makes not the slightest pretence to dramatic relevance; pure beauty is its only excuse for being. But it is in perfect keeping with the spirit of the play, and appropriately ends with the longest single movement in the entire score, an elaborate and thunderous paean to the text, 'Triumph, triumph, victorious Love'. It is a triumph of the baroque spirit as well.

Though it would be impracticable and very difficult to give a detailed analysis of this masque, a few of its special beauties may be noted in connexion with Purcell's genius for the stage. Here, at the summit of his powers, he was given that rare opportunity in his theatrical associations to create a self-contained musical entity of considerable proportions, and one can sense his joy in almost every page. No other score better illustrates his seemingly unending inventiveness in setting texts which to the ordinary mind would appear to be not only very similar but actually indistinguishable. Pedestrian verses never dampened the inventiveness of a great composer; indeed their very unassertiveness is rather a help than a hindrance. Only a neophyte would dream of tackling

> If the assassination
> Could trammel up the consequence, and catch,
> With his surcease, success.

Purcell's accomplishment at ringing infinite changes on a single theme may be compared with Schubert's in the *Winterreise* cycle, Purcell's being the more unusual in that most of the poems set by Schubert are already miniature (if obvious) dramas. The music for Acts II and IV of *Dioclesian* had been either ceremonial and

---

[9] The illumination of this staggering set must have been from lights within the machine itself.

ritualistic or martial. In contrast the masque was to treat of love, but love in a very special sense, in the idyllic pastoral tradition.

Betterton's lyrics, however pale, do suggest several aspects of Arcadian love—tender delights, painful languishments, revels and jollity, plus a species of all-out testimonial in the final poem where victorious Love has 'tamed the mighty Jove'. In addition there is one small-scale drama in four stanzas of a shepherd's successful wooing of a maiden, Dryden's obvious inspiration for the similar episode we have examined in *King Arthur*. Since some dozen separate lyrics still remain after we have counted this little drama, it is clear that there is a good deal of repetition of mood in what Betterton has provided. In Purcell there is virtually none. If a certain mood is to be repeated, he will cast it in a different musical form, will change the key and tempo, and will give it to different voices, so that the resulting composition, equally faithful to the designated mood, will be totally fresh and new. For example, compare the soprano duet, 'Ah the sweet delights of love', a leisurely song in A minor cast in miniature rondo form, with the brisk F-major tenor air, 'All our days and our nights', a short binary form which is completed by a contrapuntal four-part chorus of much vigour.

A more subtle contrast appears in two haunting songs of love's anguish, the soprano airs 'Still I'm wishing, still desiring' and 'O Mirtilo', the first song in the tiny drama of wooing. Both are in triple time accompanied by continuo, but the earlier one, an uncomplicated binary form in D minor, has a tessitura extremely high for Purcell (to say nothing of the soprano), straightforward diatonic harmony, and a strongly rhythmical bass line which gives it the character of a slow dance. By constructing the other song, the G-minor 'O Mirtilo', on a free and variable bass line and making use of seventh chords and chromatic alteration, Purcell can emphasize the effects of tender languishment in the limpid soprano line. Each of the seventeen separate numbers of the masque allows of this sort of differentiation in a greater or less degree depending on its length and elaboration.

One of the greatest delights of the masque, a rollicking Bacchanalian ensemble for two bassos and chorus, is an example of an English type of melody very frequent in Purcell, vaguely reminiscent of folk song, though more sophisticated and more scrupulous in the fitting of words to melody. It is born of the demands of the English language and sounds like the songs of no other nationality. Definition cannot go much beyond this unsatisfactory impressionism, though it may be suggestive to try to imagine songs like *Der Erlkönig* or *Tom der Reimer*, or even better some negro spirituals, in other languages. This peculiarly English tradition did not much outlast Purcell as we can tell at once by comparing these 'folk airs' (which are not folk airs) with the ballad of the post-Handelian period. Pretty as they are, they have lost this individual quality and could as easily be Italian or German or good Stephen Foster. Purcell's numerous catches and rounds, in the main outside his theatre scores, are even more striking instances of this indigenous Englishness. There is no more delightful instance than in this drinking ensemble, 'Make room for the great God of Wine', of Purcell's manner of humanizing the classical deities. Here are the words which Bacchus sings:

Give to everyone his glass,
Then all together clash, clash, clash.
Drink, and despise the politic ass.
The mighty Jove who rules above
Ne'er troubled his head with much thinking,
He took off his glass, was kind to his lass,
And gained heav'n by love and good drinking.

Bacchus never appeared thus in the operas of Lully or Cavalli.

The exhilarating chaconne movement which ends the score was probably suggested by the more elaborate one from Grabu's *Albion and Albanius*, a work Purcell was perhaps challenging by printing his *Dioclesian* score in a similar format; at that time it was extremely rare to print the music of any opera.[10] It is built on a ground bass of four bars which had been used by Monteverdi and later by Blow (who called it 'Morlake's Ground'), and is a massive construction alternating the various instruments of the orchestra in staggered entries with all the vocal resources of the company. After elaborate contrapuntal and harmonic adventures, including a ravishing alteration to the tonic minor at the line 'Thou hast tamed almighty Jove', the last sixteen bars, a straightforward homophonic chorus in dominant and tonic harmonies, are a dignified reassertion of the predominant C major tonality of the

[10] Dent: *op. cit.*, p. 203.

score, and a ringing close to words which show once again that great verse is not required for a great musical text:

> Then all rehearse in lofty verse
> The glory of almighty Love.
> From pole to pole his fame resound,
> Sing it the universe around.

3

The other Fletcherian romance to be converted into an opera was almost the last of Purcell's scores, *Bonduca*. It was an adaptation by George Powell[11] and was brought out in the autumn of 1695, a month or two before the composer's death, at the Theatre Royal in Drury Lane. The auspices were bad; a bitter rivalry had sprung up with the newly re-opened Lincoln's Inn Fields Theatre to which Betterton had drawn most of the best actors. To judge from the Prologue to *Bonduca*, spoken by Powell himself, he and his colleagues, in particular the manager Christopher Rich, hoped to boost Drury Lane's declining fortunes by importing some of the operatic paraphernalia from the dark Dorset Garden theatre where nearly all the extravaganzas had been originally produced.

> . . . Nay, we are bringing
> Machines, scenes, operas, music, dancing, singing;
> Translated from the chiller, bleaker Strand,
> To your sweet Covent Garden's warmer land.
> To us, young players, then let some smiles fall;
> Let not their dear antiquities sweep all.

Actually *Bonduca* has only one big operatic sequence, but the company was now in a position to put on the more elaborate operas like *Dioclesian* and *King Arthur*, to which they had both the rights

---

[11] In the preface Powell claims that he is merely publishing the play for a friend, 'a much abler hand than my own'. He continues with a not unusual disclaimer: 'This undertaker, who bestowed but four days labour upon it, being above the interest part of an author; and likewise a person of that modesty, as to affect no plumes from poetry, he was generously pleased to put it into my hands to usher it into the world.' His grammar would appear to offer proof of his haste.

and the scenery. And even in *Bonduca* opportunities abound for noise and spectacle. It is another heroic romance in the vein of *The Prophetess*, but can claim in addition a slight aura of patriotism, for it is a Druid-Roman play which reaches its musical climax in the rousing, 'Britons, strike home!' The protagonists are on one side the Briton queen Bonduca with her leading general Caratach, and on the other the Roman general Suetonius. In spite of heroic fighting by Caratach and the Britons, the Romans eventually triumph, leaving Bonduca and her two daughters to swallow poison and, the last pitch, Caratach to stab himself rather than outlive his country's liberty. Suetonius pronounces the benediction in a noblest-Roman-of-them-all speech over the body of his brave antagonist, and the curtain closes on a dead march.[12] A very large group of subordinate characters, all involved in deep intrigue, surround these principals, but none of them is involved in the great musical scene and, to tell the truth, none is necessary to the main action. *Bonduca* is a splendid example of the effectiveness of dramatic irrelevance, a play naively constructed of many exciting and quite detachable scenes which show off to advantage a number of familiar types—the noble warrior, the fearless Amazon, the cowardly boaster, the blunt crude soldier, the remorseful defector, in other words most of the people we met in *The Prophetess*. In spite of the accumulation of deaths at the end, the drama belongs to the world of tragi-comedy. There is a pathetic death scene for Caratach's little nephew, suggested by the famous episode in *King John*. Buffoonery involving the braggart Judas (Powell's Macer) riddles the play, but the predominant impression of irresponsibility in his scenes precludes any of the harsher discords of low-life found so abundantly in *Measure for Measure* or the comedies of Ben Jonson. Realism is nowhere. Pathos and laughter are both pushed as far as possible without any attempt at reconciliation, another example of the unresolved tensions beloved of seventeenth-century art. In the Restoration, partly owing to French influence, tragedy and comedy had split, but the taste lingered on in the constant revivals of Beaumont and Fletcher, and in the dramatic operas. Fletcher's chief inspiration is *Antony and Cleopatra*: the language is rife with echoes; two of his most thrilling scenes, the defection of Pennius (Enobarbus) and

---

[12] In Fletcher Caratach is willing to go to Rome as an honoured prisoner.

the suicide of Bonduca and her daughters atop a monument, are brazenly borrowed; but nothing is woven into a fabric of any sort of consistency. In short, it is a play that the Restoration would find practically irresistible.

The changes that Powell thought fit to make in Fletcher are interesting revelations of theatrical taste at a period just on the brink of the sentimental inundation. The scale is a little less prodigious than Fletcher's, that is, he has slightly reduced the characters and episodes, but this may be owing solely to lack of money and other resources. His company was inexperienced, and he had to find time for Purcell's music. One particularly inclines to such an opinion upon discovering the excision of Fletcher's most theatrical character, the defecting Pennius. By dropping him, however reluctantly, Powell can cut out some six scenes without damaging the continuity in the slightest. He also throws out some of the intrigues of the Roman soldiers in order to make room for his own creative plum, a love triangle involving two British soldiers and Bonduca's elder daughter Claudia. This is sheer melodrama, the favoured lover a paragon, the rejected one an odious monster; but as it adds romance and a certain titillation, it is more conventionally popular than what he sacrificed, and just half as long.

The only serious loss is in the verse, which in Fletcher is nearly always vigorous and credible, no matter how windy it may occasionally become. When Powell abandons Fletcher he can supply in his place only claptrap or something unwarrantably suggestive and lewd.[13] Two quotations will show what has happened to the Restoration's ear and, one is tempted to add, its sense of humour. In the first the villainous Comes, repulsed by Claudia, contemplates rape:

> Ye gods! ye gods! How it would fire my soul
> To clasp this lovely fury in my arms!
> Whilst scorning to be pleased, she'd curse the pleasure;
> Till with a sudden rapture seized she'd melt away,
> And springing give a loose to lusty joy.

[13] An appalling example of bawdy in the mouth of a babe is the Epilogue 'Spoken by Miss Denny Chock, But Six Years Old'. Telling the gallants of the audience that she is too young to ask favours of them because she is not old enough to grant them in return, she displays a precocious knowledge of the whole armoury of whoredom.

And here, Claudia, having watched her lover die of his wounds, appeals in vain to the gods:

> Help, help! Where now are all those gods
> The poets in their wild fancies dreamt
> Were in the woods? No kinder power to hear
> A virgin's prayer? No Aesculapius near, or
> Great Apollo?

The supernatural introduction of Aesculapius and Apollo one would have expected only from Fielding or Sheridan.

The music to *Bonduca* shows Purcell at the top of his bent. The impressive three-part overture makes a more extensive use of chromatic harmony than any other, and the deeply melancholy adagio is a superb inspiration. This is followed by what amounts to a miniature suite, six short instrumental numbers, all in binary form and sufficiently varied. Any relation to the mood of the play is quite accidental. There is an ingenious little catch in Act II, 'Jack, thou'rt a toper', which serves as a relief to the derring-do of battle, after which we move on to the big operatic scene of incantation and sacrifice in Act III. Operating on an aesthetic forbidding the principals to sing, the Restoration opera depends more heavily upon the sacrificial scene than upon anything else. Since there is almost no heroic play into which such a scene could not be easily introduced somewhere, it is hardly a surprise to find it an important aspect of Purcell's dramaturgy.

Although this is not the place to trace his development of the type, we may profitably compare the *Bonduca* scene with that from *King Arthur* four years earlier. They both follow the same general pattern of a majestic call to sacrifice, followed by a more lyrical passage to one or more gods, then a rousing episode—in *King Arthur* a bacchanale, in *Bonduca* a call to arms, and finally the battle song. It is easy to see that dramatically the two scenes are about on a par; *King Arthur* may be the more exciting in that there are two choruses, the fighting song 'Come, if you dare' being sung by Britons who have surprised the unwatchful wassailing Saxons. Musically *Bonduca* is considerably more mature and interesting. After the customary 'symphony' or introduction for strings, the chorus begins an imitative movement of solemn dignity in C minor to the words,

Hear us, great Rugwith, hear our prayers,
Defend thy British Isle.
Revive our hopes, disperse our fears,
Nor let thine altars be the Roman spoil.

In the course of this they are interrupted in turn by four soloists,
each of whom sings a single line ending with a cadence in a new
key—B-flat major, F minor, G minor, and back to C minor.
Despite the serene beauty of this music, Purcell maintains a sense
of apprehension by the chromatic harmonies resulting from
constant use of suspensions, and by the fact that the only long and
evenly flowing vocal line of the movement, given out by the bass
soloist, is deferred until just before the final choral response. In
contrast the first *King Arthur* number, 'Woden, first to thee',
merely employs F-major harmonies, two male soloists, and a
homophonic chorus in a predictable fashion. Similarly the
following 'To Woden thanks we render' is a simple antiphonal
duet in very elementary rhythm, its cheery F major but once
touching briefly upon D minor. In *Bonduca* the corresponding
'Hear, ye gods of Britain' is a bass solo somewhere between arioso
and aria of continuous rhythmic and harmonic surprise as the
music follows closely the sense of the text. The lyrical movement,
a duet for sopranos and flutes on a ground of four bars, has no real
counterpart in *King Arthur*, though the point of repose it brings
to the scene is analogous with the chorus 'Brave souls'. The tenor
recitative, 'Divine Andate! President of War', is an anticipation
of the Handelian manner, though in its avoidance of Handel's
monotonous quavers it is rhythmically more lively, and it introduces a coloratura passage that Handel would have saved for the
aria. Then comes a thrilling C-major call to arms, replete with
trumpets and strings sounding antiphonally with soloists and
chorus, before the climactic swing into 'Britons, strike home!'
Like 'Come, if you dare', this is a bounding triple-time movement
of irresistible thrust in binary form. There is no choosing between
these two rousing numbers, but at least one small difference is
worth noticing. In 'Come, if you dare' the division of the binary
form is a very normal one of fourteen and sixteen bars, which can
further be broken down into eight-six and eight-eight. 'Britons,
strike home!' is a much more unusual nine to nineteen with the
second division breaking up into nine and ten, the added measure

allowing for a vivid variation and also bringing the harmony from A minor back to C major. As statistics this is tedious enough, but as an indication of the continuing development and originality of Purcell's musical ideas it is significant. We remember in blank dismay that within a few months he was dead at the age of thirty-six.

Unfortunately for *Bonduca*, Purcell was employed for only one more scene, and in that for but one song. In the last act the extravagance of carnage and suicide is momentarily relieved when Bonvica, the queen's younger daughter, wanders in to sing a lament, 'O lead me to some peaceful gloom'. This song seems to me one of Purcell's rare failures, for its opening mood, beautifully conveyed by haunting chromatic harmonies, is abruptly and rather absurdly shattered with a bravura pictorial passage on 'Where the shrill trumpets never sound', only defensible on the grounds of extreme baroque contrast, or if we imagine the poor girl to have become unhinged. This supposition is made unlikely by the final section, 'There let me soothe my pleasing pain', an undistinguished triple-time air, repetitious and altogether too suave for the occasion.

Remembering the superb adagio of the overture, we must regret that Purcell supplied no funeral music to bolster the last tribute which Suetonius (a student of *Antony and Cleopatra*) makes to Bonduca:

> Desperate and strange!
> Give her fair funeral; she was noble, and a queen.

It is of course possible that some music is lost, for this is a very clear musical cue.

Dioclesian and *Bonduca* so perfectly suited the late baroque taste for exotic romance heightened by musical episodes combining ceremonious grandeur with surprising livelier moments, the whole drawing added impressiveness from an aura of pseudo-history, that their immediate success and continued performance into the eighteenth century are not hard to understand. The fact that of the two *Dioclesian* enjoyed considerably longer popularity—it was frequently performed during Garrick's long régime—is undoubtedly due not to any intrinsic superiority in the play but to its much more extensive musical score. It was Purcell who preserved Fletcher. Through music the amount and kinds of experience were infinitely increased and expanded, and a meretricious play was elevated to a work of art.

CHAPTER VI

The Indian Queen

I

THE LAST YEAR of Purcell's life brought an outpouring of inspiration so remarkable that for a suitable comparison we should have to go to Mozart or Schubert. Like Mozart he was literally composing upon his death-bed. Having promised Thomas D'Urfey an aria for the third part of *Don Quixote in England*, he rallied his waning strength to produce the famous song of love betrayed, 'From rosy bowers'. It is a song haunted with twilight visions, reaching its climax at the words,

> Ah! 'tis vain, 'tis all in vain,
> Death and despair must end the fatal pain.

In the clashing dissonances at this moment in the song the dying composer poured forth a last cry of protest at the tragedy of life. He died a few days later on 21 November 1695, and was buried in Westminster Abbey where for nearly half his life he had served as organist. During this ultimate year he wrote music for nine theatrical productions, including three of his most important scores, those to *Bonduca*, *The Tempest*, and *The Indian Queen*; with the exception of 'From rosy bowers' there is no telling the order in which any of this music was composed. Later on we shall see that in certain respects *The Tempest* is the most advanced from a technical point of view (which does not necessarily make it his best music), but the fact that he did not set the final masque to *The Indian Queen* makes one wonder if this may not have been his last score.[1]

[1] The matter is further complicated by a pirated edition of the score, impudently dedicated to Purcell himself, which presumably appeared just before he died. The final masque, set by his brother Daniel Purcell, was not published until the next year, but nevertheless may have been sung at the first performance.

If this be the truth it is most fitting, for *The Indian Queen* is the only case in which Purcell can be said to have made an opera out of the heroic play. Though the other operas are bristling with heroics, *The Indian Queen* is the pure product, virtually a prototype of the most popular of the Restoration dramatic genres. Thus the last score in a sense forces him to a retrospective view of his life span: the heroic play had come into being at about the time Purcell was born, had flowered luxuriantly during his lifetime, and in every important respect goes to the grave with him.

In 1664, when the composer was not yet five years old, *The Indian Queen* was brought out in great splendour at the Theatre Royal in Brydges Street. John Evelyn, who saw it on 5 February, called it 'a tragedy so beautiful with rich scenes, as the like had never been seen here, or haply (except rarely) elsewhere on a mercenary theatre'. A week earlier, on 27 January, Pepys had found the street 'full of coaches' for the play, and heard it was 'a fine thing', an opinion in which he concurred when he saw it four days later. The authors were Dryden and his brother-in-law, Sir Robert Howard. It was Dryden's first heroic play and set the model for all the rest. Though records are scanty, there can be little doubt that it was one of the most popular works throughout the period, and certainly a very influential one. As late as 1692 it was reissued three times, and in 1695 Christopher Rich brought it out as an opera at Drury Lane.

The setting of this bizarre play fluctuates between Peru and Mexico, countries Dryden knew scarcely better than Antarctica, a fact which in no way damages the story.[2] This centres around two inordinately heroic rivals, the Peruvian general Montezuma, the grandest of the grand, and his friendly enemy, the Mexican prince Acacis. It is characteristic that though Acacis is Montezuma's prisoner he can still say of him:

> Like the vast seas, your mind no limits knows,
> Like them lies open to each wind that blows.

[2] The romantic episodes of Mexican and Peruvian history Dryden took from De Gomberville's *Polexandre* (1641), translated into English by William Browne in 1647. Though the history is fictional, much of both character and plot of *The Indian Queen* and its sequel, *The Indian Emperor* (1665), came from here.

Unfortunately they are in love with the same princess, the divine Orazia, who is the Inca's daughter. Her impeccable taste leads her to choose the grander of the two heroes, Montezuma, but there are obstacles aplenty in the way of their love. First her own father insultingly rejects Montezuma as her suitor because he is not of royal birth, an action so infuriating to the proud hero that he at once changes over to the Mexican side, where

> The troops gaze on him, as if some bright star
> Shot to their aids, call him the god of war.

Not the troops alone gaze upon him rapturously, but also the usurping Mexican queen Zempoalla, the *femme fatale* and title character of the play, who presumably gave birth to Acacis in her extreme youth. She would like to have Montezuma for herself as well as for her army; consequently, when he subdues the Inca's forces in battle, she determines to put Orazia to death, or, as she puts it, to sacrifice her to the gods. Montezuma and Acacis rescue Orazia and her father, for which act they are themselves made Queen Zempoalla's prisoners. At this juncture appears the villain of the play, Traxalla. He is the queen's general and former paramour—apparently they always go together with Zempoalla, who believes that only the brave deserve the fair—and quite as stormy as his companions. Having fallen in love with Orazia at his first sight of her, he demands of the queen that she be saved and the disloyal Montezuma be sacrificed instead. It is here that the tormented and indecisive queen ('I attempt from love's sickness to fly') must consult her High Priest, and also here of course that the producer consulted Purcell, for there follows one of those scenes of incantation and ritual dear to the Restoration heart. After a passage of atmospheric verse that proves he had read Spenser's Cave of Morpheus, the High Priest in one of Purcell's great arias, 'Ye twice ten hundred deities', summons the God of Dreams. Like the Frost Genius in *King Arthur* this spirit rises slowly from the earth, and in gently melancholy measures warns Zempoalla that she should not attempt to peer into the future. Dryden and Howard provided several songs for this scene, the words not corresponding exactly with Purcell's settings of thirty years later, but we know nothing of the original music.

I shall not attempt to trace the intricacies of the last two acts which are replete with intrigues, reversals of fate, battles, sudden deaths, and of course many high-flown speeches on love, honour, friendship, and the nature of life. Among the wealth of surprising turns in the finale, the honours go first to the suicide of Acacis, committed in his wish to leave Orazia (not his to leave) with Montezuma and in the notably obscure hope that sacrificing himself will preclude all further sacrifices; secondly, to the victorious entrance of the rightful queen, who turns out to be Montezuma's long-lost mother, which of course makes his blood sufficiently blue to marry Orazia and be King of Mexico; and, finally, to the suicide of the rejected Zempoalla just at the point when she is offered her life along with several speeches of praise. But she is too noble to accept:

> The greatest proof of courage we can give,
> Is then to die when we have power to live.

Nothing remains except for Montezuma, with one auspicious and one dropping eye, to pronounce a benediction that shows us how a play so wildly remote from realism could yet exert a strong appeal to the reason:

> Come, my Orazia, then, and pay with me,
> Some tears to poor Acacis' memory;
> So strange a fate for men the Gods ordain,
> Our clearest sunshine should be mixed with rain;
> How equally our joys and sorrows move!
> Death's fatal triumphs joined with those of love.
> Love crowns the dead, and death crowns him that lives,
> Each gains the conquest which the other gives.

Dryden's mastery of the epigrammatic paradox is seen at once in the closing couplet, but, as Dobrée has observed, many of Dryden's phrases which detached from their settings seem to be epigrams, in their place 'merely appear as slightly stronger statements, which is in itself a tribute to the high standard of his dramatic writing'.[3] Certainly in Dryden there is always a good deal more than the mere loud rodomontade of the usual heroic play. It is this denser texture that leads one to believe that *The Indian Queen*, though first published under Howard's name alone,

---

[3] *Restoration Tragedy*, p. 108: London, 1929.

had been rather fully reshaped by the greater poet. Sir Walter Scott said that the characters of Montezuma and Zempoalla were Dryden's 'for certain', as was the lyrical incantation scene, but his evidence seems to be instinct only. At any rate it was *The Indian Queen* that began the widespread popularity of the heroic play, a species that had for several years been struggling to find its proper form in the plays of Davenant and Orrery. Once Dryden entered the arena triumph was assured.

The aesthetic of the heroic play and its debt to Davenant we have discussed in the opening chapter. For Dryden's taste Davenant was not sufficiently elevated, and did not seem to understand that the drama should approach 'the greatness and majesty of an heroic poem'. Dryden agreed with the contention of Hobbes that the heroic poet should raise admiration for three virtues—valour, beauty, and love. He is not 'tied to a bare representation of what is true, or exceeding probable', but rather should 'let himself loose to visionary objects'. He does not depict man as he is, but 'far above ordinary proportion', as he ought to be or as he would like to be. It is a dream world geared to a nobler pitch, the essence of Dobrée's often-quoted remark that the basis of Restoration tragedy is the romantic idea: 'Art provided what life denied'.[4]

What Dryden sought was exaltation. The flamboyant plots serve not only to provide challenges worthy of the magnificent heroes whom we are constantly called on to admire, but to take the audiences out of themselves, thereby stimulating the divine imagination. At its best it is in a very real sense a formal and intellectual drama, a drama deliberately planned to reflect not life around us but life above us. It is for this reason that the characters are simplified and typed at the same time that they and the circumstances in which they are involved become increasingly exaggerated. They must stand for more than themselves. And it is for this reason too that so often in Dryden's plays we find characters giving utterance to dilemmas which, however unrealistic the situation and the expression, must always appeal to the reason. It is a cruder form of what Racine brought to the zenith of refinement, and it reveals the purely formal interest of so much heroic drama. One example is Montezuma's final speech; a better is

[4] *Ibid.*, pp. 20, 29.

Orazia's soliloquy in Act IV which occurs just after she has told
Montezuma, now beloved by the Indian Queen, that she had
rather see him dead than married to another woman:

> How are things ordered, that the wicked should
> Appear more kind and gentle than the good!
> Her passion seems to make her kinder prove,
> And I seem cruel through excess of love:
> She loves, and would prevent his death; but I
> That love him better, fear he should not die.
> My jealousy, immortal as my love,
> Would rob my grave below, and me above,
> Of rest.—Ye gods, if I repine, forgive;
> You neither let me die in peace, nor live.

This kind of interest indicates perhaps the clearest difference
between Dryden's heroic play and Fletcherian heroic romances
like *The Prophetess* and *Bonduca*. Although both types are built
around the heroic ideal, Fletcher's plays are nearer to the paler,
less intense world of tragi-comedy, and stand somewhere between
the Elizabethan romantic comedy and the Jacobean thriller.
Their plots, full of effective and detachable stage scenes, are busy
rather than intricate in Dryden's sense, their actions are less
violent, and the characters are not so varied and of course not
nearly so exaggerated. Their settings are of the antique world,
Rome and Britain, or often Arcadia, not of Turkey or India or
Mexico. The experiences of the plays are as unreal as those in
Dryden, but neither the conception nor its expression appeals
much to the intellect. It is for this reason, I think, that Fletcher's
plays make better vehicles for operatic treatment in the manner
available to Purcell than does the pure heroic play. The appeal is
less unified, there is less that will be interrupted by music. Even
more important, the kind of musical expression that the heroic
play demands belongs to another operatic tradition entirely; it is
what we see in the passionate world of Monteverdi or two hundred years later of Giuseppe Verdi, but very seldom in theatre
music of Purcell or of any Englishman. *Dido and Aeneas*, as well
as a great deal of his religious music, shows what he could have
done had he been given the chance, but he was not.

Before turning to Purcell's score we might ask a final question
about the heroic play. In the face of the lofty conception that

dictated its point of view, and of the expert craftsmanship of Dryden, why has it disappeared from the stage apparently for ever? Rather than embark upon a sea of reasons, I shall quote two separate statements by Professor Dobrée, each capable of infinite illustration and elaboration. 'The gloriously abstract principles of Hobbes and Davenant', he writes, 'were forgotten by the playwrights, who, in trying to humanize the drama, brought it nearer to life, and so turned a not indefensible unreality into falsity.' In short they degenerated into sentimentality. Although this is not true of Dryden, Dryden has disappeared as well. That is because his heroic drama 'mapped out not the actualities of human emotion, but its ideals; which was unfortunate for itself, since, while feelings remain unchanged, ideals are various'.[5] This is at least one reason why *Othello* is still alive and *The Indian Queen* is still dead.

2

It is not surprising that a work of Purcell's maturity like *The Indian Queen* should contain some of his most beautiful music, but considering the restricted limits within which he had to work one is surprised at its variety. In the first place, opportunities for spectacle were limited. The production was not a Dorset Garden extravaganza and there are no signs of machines. This was probably owing to the straitened economy caused by Betterton's secession, for Rich, being the patentee of the Theatre Royal, would have had access to the dark Dorset Garden's machinery, but in this case could not afford to utilize it. To revive *King Arthur* and *Dioclesian* (which he soon did) was one thing, since the paraphernalia of the original productions would still have been intact, but quite another to convert *The Indian Queen* into a *tragédie à machines*. The play's first appearance in 1664 had been before the heyday of the grandest machines on the English stage, and the 'splendours' that delighted Evelyn and Pepys were doubtless elaborate groupings of many supernumeraries dressed in exotic costumes. But more important, as the précis of the plot may have suggested, there was absolutely nothing Purcell could do, overtures aside, except in scenes that admitted of some sort of ritual

[5] *Op. cit.*, pp. 43, 91.

ceremony. In a story so desperately complicated not much time could really be spared for these, and when they were allowable not even Dryden could devise much variation in them. Purcell could.

The first surprise, however, comes after the overture when the composer takes the step unusual for the English theatre of setting the prologue to music. Actually the prologue itself is quite novel, being in dialogue form between a couple called simply Indian Boy and Girl. Her name is later given as Quevira. The orchestra gives out a lively C-major trumpet air which wakens the sleeping boy. He speaks of a prophecy telling of a race of strangers who will come to conquer their innocent pastoral world. In his opening aria, light, airy, and elaborate, he sings joyously of nature's bounteousness and sets the idyllic tone of the entire movement. Like the girl's reply, an ingenious air for soprano and two flutes, it is constructed over a strongly marked and melodious continuo line which, because its longest phrase is many times repeated, gives almost the impression of a ground. After a recitative from the boy, they sing a duet of welcome to the strangers in G minor; Quevira is momentarily fearful, but the boy reassures her and they join in a joyful C-major duet, after which the orchestra repeats the trumpet air and the prologue is over. This little movement, which might take about ten minutes to perform, is assuredly no world-shaker, but it draws us into the world of opera, displays a charming innocence, especially in the light of the tempests to follow, and serves notice that the score will be full of imagination and surprise.

Quevira was sung by the famous boy soprano, Jemmy Bowen, usually called 'The Boy', for whom Purcell wrote some ingratiating florid music. In the supplement to Theophilus Cibber's *Lives* we are told of the youth that 'when practising a song set by Mr Purcell, some of the music told him to grace and run a division in such a place. O let him alone, said Mr Purcell, he will grace it more naturally than you or I can teach him.' Lest this make Purcell appear to encourage free bravura invention, it should be noted that he usually wrote out his vocal graces in full, but the story may suggest how he hit upon the idea of setting the prologue. Jemmy Bowen was a member of the company, and this was the composer's happy thought for using him.

The first musical scene in the play itself does not come till Act II, and it is apparently Purcell's interpolation.[6] In effect it is a miniature masque in which Fame and her followers singing Queen Zempoalla's praises cast out Envy, who 'flies from the place where Flattery reigns'. It is, of course, detachable, but it suggests to me that Purcell with unerring dramatic instinct had put his finger on the place where the play was weakest, the Indian Queen herself. Though the play is named for her, and at the end the entire dramatis personae, or at least those who are permitted still to live, praise her extravagantly, neither her speeches nor her actions justify any of it. Purcell, by centring all the music around her, considerably remedies this error, for she thereby not only becomes the most important character in the opera but she also becomes associated in our sympathies with beauty and even, in the instance of 'I attempt from love's sickness to fly', with tenderness. Again it is the composer who is the dramatist.

The masque is preceded by a 'symphony' identical but for key with one in the Queen Mary birthday ode for the previous year, 'Come, ye sons of art', another indication that the incidental music for these plays is more often than not mere decoration. A curtain then rises and 'Zempoalla appears seated upon a throne, frowning upon her attendants'. Fame, an alto, sings a brisk little binary tune, repeated by the chorus in simple four-part harmony, 'I come to sing great Zempoalla's story'. The key of C major is dictated by the scale of the natural trumpet which answers antiphonally the oboes and vocal parts. This orchestration is rich for the period, though as usual in Purcell the trumpets and oboes are not so much regular constituents of the orchestra as they are obbligato instruments for special colour effects. Indeed the burden of the accompaniment rested nearly always upon the harpsichord. Even the strings in an average opera band at the end of the seventeenth century played too crudely to be entrusted with the delicate task of supporting a singer, hence we see them most often in the opening 'symphony' and the concluding ritornello, or else playing

[6] It occurs in the only authority for the dialogue of the opera, a manuscript in the British Museum (Add. 31449). It is reduced from the play to allow for the musical scenes, and contains all the music and lists the cast. By the absence of any actor who seceded with Betterton to Lincoln's Inn Fields in April, we know that the opera appeared after that date.

antiphonally with the continuo.[7] Purcell is far more trusting of his instrumentalists than are most of his contemporaries.

Following immediately upon this jolly strain, the basso, Envy, sings,

> What flattering noise is this,
> At which my snakes all hiss?

On each repetition of the lines the followers of Envy utter the single word 'hiss' and 'this', a bit of musical imitation bound to make a striking effect on the stage. The melodic line follows a fairly predictable pattern alternating between the tonic C minor and the relative major, but the picturesque 'hiss' continues to startle us. Fame makes another buoyant entry and Envy, departing, replies scornfully, the movement attaining a neat compactness by a reprise of 'What flattering noise' as Envy leaves, followed by a reprise of the opening air for full chorus and orchestra. Musically the episode is a trifle jejune and blaring, especially for Purcell's maturity, but on the stage the contrast between the bright C-major songs of Fame and the darker hues of Envy, as well as the balletic movements that must have accompanied the music, would make their point.

The great operatic scene of *The Indian Queen* is in the third act and repays careful attention, for here Purcell touches the feelings in a way that Dryden never does. Zempoalla, tormented by unrequited love for Montezuma, has had an evil dream and in her anguish calls upon the High Priest, Ismeron, for help. To interpret the dream he summons the God of Sleep in the famous bass air, 'Ye twice ten hundred deities', which Dr Burney called 'the best piece of recitative in our language'. It is composed of four very different parts, each calculated to illustrate the exact mood of the words, yet they are held together by the G minor tonality.

After the sonorous opening declamation comes a freakish air for the conjuring with highly illustrative description on such words as 'swelled', 'glide', 'twisted', and, most amusingly, 'pants' (certainly studied by Handel), heightened by string obbligato. Just as this kind of literalism is on the verge of becoming tiresome there is a magical change at the words,

---

[7] E. J. Dent in Grove's *Dictionary of Music*, vol. VII, p. 450: London, 1954.

Ismeron:

Bass

From thy sleep - - - ing man·sion rise, And o-pen, and

Strings

o-pen thy un-will - - ing eyes, While bub — bling

springs their mu — sic keep while bub-bling springs their

mu — sic keep, That use—to lull—thee, use—to lull—thee, lull—thee

in thy sleep

From thy sleeping mansion rise,
And open thy unwilling eyes . . .

eight bars of chromatic steps up
the whole octave in the smooth-
est legato. The device is the same
that Purcell had used in the Frost
Scene in *King Arthur*, but besides
the marked difference in rhythm
and mood, the modulations are here free of all dissonance.
The music then falls quietly into an air to dreams of heavenly
serenity, perfect complement to the fantastical arioso. Its art
defies analysis, for the basis of the song is absurdly simple—
groups of three notes alternately ascending and descending with
the bass first anticipating the melody and then going its own way
sometimes in parallel, sometimes in contrary motion. The harmonies are strictly diatonic and unadventurous, yet the effect is
sublime. The God of Dreams sings a languishing air to an oboe
obbligato, 'Seek not to know what must not be revealed', with an
intricate rhythm and occasional stunning dissonances. Its delicate
airiness and the timbres of voice and oboe make a striking contrast
to the High Priest's song. The god leaves on a swifter passage
where the oboe is used antiphonally rather than for harmonic and
colouristic purposes. The effect of this entire episode is of course
to invest Zempoalla's torment with dignity and beauty, and to
raise her dramatic temperature many degrees.

Nor is this all. After some spoken dialogue in which Zempoalla
expresses her fears at the god's warning, a spirited trumpet overture shifts the mood, and Ismeron calls upon two Spirits of Air
to bring the queen's soul 'back to its harmony' with music. Their
duet, 'Ah! how happy are we', on a fascinating four-bar ground,
is meltingly lyrical and faintly touched with sadness. The mood is
idyllic, a plateau of peace and innocence, as it were, surrounded
by a darker mystical world. A vigorous chorus breaks in upon
them, after which a soprano sings perhaps the most famous song
in all Purcell, 'I attempt from love's sickness to fly'. Although
comment upon its melody would be idle, its function in the scene
is not always understood. Mr Holland, one of Purcell's ablest
commentators, has complained that its sentiments ('I am myself

my own fever and pain') are scarcely calculated to soothe the already overwrought Zempoalla,[8] but surely the song is in the convention of the spoken thought, like Maximinian's 'What shall I do to show how much I love her?' from *Dioclesian*. Expressing the frustrating anguish in her heart, it would be rendered by Zempoalla herself were she a singer; as it is, we accept the sentiments as hers. During this entire musical episode our sympathy for the queen is at its strongest, which shows Purcell's understanding of the power of association. We should never feel this way from what she says and does. It is possible to think of the music as dramatic in yet another way, as dramatic irony, for its characteristics of beauty and purity could suggest a possible happy outcome for the queen.

The last operatic episode opens Act V.[9] Something of the spectacle may be grasped from the original stage direction: 'Scene opens and discovers the Temple of the Sun, all of gold, and four priests, in habits of white and red feathers, attending by a bloody altar, as ready for sacrifice. Then enter the guards, Zempoalla, and Traxalla; Inca, Orazia, and Montezuma, bound. As soon as they are placed, the priest sings.' The episode is short, is quite different from anything else in the score, and in conception is the most dramatic of the opera. It is in contrasting halves, the first a massive homophonic chorus, 'While thus we bow before your shrine', in the major, followed by Ismeron's stately recitative, 'You who at the altar stand', with the chorus answering on 'All's prepared' and 'All is done'. No saints entering the gates of heaven could sound more assured. But suddenly the entire musical and dramatic climate is altered with a change to the 'horror key' of F minor in a grimly dissonant contrapuntal chorus, the only example of such texture and harmony in the opera. By the time it has come to a grinding halt with the reiterated phrase, 'There's nothing to be trusted here below', the doors are open wide for chaos, and for the violent denouement of the play.

The Masque of Hymen at the end is not Dryden's but is a conventional afterthought of the producer in 1695. We do not

[8] *Henry Purcell*, p. 171.
[9] A single song for the fourth act, 'They tell us that ye mighty powers above', reflects Orazia's feelings, but there is no indication of where it occurs or how it is introduced.

even know who wrote the verses, and the mildly pleasant music of Daniel Purcell need not be perpetuated. The pallor of its hues is apparent the moment we place it beside the Masque of Hymen in *The Fairy Queen* or the Masque of Love which closes *Dioclesian*.

3

The Indian Queen can be described as an opera of love versus patriotism in a remote and exotic setting, an example of the kind of plot that the most prolific of all operatic librettists, Pietro Metastasio, used over and over again during the next century. Although we have now looked at its story and its music, I have said very little about its peculiar dramaturgy since that can be treated most revealingly in comparison with a more famous opera on the same subject of love versus patriotism in exotic surroundings—in fact, the most popular ever written. This work is of course *Aida*, which Verdi wrote in 1871 at the request of the Khedive of Egypt soon after the opening of the Suez Canal. Most readers will remember that the story concerns the Ethiopian princess Aida, a captive in war who has become the favourite slave of Amneris, the daughter of the Pharaoh. She is secretly beloved by the mighty Egyptian warrior Rhadames, whom Amneris also loves. When Aida's father, the fierce Ethiopian king Amonasro, is captured, he forces Aida to wheedle the battle plans from Rhadames. They are overheard by Amneris and the High Priest, and Rhadames is condemned to burial alive, scorning the distracted Amneris' offer of escape. Aida, remorseful, conceals herself in the tomb and dies with her lover as Amneris in the temple above prays for the peace of his soul.

So brief a précis cannot begin to suggest all the similarities in the two stories, but the striking parallels in dramatis personae will be noticed at once. Montezuma corresponds to Rhadames, while Orazia, the princess torn between love and her father's stern edict, is kin to Aida; and Zempoalla, the furious rejected queen, to Amneris. The stone-hearted Inca corresponds to Amonasro, Ismeron to the High Priest Ramfis, and Traxalla (less closely) to Amneris' lord, the Pharaoh. Only Acacis, the heroic magnanimous rival, is missing. The formal nature of the heroic play demanded that the female rivalry be balanced by the male rivalry; Traxalla is thrown in for good measure. But what binds the works even closer together is the fact, only recently discovered, that the *Aida* libretto stems from a libretto by Metastasio, *Nitteti*, set first by Conforto in 1756 and subsequently by some two dozen other composers.[10] Nitteti is Amneris, but the Aida figure, a servant and shepherdess (!) named Beroe, far from Ethiopian turns out to be the true princess of Egypt, while it is Nitteti who is found to be the daughter of shepherds. This welcome news, revealed in the last act by a long-lost papyrus, rescues the lovers from their tomb and allows them to be married. The *deus ex machina* ending is, of course, much closer to the heroic play than the sombre finale in Verdi; indeed most of the Metastasian schemes of intrigue leading to exciting tableaux or climaxes for musical exploitation are pure heroic.

It can be easily seen that the plot of *Aida* is almost as unreal as that of *Nitteti* or of *The Indian Queen*, and that only the nineteenth century's love of tragic endings kept it from being every bit as unreal. All its ingredients are straight out of the drama of nearly two hundred years before, and are geared to the nobler pitch. It is this condition that accounts for a curious dichotomy in *Aida*, one which will serve to clarify the heroic dramaturgy. The outstanding feature of the heroic world is just what the adjective implies—it is a world of heroes (and of their opposite, villains), not a world of human beings. The sentiments breathed by these aggrandized beings are what they ought to breathe in such a world, not what frailer mortals actually breathe in this one. When Oswald challenges King Arthur to decide the battle by single combat, it never occurs to Arthur or Dryden or the spectator that he should refuse. The realistic commentary upon this bit of heroics is the reply of Octavius to Antony's challenge in Shakespeare, or of Henry IV to Hotspur's. When later and lesser dramatists than Dryden—Otway and Rowe, for example—tried to humanize the heroic world, to bring it nearer to ordinary life, it immediately collapsed into sentimentality. The grand artificiality is what sustains the nobler pitch. Dryden arranges his episodes to lead up to climactic passages on some exalted theme

[10] F. Perez de la Vega: *La Prosapia de Aida*: Mexico City, 1950.

that will take the audience out of themselves. Such a passage occurs in the fourth act after the noble Acacis at a great risk frees Montezuma and Orazia from the Indian Queen's clutches, and then insists that Montezuma, his closest friend, fights him for Orazia's hand. It is the turning point of the play.

> ACAC. That which my honour owed thee I have paid;
> As honour was, so love must be obeyed.
> I set Orazia as thy captive free,
> But as my mistress ask her back from thee. . . .
> MONT. Oh tyrant love, how cruel are thy laws!
> I forfeit friendship, or betray thy cause.
> That person whom I would defend from all
> The world, that person by my hand must fall.
> ACAC. Our lives we to each other's friendships owe;
> But love calls back what friendship did bestow:
> Love has its cruelties, but friendship none;
> And we now fight in quarrels not our own.

The action is frozen into a striking tableau while we hear elevated sentiments on Love, Honour, and Friendship. The deeds and feelings are separated. There is no psychological motivation in the modern sense and no realism. In exactly the same way are the big scenes in Metastasio led up to: they culminate in an 'aria situation'. And we find ourselves also in exactly the same world of the stately conflict of love and honour against a background of thrones, priests, warriors, and captives.

In *Aida* Verdi is unable to enter wholly into that world. True, *Aida* is fairly riddled with consecrations and triumphals—Verdi even brings a large brass band on the stage with the warriors and elephants (if available) in Act II—and there are ballets of priestesses and of Nubian slaves, all these with generous splashes of local colour. But it is in his treatment of the principals that Verdi betrays his uneasiness with all this pageantry, for they are in another tradition altogether, that of the Italian *verismo* opera of the late nineteenth century. He attempts to make them real-life figures acting in a manner that would not be out of place in a modern play, and this does not suit either his story or his setting, nor does it coalesce very well with all the spectacular apparatus. The turning point of the opera is an excellent illustration, the scene in which Amonasro forces Aida to submit to his will and promise to extract the battle plans from Rhadames. Verdi carefully prepares for Amonasro's entrance by giving to everything before —Amneris' scene with the priests, Aida's 'O patria mia'—a feeling of waiting, of expectation.[11] When he suddenly appears the effect is startling, Aida's 'Ciel! mio padre' at once signalling an accelerated tempo. Verdi's prime concern during the duet which now ensues is psychological realism, to give distinctive personalities to his characters and to make their motivations and actions thoroughly believable. Amonasro's autocratic sternness is conveyed by his opening recitative, hammering on a single note in 'A te grave cagion m'adduce, Aida'. He appeals first to Aida's pride, as he begins now to manipulate her emotions that he may establish some control over her. (In Dryden the Inca simply gives an order to Orazia, and she and we must accept.) He works on her nostalgic memories of her homeland, and the woodwinds of 'O patria mia' are heard in the orchestra, indicating that Amonasro has overheard her aria. Aida, succumbing to his power, repeats his phrases and then develops them further. He changes the mood as he begins to speak of the Egyptian atrocities, but does not yet make his demand, hoping to arouse her feelings to the point where she will have no wish to resist. In this, however, he fails, and must finally resort to fury as he charges her with being disloyal to her country and her gods. Verdi summons the brasses to sharpen the realism of Amonasro's thunderous picture of the horrors of war, a thrilling *verismo* passage. By evoking finally the image of her mother's ghost rising from Ethiopia's ruins to curse Aida, he breaks down her resistance. Aida, weeping and spent, for a moment is too overcome to sing, so the 'cellos sing for her; gradually she joins them brokenly, but they must complete her phrases, indicating the terrible strain she is enduring. The victorious Amonasro now sweeps into one of Verdi's most inspired melodies at the words, 'Pensa che un popolo vinto, straziato'. It is the lyrical climax of an episode which is an excellent example of psychological and dramatic realism.

How different this is from Dryden and Purcell, and from Metastasio! Verdi has taken what by 1870 he would consider an old-fashioned story (doubtless suitable to an Egyptian audience),

---

[11] In the analysis of this scene I am indebted to Katherine Griffith's article, 'The Decisive Moment': *Opera News*, vol. XXII (25 November 1957), p. 10.

and has been only partially able to accept it for what it is. The style of *Il Trovatore* or *Ernani*, blissfully at home in broad splashy spectacle and unpsychological motivation, would have been infinitely more suitable to the libretto, and would have made an opera of greater unity of effect. It is significant that in his last two operas, *Otello* and *Falstaff*, he and his librettist Boito greatly simplified Shakespeare in the interests of psychological realism.

Verdi's use of the sacrificial scene in the first act is exactly analagous to Purcell's in *The Indian Queen* and most of his other operas, whereas the triumphal scene, waving the ensemble towards the end, serves precisely the function of similar episodes in *Dioclesian*, *King Arthur*, and *Bonduca*. Here is the world of the heroic extravaganza, and nothing Verdi is able to do can weave it into the *verismo* technique of the purely dramatic episodes in *Aida*, though these two scenes do control the mood or tone of the whole work just as they do in Purcell. In other scenes where the sacrificial element is important but not central he uses it as a background which he is able to blend in masterly fashion with the more vital dramatic action. The outstanding example is in the Amneris-Rhadames scene in Act IV, but the liturgical note is impressively though briefly employed at the opening of the Nile Scene and during the last few moments of the opera. Except in *Dido* Purcell, as we know, was denied the use of this choral background against which the principals could sing, and had to content himself with writing in essentially unintegrated blocks.

The other way in which Verdi attempts to turn *Aida* into an integrated whole is one not really denied Purcell, I suppose, but one neither he nor any other composer before the romantic period ever gave much thought to. This is the use of local colour, in *Aida* plaintive oriental strains that do service most effectively for Egyptian atmosphere. In fact it is so easy to do that in the hands of composers less gifted than Verdi it quickly becomes a tawdry substitute for musical thought, the most frantic illustration being in *Turandot*. But in *The Indian Queen*, as Westrup says, the action might be taking place in St James's Park for all the music tells us. Atmosphere was managed by scenes and costumes; the poet and composer 'contented themselves with rising to the emotional heights suggested by the theme'.[12] This indifference to atmospheric

[12] *Purcell*, p. 142: London, 1947.

colour is still the rule a hundred years later when Mozart wrote *Die Entführung aus dem Serail* and *Die Zauberflöte*. Purcell comes nearest to it in that pictorial or descriptive writing where he is illustrating a single word, of necessity a momentary touch, or in several beautifully sustained longer passages when he calls up emanations of such elemental states as sleep, mystery, or night. As we saw with the Sorceress in *Dido*, the mere fact that her speeches were set to music instead of being spoken was thought sufficient to give them a supernatural flavour, hence the witches can sound like rustic revellers without any cause for surprise in the audience. The care Verdi took in weaving a superficial orientalism into the score of *Aida* does give it a certain kind of consistency, but he cannot escape the consequences inherent in the naively bold heroic-play technique of effects without cause. *Aida* is undoubtedly a greater work of genius than *The Indian Queen*, but unlike the earlier work it sits uneasily in its greatness.

4

Since the present chapter has had so much to say about scenes of ritual and sacrifice, probably the one indispensable staple of Purcell's operatic artillery, this is the place to speak of these scenes as a group. The ceremonial scene, often the only musical episode in a play, sometimes assumes an important role in baroque dramaturgy, for it contributes that spaciousness and dignity essential to the heroic proportions of a form too prone to mere noise and smoke. In the best instances its function of lending a wider perspective to the derring-do of the protagonists is like that calm massive façade against which the Trevi Fountain is built, where the flamboyance of Neptune and his denizens is both controlled and ennobled by the imperturbable wall of stone of the Palazzo Poli. The impressiveness of these scenes is not limited to the music alone, but owes a great deal to the many visual possibilities in costume, setting, and the dance.

As might be expected, it is here that Purcell's theatre music comes closest in style to the large output of sacred music that he had been writing since his teens and which is itself 'dramatic'. His masters in the anthem were Locke and Blow and especially

Pelham Humphrey, who at the expense of King Charles II had studied both in France with Lully and in Italy where Carissimi and Cesti had brought the sacred cantata to a high level of refinement.[13] Humphrey was able to combine in his own music, which is nearly always sacred, the expressive declamation of Lully's operas, with its choral effects and strong rhythmic sense, with an Italian sweetness and pathos. His addiction to 'false' relationships and violent pictorialism along with the careful observance of verbal inflections in his musical rhythms show that he was also much influenced by the English idiom of Lawes and Locke. To this remarkable young composer, who died in 1674 when he was only twenty-seven, is due the shaping of the English anthem into a short cantata for instruments, solo voices, and chorus. His anthem, 'By the waters of Babylon', long mistaken for a composition by Purcell, shows how they are imaginatively combined into a dramatic whole. A stately recitative for the basso is followed by an excited turbulent chorus of mocking Babylonians, after which comes a languishing trio, 'How shall we sing the Lord's song?', and the brief concluding chorus. On a small scale it is theatrical in much the same manner as Verdi's *Requiem*, a score in which every page reveals the operatic composer. Harmonically Humphrey's style is signalized by the simultaneous use of major and minor tonalities, the augmented and diminished steps of the melody seeming to contradict the full tonal cadences. As Bukofzer has expressed it, 'The peculiar effect of the English idiom can be described as the clash between the chromatic, or rather non-tonal melody and an essentially diatonic harmony.' To see how profoundly Purcell fell under this influence we need go no further than the score nearest at hand, the final chorus of *The Indian Queen*.

Purcell's sacrificial scenes date back to his very first work for the stage, Nathaniel Lee's *Theodosius* in 1680, where his experience in the sacred anthem immediately puts him at his ease. In the second act of *Psyche* Locke had written a ceremonial episode that could have served as his model, but its stolid unmelodic declamation the twenty-one-year-old Purcell easily outstrips. After *Theodosius*, extended scenes of ritual are found in the following works,

[13] In this paragraph I draw upon Bukofzer, *Music in the Baroque Era*, pp. 188 and 200, and Watkins Shaw in *Eight Concerts of Purcell*.

and the dates are significant: *Circe* (1685), *Dioclesian* (1690), *King Arthur* (1691), *Oedipus* (1692), *Bonduca* (1695), and *The Indian Queen* (1695). For all but two of them the framework is practically identical—a stately passage of invocation for the priest (or priests) and chorus, a more lyrical and romantic passage most often for the soprano with instrumental obbligato, and finally some sort of rejoicing or triumphal movement involving all available musical forces. *King Arthur* is an exception in that there is a double invocation and no middle section of languishment, and that the chorus is used in every number of the scene; the difference in *The Indian Queen* is that the extended ritualistic scene of Ismeron and the God of Dreams in Act III is closer to the masque, while the ceremonial of Act V is very brief. But what is most striking in this group is that we have a collection of several dozen individual numbers in which, despite frequent similarity of style and construction, Purcell never once repeats himself, and of which even the least is beautiful. Their freshness and variety are extraordinary.

Of individual numbers there is no need to speak at length, especially since many have already been treated in our consideration of the major scores, but it is always fascinating to see how increasingly inventive and ingenious Purcell becomes. The distance between *Theodosius* and *Bonduca* is vast: it is no less than that between the most competent composer of his period and the nonpareil of English music. In the *Theodosius* scene two daughters of the king are preparing to take the veil. It opens as we should expect with an invocation of stately beauty from the priest with trio response, and is followed with gently melancholy solos for each soprano, and a brighter conclusion for priest and chorus. Despite lovely moments it is on the whole unadventurous, all the numbers are in the same key of G minor, the accompaniment is for only continuo and two recorders (obviously all that was available), and, most surprising, there is virtually no repetition of words anywhere. We have seen over and over that one of Purcell's notable accomplishments was throwing off the subservient attitude towards poetry of composers like Lawes and Locke who had attempted 'just note and accent' by exact syllabic declamation. Largely by repetitions of single words or phrases Purcell achieved the uneven line lengths and rhythmic variety that are so characteristic of his mature style, and which enabled his vocal music to take on larger proportions than that of any previous English composer. Hardly a hint of this creeps into *Theodosius*. Besides the ceremonial scene in Act I he has written single songs to be sung between each act. The plan is naive and decorative—there is not the slightest attempt to introduce them into the play itself—and we are not much put off by the fact that they are pure Restoration pastoral though the drama takes place at Constantinople in the first century. One of them, 'Hail to the myrtle shade', a duet for soprano and alto, is meltingly melodious.

Five years later, though he had done almost no stage music in the interim, his dramatic style is considerably more advanced. For a revival of *Circe*, a dismal rhymed tragedy by Davenant's son Charles, he supplied a long sacrificial scene in which he does a good deal with key contrasts and with more elaborately planned choruses. In the opening invocation a persistent figure on the words 'we must, we must' pulls the whole episode together, achieving a sense of organization not to be found in anything in *Theodosius*. He does it again in the next number, an alto aria 'The air with music gently wound', by means of a ground bass, and in addition manages a subtle variation by having the chorus come in on the same melody but abandoning the ground. The first part of the scene is predominantly major and pleasant, and shows that Purcell has not fully exploited the moods of the text; but after an interruption by Circe, a garrulous goddess who summons Pluto and attendant horrors, the mode is mostly minor with frequent chromaticism. The final number, 'Pluto, arise!', is a highly charged recitative for basso with rich harmonies scored for the entire orchestra. The verses are deplorable—one number begins, 'Their necessary aid you use'—but the music serenely transcends them and foretells the splendours to come.

In looking at the chronology of these scenes we note that the three earliest use only the bass with the chorus in the opening invocations, and that by the use of rests and off-beat entries all three give somewhat the same impression in their vocal lines and their rhythms. With *King Arthur* he ventures to two soloists with chorus and adds a second invocation, though sticking to fairly conventional F-major harmony, but in *Oedipus* the next year we find three soloists with the chorus in dense chromatic harmonies, and in *Bonduca* four.

The same clear progression from competence to complex brilliance appears in the lyrical airs of the middle sections of these scenes. The soprano aria in *Dioclesian* has a flowing ease and an insinuating quality lacking in the stiffish *Theodosius*, whereas the comparable song in *Bonduca* adds a second soprano, a ground, and two flutes. The ground of the alto solo in *Oedipus*, 'Music for a while', is far more complex than that of the related air from *Circe*. Indeed in the *Oedipus* scene, consisting of only three numbers but each of them extensively developed, Purcell has achieved technical perfection. The layer upon layer of descents on the words 'ten thousand fathoms low' in the invocation, the relation between ground and voice in the alto solo, and in the final number the changes rung upon a simple descending scale and upon that old friend, the I_4^6-V-I cadence—all these are virtuoso strokes of the first order. Yet in comparison with the longer episodes in *Bonduca* and *The Indian Queen* they are deficient in providing some prevailing unity of mood. They remain three separate pieces held together only by their common C minor tonality, and indeed the second of them is unabashed decoration, mere 'entertainment' and relief from the horrors (in more than one sense) of Dryden and Nat Lee's play. Thus the *Oedipus* scene, for all its very great beauty, is a good example of how the Restoration audience took its music, and shows us why opera as conceived in the serious sense of a Monteverdi or a Gluck was not possible for Purcell in the commercial theatre. How great a tragedy this has been to the world is all too plain when we look at the isolated, lonely *Dido and Aeneas*.[14]

[14] In addition to these scenes of ceremonial Purcell wrote dozens of incidental songs scattered over nearly forty plays. Some of them are discussed by Westrup: *op. cit.*, ch. 12.

CHAPTER VII

The Tempest

I

THE FLOOD OF MUSIC pouring from Purcell's pen during the last year of his life seems almost frenzied, as though he sensed that he was a doomed man with far more to give than time to give it in. I think it not too fanciful to say that one feels this quality not only in its sheer mass—for the theatre alone he provided music to nearly a dozen plays, three of them major scores—but in the nature of some of the music itself. On the one hand there is a new burst of gurgling exuberance, as in the Neptune arias at the end of *The Tempest*, the last feverish excitement of creation, and on the other a deeper poignance, a harsher dissonance, as in the concluding chorus of *The Indian Queen* or the final song, 'From rosy bowers'. Although it now seems impossible to trace the exact chronology of these ultimate compositions, *The Indian Queen* and *The Tempest* are unquestionably the two last works on a large scale. In some ways *The Tempest* is as suitable a valediction for Purcell as it was for Shakespeare, for here he takes his farewell of one style, seen most beautifully in the setting of 'Full fathom five', and experiments with a new Italianate manner which was to dominate English music during the early eighteenth century. As with Shakespeare, it is perhaps his least characteristic work yet to many judges his most beautiful. And how fitting that great genius should in its farewell do something totally unexpected.

It is amusing that the most popular play of the Restoration so far as we now can tell was not by a contemporary playwright at all but was Shakespeare's. More accurately a distant cousin of Shakespeare's, for it is an operatic version of *The Tempest* sub-titled *The Enchanted Island* and adapted by Thomas Shadwell in 1674 from a slightly earlier adaptation by Dryden and Davenant. From the first it was a big thing. At the opening performance in Lincoln's Inn Fields on 7 November 1667, Pepys found himself amidst 'a great many great ones. The house mighty full; the King and Court there: and the most innocent play that ever I saw; and a curious piece of music is an echo of half-sentences, the echo repeating the former half, whilst the man goes on to the latter; which is mighty pretty.' Anyone who has read the play must be startled by Pepys' notion of innocence, but his notice does suggest the importance of the music even in the Dryden-Davenant version, called merely 'A Comedy'. Much bigger things were in the offing, however, for the larger stage and elaborate machinery at the new Dorset Garden Theatre prompted the managers to put on a downright extravaganza. The most valuable contemporary reference to it is again that of John Downes, the prompter of the Duke's Company for over forty years, who leaves us in no doubt about its success:

> The Tempest, or Enchanted Island, made into an opera by Mr Shadwell, having all new in it; as scenes, machines; particularly, one scene painted with myriads of ariel spirits; and another flying away, with a table furnished out with fruits, sweet-meats, and all sorts of viands; just when Duke Trincalo and his companions were going to dinner; all things performed in it so admirably well, that not any succeeding opera got more money.[1]

Shadwell's opera absorbed the Dryden-Davenant alteration from which it differs very little except in a more extensive use of music and spectacle. Despite the lavishness of the court masque, the general public had had very little splendour before the opening of Dorset Garden on 9 November 1671, and *The Tempest* outdid that theatre's former outdoings. Many contemporary allusions testify to its immediate and continued popularity, and to various

[1] *Roscius Anglicanus*, p. 34: London, 1708. There has been much controversy over Shadwell's part in the enterprise, a few scholars favouring Dryden or Betterton as the operatic arranger. The extensive bibliography may be found in Nicoll: *A History of English Drama*, vol. 1, p. 430: London, 1952. The latest and completest summary of both the bibliographical and musical problems of the 1667 and 1674 productions is by J. G. McManaway: 'Songs and Masques in *The Tempest*': *Luttrell Society Reprints*, no. 14 (1953), pp. 71–96.

special performances and revivals. It was to a new production in 1695 that Purcell was engaged to write an entire new score with results so successful that it eclipsed the older music and served all eighteenth-century performances up to the advent of Dr Arne fifty years later. Even then Arne merely added new numbers, the bulk of Purcell's score being retained.

With *The Tempest* we enter the troubled waters of Shakespearean adaptations, upon which the perfect commentary is Shadwell's own second act verse, 'Arise, ye subterranean winds'. Since many articles and at least two important books[2] have been written on this subject from various points of view, little need be said here except as it relates to Purcell's Shakespearean operas. On at least one point all critical sensibilities have been sufficiently bruised to unite in a common attitude—a kind of amused horror that the Restoration could have felt the need to make such tasteless revisions, and could have liked them so well after they had been made. Yet in the light of a great many factors it would probably be more remarkable had the plays *not* been revised than otherwise. Although there is no defending things like Tate's *King Lear*, we must make an effort to look upon the operas at any rate not as adulterations of Shakespeare but as works in their own right with genuine and individual attractions. That these consist in various musical and scenic effects rather than in the texts is after all true of nearly every musical play ever written and of most genuine operas as well.

Viewed against the background of the whole century the desire to 'improve' Shakespeare during the Restoration is perfectly normal. He was not yet sacrosanct but rather was popular in the broadest sense of the term, belonging not to connoisseurs but to the public. Furthermore many of the physical conditions of stage performances had been so altered that some corresponding changes in the texts were thought necessary to accommodate them. The long, bare apron stage of the Elizabethan theatre, which forbade any kind of decorative production, had shrunk considerably, and as a consequence the proscenium arch came to be regarded more and more as a picture frame. The greater attention given to the look of the production was therefore natural,

[2] G. C. D. Odell: *Shakespeare from Betterton to Irving*: New York, 1920; and Hazleton Spencer: *Shakespeare Improved*: Cambridge, 1927.

and the coincidence of elaborate machinery commercially popular in France and in Italy (and in part transferred to the English commercial theatre from the court masque, as we have seen earlier) tended to exaggerate that attention. The audience, too, was a small and aristocratic one which had largely formed its taste on the splendours of the masque and would not be satisfied with Puritan austerity in production. The enormously reduced size of this audience and the consequent necessity for a perpetual change of bill dictated a shortening and simplifying of the plays. There is a limit to what a small group of actors can learn and execute. The introduction of actresses meant a different emphasis in Shakespeare's female roles and a doubling of the cult of the star. Equally important was the gradual emerging taste of the Enlightenment and the desire to emulate French clarity and sophistication which was accompanied by a strong distaste for Jacobean and metaphysical excesses. Of the many directions illustration might take, one quotation from Dryden must suffice:

> Yet it must be allowed to the present age that the tongue in general is so much refined since Shakespeare's time, that many of his words, and more of his phrases, are scarce intelligible. And of those which we understand some are ungrammatical, others coarse, and his whole style is so pestered with figurative expressions that it is as affected as it is obscure.[3]

To our earlier discussion of the heroic taste and of the changes the Restoration wrought in Beaumont and Fletcher, all pertinent here, nothing need be added. No one will claim that *The Tempest* is better off for being converted into an opera, but neither should we be appalled at the Restoration for enjoying such a work. Will not some future age look back in wonder (if not anger) at a period which applauded musical adaptations of *Pygmalion* and even *Anna Christie*? And before losing all patience with Restoration perversity it is prudent to remember two facts. First, only about half a dozen of the Shakespearean alterations were especially successful; at least three of the greatest plays—*Hamlet, Othello,*

---

[3] Preface to *Troilus and Cressida, or Truth Found too Late.* A similar attitude is suggested in the prologue to the play, where Betterton, representing the Ghost of Shakespeare, declaimed:

> Untaught, unpractised, in a barbarous age,
> I found not, but created first the stage.

and *Julius Caesar*—appeared season after season with no alteration beyond extensive cuts. Second, it is only in our own time that the movement to present Shakespeare in a complete text and with some approximation to Elizabethan practices has made any headway. The nineteenth century had its own ways of smothering Shakespeare quite as efficiently as the Restoration.

From a musical point of view *The Tempest* is in a class apart among Shakespeare's plays. It is in a very special sense a play to be seen and heard. Everyone will recognize its frequent proximity to the masque, not merely in the ceremonial of Ceres from Act IV, and the traces of the antimasque in the animals that drive off Caliban and his drunken friends, but also in the way that music pervades the moods of the play. After the harsh realism of the opening scene we fade into the strange sounds of the island with the songs of Ariel constantly evoking or reinforcing the magical atmosphere. In addition a good deal of instrumental music is called for, all of it important to Shakespeare's conception of the dream-like world of the imagination. It is not too impressionistic to say that some of the scenes, especially those of Ferdinand and Miranda, are like slow movements from a ballet, rarefied and symbolic. Consequently, to plan a production of *The Tempest* with an operatic slant is not a far-fetched idea but is in fact harmonious with Caliban's great speech beginning,

> The isle is full of noises,
> Sounds and sweet airs that give delight and hurt not. . . .

But the chief interest of Davenant, and especially Dryden, was something different. On a subject that has been so widely discussed elaboration is unnecessary. To the uninitiated reader a statement from Dryden's preface will give the clue:

> Sir William D'Avenant, as he was a man of quick and piercing imagination, soon found that somewhat might be added to the design of Shakespeare, of which neither Fletcher nor Suckling had ever thought: and therefore to put the last hand to it, he designed the counterpart to Shakespeare's plot, namely that of a man who had never seen a woman; that by this means those two characters of innocence and love might the more illustrate and commend each other.[4]

[4] Although the play had come out in 1667 it was not published until 1670, two years after Davenant's death, hence the tone of Dryden's encomiums.

Dryden tells us that the 'comical parts of the sailors' were also Davenant's invention 'and for the most part his writing', and implies that everything else was his own. These include a sister for Miranda named Dorinda, Caliban's sister Sycorax, and a sweetheart for Ariel called Milcha. Thus is the Restoration passion for balance satisfied, a balance comparable to that which permeates baroque architecture and decoration, a mass or cluster on one side always having its counterpart, not necessarily a duplicate, on the other. These additional characters also provide generous opportunities for introducing bawdy or near-bawdy dialogue. The sisters' ignorance of 'that thing' man, and Hippolito's of 'those dangerous enemies of men called women' provide an Open Sesame to doubles entendres. In his imposing edition of Dryden's works Sir Walter Scott said that Miranda and Dorinda speak the language of prostitution before they ever see a man. The following exchange gives some idea of the possibilities lurking in their innocence.

> MIRANDA (*to Dorinda*): If children come by lying in a bed, I wonder you
> And I had none between us.
> DORINDA: Sister, it was our fault, we meant like fools
> To look 'em in the fields, and they, it seems
> Are found only in beds.
> HIPPOLITO: I am o'erjoyed that I shall have Dorinda in a bed. . . .

To call this bawdy is certainly extravagant, but it exhibits a leering archness utterly alien to Shakespeare. From Dryden, a nonpareil at elegant smut, the indecencies spring, for Davenant was almost prudish when he had to deal with verbal grossness.

Hazleton Spencer's summary tells everything that the modern Shakespearean idolator feels: 'Gone is the noble serenity that makes us eager to regard *The Tempest* as Shakespeare's farewell message to the world; in its place we have a licentious farce.'[5] But to one interested in the widely various manifestations of the baroque spirit, the play is a fascinating illustration of the baroque passion for piling into a single work so wide a diversity of appeals as to land it straight in the lap of the grotesque. Still, the utter delight of some of the *grotesquerie* is unmistakable, especially in Trincalo's besozzled wooing of Sycorax, whom he calls 'dear

[5] *Op. cit.*, p. 203.

blobber-lips . . . my fair fuss . . . Queen Blouze the First'. 'She
wants a little breeding', he adds, 'but she's hearty.' Regrettably
Sycorax is not long in absorbing the authentic Restoration flavour;
so unabashed are her overtures to other visitors on the island that
her newly gained husband exclaims: 'Well, I must be rid of my
Lady Trincalo, she will be the fashion else; first cuckold her
husband, and then sue for separation, to get alimony.' To lament
that this is not like Shakespeare is to be both irrelevant and obtuse.
What is more, Dryden and Davenant by stripping Prospero of his
omnipotence have even been able to kindle a spark of dramatic
interest lacking in the original. When Hippolito is thought to be
slain in a duel with Ferdinand, Prospero's grief is genuine and his
helplessness to bring him back to life strikes one as touching. Of
course it is all a mistake—Hippolito has fainted from lack of blood
and Ariel restores him with healing herbs—but for a moment the
play embraces a human dilemma quite absent from Shakespeare.

It is more an entertainment than a play, however, and if the
alterations, however understandable, seem regrettable, the
music is always there as compensation. Ariel's familiar songs,
originally set by Shakespeare's contemporary Robert Johnson,
were reset in the Restoration by John Banister, who also supplied
music for two new texts, Ariel's 'Dry those eyes which are
o'erflowing' and the duet with Ferdinand, 'Go thy ways', which
had so enchanted Pepys. 'No more dams' and 'The master, the
swabber' were not set, but, doubtless as in Shakespeare's time,
were bawled out to some old ballad tune or else extemporized
by the actor. The masque of Ceres is unaccountably dropped—
perhaps it was too stately and pale—but a vigorous substitution is
made at the entrance of the conspirators earlier on, 'A dialogue
sung in parts' by two devils in Act II beginning 'Where does
proud ambition dwell?' The stage direction then reads: 'Enter the
two that sung, in the shape of devils, placing themselves at the
corners of the stage'. They are joined by Pride, Fraud, Rapine,
and Murder, who do not sing, 'after which they fall into a round
encompassing the Duke, etc., singing:

> Around, around we pace
> About this cursed place,
> Whilst thus we compass in
> These mortals and their sin.'

This is so close to what Davenant provided for the witches in his operatic *Macbeth* that one can assume it is his rather than Dryden's. The music has not survived, nor has that for the saraband danced by Ariel and Milcha at the end.

There is little more music here than in Shakespeare's own play, and certainly not enough to justify the title 'opera' even in the very free Restoration sense. With Shadwell it is another matter. Except for a few cuts and some transpositions of scenes and speeches, the non-musical part of the text is practically the same as the 1667 version; in fact for two centuries it was published in editions of Dryden and Davenant as their work.[6] But he added a great deal of music by four different composers, all of them very celebrated at the time, which proves that the production of Shadwell's opera, quite apart from the truly dazzling scenic splendours, was one of the most important theatrical events of the Restoration. Locke, Composer-in-Ordinary to the King, wrote eleven separate instrumental numbers, five of them act tunes, the remainder played before and at the opening of the curtain. Draghi, probably organist to Catherine of Braganza and popularly known as 'Signor Baptist', furnished all the dance music, the only part of the score that has not been preserved. Humphrey, Master of the Children, did most of the new vocal music to some of the verses Purcell was to set twenty years later. They include the greatly expanded scene for the devils in Act II in which the four allegorical figures become singers, the song 'Where the bee sucks', and a large-scale masque of Neptune and Amphitrite at the end. The fourth composer was an Italian then residing in London, Pietro Reggio, who set the thunderous aria at the end of Act II, 'Arise, ye subterranean winds'. Most of Banister's music was

---

[6] Before Montague Summers' reprint in *Shakespearean Adaptations* (1922) the 1667 version was printed only twice, in 1670 and in Tonson's folio Dryden of 1701. All other printings are really the Shadwell opera, though not recognized as such until an article by Sir Ernest Clarke writing in the *Athenaeum* for 25 August 1906. The publishers of the Shadwell opera in 1674 (and subsequently in 1676, 1690, and 1695) did not look upon it as a new work, for they retained the prologue and epilogue of the Dryden-Davenant comedy. The only reason Dryden himself did not supply the new lyrics seems to be that he had switched to the King's Company under Killigrew, and soon began to make acid remarks about the spectacle of the other more successful house.

retained as well, making up a musical score of sizeable proportions.[7]

Other works of the period, *The Siege of Rhodes* for one, had had large musical scores, but nothing had ever appeared in the professional theatre in England which even approached the staging of the operatic *Tempest*. It is this splendour of spectacle and machinery, together with the licentious dialogue, that made it for decade after decade one of the most popular works on the London stage. Even in 1746 when Garrick revived Shakespeare's original play for a single season only, the masque of Neptune and Amphitrite remained in a new setting by Arne. When Shakespeare's play was reinstated in 1757 how much of the music was retained it is impossible to say. Advertisements throughout the eighteenth century boast of new scenes and machines, new decorations, or new dances, and occasionally, as we have seen, of new music, which invariably means that some new numbers were added to portions of the older music. In 1777, for example, Thomas Linley supplied music for an adaptation, possibly by Sheridan, which included a song, 'O bid your faithful Ariel fly', ornate and pretty but lamentably soubrettish. With Kemble's 1789 production Dorinda and Hippolito were back in full force and did not finally disappear until the middle of the nineteenth century. After Purcell there seems to be no completely new score.[8]

Shadwell's opening stage direction gives an elaborate description of an inner proscenium especially designed for the production bearing the Royal Arms of England but is more interesting for what it tells us about the orchestra.

> The front of the stage is opened, and the band of 24 violins, with the harpsicals and theorbos which accompany the voices,

[7] This piecemeal accumulation of the score, plus the existence in *The Ariel's Songs* (c. 1675), where Banister's settings appeared, of a mysterious 'Dorinda's Lament' by James Hart, printed in none of the quartos, has suggested to W. M. Milton ('Tempest in a Teapot': *ELH*, no. 14: 1947) that the operatic version grew very much like Topsy, and to call Shadwell 'author' in any strict sense would be unrealistic. The complete bibliographical history is given by McManaway: *op. cit.*

[8] Garrick's operatic *Tempest* (1756) with a score by J. C. Smith, Handel's amanuensis, is another work altogether with a text in which relatively little is taken from Dryden and Davenant. There are thirty-three vocal numbers, many with texts by Garrick. It appears to have survived for only one season. (C. B. Hogan: *Shakespeare in the Theatre*, vol. II, pp. 636–9: Oxford, 1957.)

are placed between the pit and the stage. While the overture is playing, the curtain rises, and discovers a new frontispiece, joined to the great pilasters. . . .

Both the size of the orchestra, which was doubled, and its position, ordinarily in a gallery over the stage, are unusual. The 'band of 24 violins', which would mean all the strings, was the Royal Band, and some of the singers who amounted to 'above 30 warbling voices' were imported from the Chapel Royal.[9] Room was made for the orchestra by means of a second proscenium, Shadwell's 'new frontispiece', the same arrangement that is described in *Albion and Albanius* in the next decade. The Dorset Garden stage was so deep that this was no disadvantage except perhaps on the point of visibility. The profounder significance of this change in position, as Dent observed, was that the presence of a band of instrumentalists could now be accepted as a recognized convention, a normal constituent of the mental atmosphere of the play.

An idea of what the opening scene looked like can be gathered from the description:

> Behind this is the scene, which represents a thick cloudy sky, a very rocky coast, and a tempestuous sea in perpetual agitation. This tempest (supposed to be raised by magic) has many dreadful objects in it, as several spirits in horrid shapes flying down amidst the sailors, then rising and crossing in the air. And when the ship is sinking, the whole house is darkened, and a shower of fire falls upon 'em. This is accompanied by lightning, and several claps of thunder to the end of the storm.

What could not be accomplished by the wave and cloud machines and trapezes for the flyings could be entrusted to the backdrop; some idea of it may be had from the frontispiece to the play in Rowe's 1709 Shakespeare. When the house (meaning the back part of the stage) is darkened, hanging candle-fixtures were probably

[9] The Lord Chamberlain's accounts for 16 May 1674 accord that 'it is His Majesty's pleasure that Mr Turner and Mr Hart, or any other men or boys belonging to His Majesty's Chapel Royal that sing in *The Tempest* at his Royal Highness' Theatre, do remain in town all the week (during His Majesty's absence from Whitehall) to perform that service'. This is a conspicuous example of royal patronage unusual for the time, or at any time in England.

pulled into the wings or up into the rafters. From this opening down to the final masque the scene alternates between Prospero's habitation with its walks of cypress trees and a cave and 'the wilder part of the Island . . . composed of divers sorts of trees, and barren places, with a prospect of the sea at a great distance', haunted by Caliban and the sailors. In every act there is extensive use of machinery along lines that anyone familiar with even Shakespeare's Ariel might imagine. But after the opening scene Shadwell does not really stop the clock with splendours until the masque of Neptune and Amphitrite, which we shall consider along with Purcell's music. It should be remembered that the operatic *Tempest* is by no means typical of the Shakespearean adaptations so prevalent (however short-lived) in the Restoration and the eighteenth century. In the first place, with the exception of *The Fairy Queen*, it is easily the most spectacular of them, and secondly, so far as the text is concerned it may be the worst. Hippolito has with some justification been called the silliest character ever to appear on the stage. Yet its very absurdity makes it delightful, and with the addition of Purcell's music *The Tempest* was without any doubt ravishing to the eye and the ear. It is not the text but the music and spectacle which account for its long-sustained popularity.

2

The score for this work is quite different from any of Purcell's other theatre scores. One can understand why some students of his music find it disappointing, though to Professor Westrup, the most eminent authority on the composer, it shows, along with *The Indian Queen*, 'the full flowering of Purcell's gifts as a composer for the stage'.[10] This is owing to his complete mastery of the latest developments of the Italian style, both vocal and instrumental, which he uses throughout with unfaltering technical facility. To the critics of the score this is just what is wrong. *Da capo* arias follow one upon another, nearly always with a motto beginning, a short instrumental symphony after the first vocal phrase which is then repeated and developed along fairly predictable lines, and with a faultless unity of style. What is often lacking are the strong

[10] *Purcell*, p. 140.

sense of individuality and the constant surprises that delight us in the earlier music. Certainly it is the most suave of Purcell's scores and everything in it is pretty, but its strengths lie in its formalities rather than in what most people adore in Purcell, his seemingly spontaneous vitality. When this spontaneity does appear in such songs as 'Come unto these yellow sands' and 'Full fathom five', the difference from the rest of the score is startling.

Since the music was not published for many years, and since theatre records are very meagre before the eighteenth century, we are forced, lacking other evidence, to date *The Tempest* by a new edition of the text of the play, which usually coincided with a revival. The only possibility is 1695, the last year of Purcell's life, a date that we should have been inclined to fix upon in any event because of the style of the music. Purcell's text differs from the 1674 *Tempest* in only one noticeable respect—the masque of Neptune and Amphitrite has been reduced by about half, and the lines that remain, though similar to Shadwell's, are different. The only music over which there is any question is the overture, which has not been definitely established as belonging to *The Tempest*. The manuscript (not an autograph) unobligingly says only 'Overture in Mr. P. Opera', and the key of G minor is employed nowhere else in the score, very unlike Purcell's customary practice. Nevertheless it is a beautifully finished composition in which the subject of the quick fugal movement is ingeniously inverted. Its airy grace suggests Ariel, but so do all the comparable sections in Purcell's Lullian overtures.

The actual setting of the text begins, like the earlier versions, with the duet of the devils who accost Alonzo, Antonio, and Gonzalo in Act II. Though the text is horrendous, the two bassos sing, like the witches in *Dido*, in merry, strongly rhythmical antiphonals, puckish rather than grisly devils and consonant with the spirit of Ariel who pervades the musical sections of the play. The chorus answers with a remarkable anticipation of Handel's 'Hallelujah' chorus before the devils sing a second verse in a more intricate rhythm with a glancing harshness created by two examples of false relationship. Pride, Fraud, Rapine, and Murder rise in turn and sing, but what happened to their music, if Purcell ever wrote any, is unknown. The episode ends with a gay little contrapuntal chorus with dotted rhythms and bland C major harmonies to the words 'Around, around we pace'. Its infectious charm and ingenious handling of a simple binary form make the corresponding chorus in the contemporaneous *Macbeth* score look very insipid indeed, though this music has frequently been claimed as Purcell's. These happy devils dance out leaving the shipwrecked conspirators to bless their luck, but with the splendours of Dorset Garden's trap-doors at his command Shadwell will not leave them alone for very long. 'As they are going out, a Devil rises just before them, at which they start, and are frighted.' After Alonzo's cry, 'O heavens! yet more apparitions', this devil sings the most celebrated aria in the score, 'Arise, ye subterranean winds'. As he finishes, 'Two winds rise, ten more enter and dance. At the end of the dance, three winds sink, the rest drive Alonzo, Antonio, Gonzalo off', and Act II, to the relief of the machine operators below the stage, has ended.

This massive bravura aria, as well as the equally formidable Neptune arias in the final masque, Purcell probably wrote for the marvellous basso Richard Leveridge, who by this time had begun his long career on the London stage where he continued to sing them right down to the middle of the next century. Their style of long roulades up and down the scale on a single breath the reader will know something of from an aria like 'Why do the nations?' from *Messiah*, but the fiendish virtuosity demanded for their execution leaves Handel behind. It is the first of several examples in the score of the Italian concerto style with motto beginning and longish instrumental passages repeating the vocal line, which is itself usually repeated at least once, not counting the *da capo*. In 'Arise, ye subterranean winds' (not actually a *da capo* aria) the enormous scale passages encompass two octaves, but the harmonies, all tonic, dominant, and subdominant of C major plus a brief middle section in A minor, are so simple that the showiness is easily assimilated. It is high-powered extrovert music designed to shake the traitors (and probably the basso); subtlety in structure or in harmonies would be supererogatory.[11]

It is also in this aria that the first misgivings about the authenticity of the score may arise. Mr Dennis Arundell is bluntly sceptical of Purcell's hand in the whole undertaking:

[11] Westrup (*op. cit.*, p. 146) reproduces the beginning of this aria alongside that of Reggio's paler version in the 1674 production.

It is said that towards the end of his life he began to write more in the Italian style that became typical of the early eighteenth century, but, if this is so, and if *The Tempest* with its false accentuation of the words is really by Purcell, then it is as well he did not live long enough to outgrow the music of his that we know—the strength of which lies in its truth rather than in its formalities, in its union with words and thoughts rather than in its unity of style, in its instinct rather than in its technique, and in its spontaneous vitality rather than in its considered academicism.[12]

Purcell's distinctive gift is in the setting of English words; the melodic shape seems to conform with the natural way of speaking the words, the perfect example of 'just note and accent', but it is above all a melody, not merely words sung. Mr Arundell insists quite plausibly that in 'Arise, ye subterranean winds' Purcell would have put the roulade on 'rise' rather than 'sub' and goes on to suggest that at his death he may have left the vocal line of the aria in the rough, and that his brother Daniel fit the words carelessly.[13] Further suspicions arise from the dance of the winds immediately following. Taken from Lully's *Cadmus et Hermione*, which had been performed in London in 1686, it is the only known example of Purcell's borrowing music from another composer. Though he appropriated the tune, why we do not know, he considerably changed the bass and, as a consequence, the harmony. One wonders why he should have gone to this labour when he could as easily (or more easily) have composed an original number. On the other hand, if this appropriation were also the work of Daniel one would have expected a wholesale transfer rather than the meticulous changes in harmonization. Yet in spite of these puzzling matters of detail, no one can seriously doubt that *The Tempest* is predominantly Purcell's. The Italianate manner of so much of the score may already have become conventional on the Continent, but for Purcell the departure from the style of his other theatre music was in the nature of an experimental adventure, and his excitement leaps forth in the exuberant virtuosity with which the familiar formulas are treated in the many bravura arias. Not one of his contemporaries could possibly have

---

[12] *Eight Concerts of Purcell's Music*, p. 23.
[13] 'Purcell and Natural Speech': *Musical Times*, No. 1396 (June 1959), p. 323.

produced the great concluding masque of Neptune. It is as simple as that.

The third act begins with two songs which the average listener will feel are the most Purcellian of the score and which, incidentally, are the only songs he wrote to Shakespearean words. The Italianate arias of *The Tempest* could have been at least approached (which does not mean equalled) by several other composers—they would have followed the same musical form and produced a singable line—but no one else could have composed 'Come unto these yellow sands' or 'Full fathom five'. Though it is difficult to explain why, the attempt can be made. Shadwell gives the second of these songs to the absurdly named Milcha, but no matter, they are both magical airs evocative of the supernatural in its gentlest, most delicate aspects. In common time and the key of C major, the soprano solo is in both cases followed by a choral answer. Their individuality lies first of all in the rhythms which change from phrase to phrase. 'Come unto these yellow sands', with words reduced from Shakespeare, breaks down into three divisions of two lines each:

> Come unto these yellow sands
> And there take hands;
> Foot it featly here and there
> And let the rest the chorus bear.
> Hark! hark! the watchdogs bark,
> Hark! hark! I hear the strain of Chanticlere.

To the first couplet Purcell devotes four bars, of which $1\frac{1}{2}$ are on the word 'yellow'. The four bars of the second couplet are divided $1\frac{3}{4}$ and $2\frac{1}{4}$. These are sung by Ariel. The chorus sings the six bars of the concluding couplet. Each of the three divisions has its individual rhythmic pattern, a highly complicated format for so short a song, and yet the effect is never fussy or precious. A comparison of the two songs with earlier settings by Johnson and Banister reveal Purcell as the supreme master before Mozart at combining apparently artless innocence with suave sophistication. The settings of the other composers are merely pretty. Banister's version of 'Come unto these yellow sands', for example, for the 1667 production lacks Purcell's rhythmic variety; the first two lines are sung to identical music:

Ariel:

Come un-to these yel-low sands, and there take hands; Curt-sied when you
have and kissed, the wild waves whist: Foot it gent-ly here and there,
and sweet spirits the bur-then bear....

The setting by J. C. Smith for Garrick's 1756 opera is finicky to a
degree.

The more ingenious of the two, 'Full fathom five', retains all
Shakespeare's words and begins with a chime of bells that persists
throughout. The singer's entry on the second beat is characteristic
of the discontinuous rhythms that are a feature of the song; none
of the six lines for Ariel (down to the chorus, 'Sea nymphs hourly
ring his knell') begins on the first beat. The two miniature roulades come rather surprisingly on 'corals' and 'nothing', which
Mr Arundell would doubtless call senseless, but which surely
contribute to the piquant grace of the whole. The choral refrain,

> Sea nymphs hourly ring his knell,
> Hark! now I hear them, ding, dong, bell,

has sometimes been cited as an especially appealing example of
Purcell's dissonance treatment. In the first two bars the soprano
and bass lines appear to have been conceived horizontally but not
vertically. That is, the second bar of the bass line continues the
pattern set in the first bar without reference to the different melodic conditions above. In the second and third chords of the bar
this independent movement produces a dissonance characteristic
of the madrigal style in that four successive notes of the scale are
heard simultaneously. The cadence on 'ding, dong, bell' with its
false relationship between the flat and sharp seventh is the most
atmospheric touch in the score. At a middle point in the chorus the
tenor comes in half a bar late, then gives the effect on 'ding, dong,
bell' of racing to catch up. Banister's pleasant setting, a conventional triple-time tune with the same rhythmic pattern throughout, even for 'ding, dong, bell', throws a revealing light upon
Purcell's individuality:

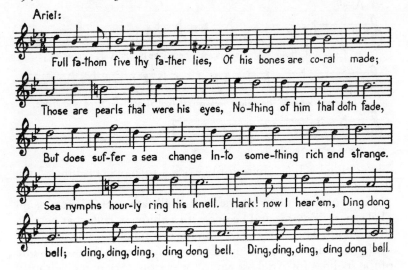

Later in the act Ariel is called upon to serenade Alonzo, mourning the supposed drowning of Ferdinand. In the song 'Dry those eyes which are o'erflowing', Purcell's technical virtuosity may possibly be running away with itself. It is a very long ornamental air of languishment for soprano with double violin obbligato constructed above one of the most elaborate grounds he ever devised, nine bars of quavers built on a descending tetrachord.

The long vocal lines must bring anguish to the throat of any but the most accomplished soprano, while the weaving of the two violins with the ground and the serenely unhurried melody is a masterpiece of the art that looks artless. The voice itself and then the violins finally take up the ground. Yet its length and elaborateness make the song dramatically pointless and unabashedly static. Banister's simple setting with its smoothly

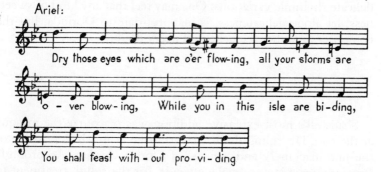

Ariel:

Dry those eyes which are o'er flow-ing, all your storms are o - ver blow-ing, While you in this isle are bi-ding, You shall feast with - out pro-vi-ding

flowing vocal line is more convincing in the situation than Purcell's ornate aria, but the latter is a perfect example of the exquisitely decorative formal block so congenial to baroque taste. Since *The Tempest* is as undramatic as a play can possibly be, Purcell's song ought, I think, to be a welcome addition to any performance in any age.

Dryden's echo duet, 'Go thy ways', was not set by Purcell— possibly the Ferdinand could not sing. The original Banister setting ended with a long passage for Ariel beginning 'Kind fortune smiles', and of these words Purcell makes a charming aria. It is very unlikely that the first part of Banister's duet (that is, as far as 'Kind fortune smiles') was retained in the 1695 production, however popular it had been with Pepys and others, because it could not easily be grafted on to Purcell's song. The duet is in F major, with its last cadence before Ariel's solo on the dominant of the relative minor, providing the obvious transition into the simple aria. Purcell's more elaborate setting in C major could hardly have been substituted.

Since the fourth act is devoted largely to the quartet of lovers there is little music. A song for Dorinda by James Hart beginning 'Adieu to the pleasures and follies of love' had been introduced into the act at some time before the publication of *The Ariel's Songs*, but it was dropped out and Purcell supplies Dorinda with 'Dear pretty youth', another example of his talent at chastening a bawdy lyric. Hippolito, having been wounded by Ferdinand in a duel, is unconscious, and Dorinda is inviting him to go to bed with her, though she is supposedly innocent of the import of her words. Purcell's setting is just saved from oversweetness by delicate rhythmic variations. One may feel that any kind of sweetness, let alone delicateness, is inappropriate to Dorinda, but the composer gives her the benefit of every doubt.

3

Shadwell's most extensive addition was of course the masque at the end. His ruling desire was to make as much as possible of the fine machinery and 'effects' of Dorset Garden. Accordingly Prospero promises to 'make amends' for the rough treatment to which he had subjected the entire dramatis personae and says, 'I'll entertain you with my magic art'. At this point the 'Scene changes to the rocks, with the arch of rocks, and calm sea. Music playing on the rocks.' At Prospero's call 'Neptune, Amphitrite, Oceanus, and Tethys appear in a chariot drawn with sea-horses; on each side of the chariot sea-gods and goddesses, Tritons and Nereides'. Alonzo, suitably impressed, exclaims, 'This is prodigious', and the masque begins. The action could hardly be simpler: Amphitrite asks Neptune to calm the sea so that the inhabitants of the enchanted island can get safely home. Neptune calls up Aeolus who in turn stills the four winds, who fly down and dance. The masque ends with rapturous rejoicing over the good weather—a delightful British touch.[14]

The original setting by Pelham Humphrey, lost for two and a half centuries, was discovered in 1920 at the library of the Paris

[14] This masque, though appropriate enough for *The Tempest*, is of course dispensable, and in the eighteenth century it was not unusual to see something else substituted for it, considerations of style not being the strong suit of professional playhouses. At Drury Lane on 12 February 1750, for example, the 'Grand Entertainment' at the end is Handel's *Acis and Galatea*, and on 27 April of the same year it is *The Savoyard Travellers*.

Conservatoire and was printed in part by Barclay Squire the next year.[15] Though the text is twice the length of Purcell's, it would have taken far less time to sing, as it is largely in Lullian declamation with no repetition of lines except in the brief note-against-note duets and choruses. The tonality is G minor and B-flat major. Historically the piece is interesting, for Humphrey is usually credited with having introduced into England this style of declamatory recitative which Lully had taken from Italy and had developed extensively in his French operas and *comédies-ballets*. It is all mildly pleasant, but far less dramatic than Humphrey's sacred music; indeed it gives point to the suspicion that in Restoration opera the scenes and machines were more important than the music.

With Purcell we are upon palpably different ground. Technically it is his most polished work and exhibits his mastery of the Italian concerto style. Beauties crowd upon beauties as each line of his reduced text is given its fullest possible musical exploitation. Nowhere else has he produced such a series of full-scale arias with such fully developed accompaniments. Since there are virtually no contrasts of characterization or developments in the stage picture, here is the one theatre score in Purcell that would lose comparatively little in a concert performance. The plan is thoroughly uncharacteristic. Of the seven separate numbers five are solos, one is a duet with choral refrain, and only one (and much the shortest) is a chorus. The tonality is limited to C major and minor. Of the five solos three are elaborate bravura arias for basso in almost identical style and three are *da capo* arias (one each for soprano, alto, and basso). Except for an oboe obbligato in the soprano's 'Halcyon days', the scoring is entirely for strings.

For Purcell this set-up is quite unusual and on the face of it singularly unpromising. It suggests no easy solution like certain of the other Shakespearean adaptations. In *The Fairy Queen*, for example, the Masque of Night offered four figures in obviously contrasting voices and moods, as did the Masque of the Seasons in the same opera. Or only a year earlier than *The Tempest*, in 1694, the masque in *Timon of Athens* (another Shadwell arrangement) was laid out upon the simple plan of a contest between love and

[15] 'The Music of Shadwell's Tempest': *Musical Quarterly*, vol. VII (1921), pp. 565–78. So far as I can discover the score has not yet been printed in full.

wine.[16] Though it seems to me a far less rewarding work than the Neptune masque, it is extremely pretty and runs along character-istic lines which insured its immediate popularity. Lord Lansdowne writing several years later in the epilogue to yet another Shake-spearean adaptation, in this case his own *Jew of Venice* (1701), said:

> How was the scene forlorn, and how despised,
> When Timon, without music, moralized!
> Shakespeare's sublime in vain enticed the throng
> Without the charm of Purcell's siren song.

Clearer evidence of how much the theatre relied upon music in these enterprises would be hard to find.

If ever a play needed stepping up in whatever manner it is *Timon of Athens*. Purcell's score clearly lightened the drabness of what Shadwell offered as ancient Greece by its melodiously spirited rivalry of Cupid and his followers against their opponent Bacchus. The masque exhibits a neat sense of unity and coherence; there are three movements apiece for Love and Wine, and in each Purcell tries to emphasize something slightly different. The double opening, 'Hark how the songsters of the grove' and 'Love in their little veins inspires', is in a delicate airy vein with flute accompaniment beautifully devised for comparing lovers' rap-tures with the gurgling joy of birds' songs. A glance at Grabu's opening, by no means unattractive, points up the wonderful felicitousness of Purcell's setting:

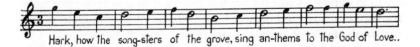

Hark, how the song-sters of the grove, sing an-thems to the God of Love..

---

[16] The textual problem is complex. The masque in Shadwell's play (1678) was set by Grabu, but Purcell's text follows Shadwell in only the first four numbers. Though the remainder of the two texts follows a similar pattern, Purcell's eschews certain crudities, for example, a song by a Shadwell 'Nymph':

> Go drivel and snore with your fat God of Wine,
> Your swelled faces with pimples adorning. . . .

The Purcell text was the work of Peter Motteux about 1692 and was partially set at that time by Franck. Purcell's own score composed in 1694 offers plain evidence of the frequency with which new music was ordered.

The following song,

> But ah! how much are our delights more dear,
> For only humankind love all the year,

is a good instance of his employment of a minor mode in the affective vein for the expression of happiness. Even more affective is the tenor arioso, 'The cares of lovers', in which the swain expresses his aromatic pains by means of a free-moving bravura recitative. The massive chorus, 'Who can resist such mighty charms?', Westrup justly maintains would not be out of place in a Handel oratorio, so lofty is the style. The least individual number of the score is the finale, a duet for Cupid and Bacchus, where Purcell simply could not think of a mood that would suggest a combination of these rival qualities. The words Motteux provided may have discouraged him beyond repair:

> Come, let us agree, there are pleasures divine
> In wine and in love, in love and in wine.

But the *Timon* music cannot qualify as one of the great scores because in spite of ingenious small differences in each number, only three moods are really possible—the joys of love, the joys of drinking, and the pains of love, the latter subject being developed by both parties though with differing emphasis. Presumably the pains of drink is not a suitable subject for music, or at any rate not in Purcell's eyes. The score of a dozen numbers can scarcely avoid an impression of repetitiveness, nor is there, apart from the one great chorus, any inspiration of that spacious splendour which is the masque form's *raison d'être*.

What, then, of *The Tempest*? In a concluding static block given over to the sole business of rejoicing, how can there be any of those contrasting or conflicting currents so necessary for dramatic life? And how can the attention be captured for half an hour or more after everything is over? For dramatically nothing is left, neither in the action of the play nor within the action of the masque. Here are none of the miniature comedies of wooing or the exploring of the many-sidedness of love or patriotism that we remember from *Dioclesian* and *King Arthur*. Here is only jubilation. Yet here also is the richest part of the score and incontestably the most interesting part of *The Tempest*. The interest, in other words, is purely musical.

What first strikes us is its amplitude. After a few lines of greeting between the monarch of the sea and his consort, the dimensions of the music are sounded at once in the elaborately ornamental aria for Neptune,

> Fair and serene, like thee, my queen,
> The region of the air shall be.
> At Neptune's call the winds shall fall,
> Nor longer vex the region of the sea.

It establishes with calm authority that note of confident strength and positiveness peculiar to this score. The singer repeats the verses three times in a form almost strophic, the difference being that the long scale passages suggesting the wind vexing the sea are in each case slightly different and end on different cadences, moving from E-flat major to G minor to the tonic C minor. The strophic repetitions emphasize the rocklike solidity of Neptune, the coloratura his dashing exuberance.

The chorus of Nereids and Tritons moves to the major to answer him in a gently lilting triple-time song suggesting the lapping of waves and a halcyon existence. This chorus can illustrate the manner and extent of Purcell's reducing the original Shadwell text. The lines Humphrey set at this point are as follows:

> Be calm, ye great parents of the floods and the springs,
> While each Nereid and Triton plays, revels, and sings.
> Confine the roaring winds, and we
> Will soon obey you cheerfully.
> Tie up the winds, and we'll obey,
> Upon the floods we'll sing and play,
> And celebrate a halycon day.

All this Purcell's chorus reduces to only two lines:

> The Nereids and Tritons shall sing and shall play,
> And nature shall smile on this happy day.

The phrase 'halcyon day', on the other hand, he took as the inspiration for the soprano air whose counterpart is not in Shadwell.

Neptune summons Aeolus to protect the voyagers as they leave the Enchanted Island and sings a second mighty aria:

> While these pass o'er the deep,
> Your stormy winds must cease.

Here we find Purcell exploiting to the full the Italian style built on the motto beginning with constant alternation between voice and strings and with the vocal line given out in the major with tonic cadence, repeated with dominant cadence, repeated again in the minor, and so on. In the slower middle section much use is made of long sustained notes for the voice with considerable instrumental activity beneath it. So predictable a formula cries out for the most fertile musical imagination if monotony is to be averted. The three Neptune solos are singularly successful in this respect, even though the roulades make less effort at pictorialism or dramatic aptness than is usual for Purcell. In this particular aria almost identical patterns on 'stormy', 'wat'ry', and 'bless' tell their own story. The real drawback, however, to a successful realization of the score today is the staggering professionalism required of the singers. A basso coloratura of the accomplishment of Leveridge has not appeared in the world since the retirement of Plançon early in the present century. The heavily aspirated hooting that one has resigned oneself to in performances of *Messiah* makes butchery of the more delicate Purcellian line which cannot stand up under the assaults that Handel miraculously survives.

Another soloist appears with Aeolus, an alto, who answers Neptune in more coloratura, but whose merry 'Come down, my blusterers', by means of insinuating rhythms and a beguiling vocal line, achieves characterization of a very different sort from the majestic lord of the sea. The first *da capo* aria of the masque, it has a double middle section, the first part in triple time and the tonic C major, the second moving to E minor and the brisk common measure of the opening.

Except for her few bars of initial greeting to Neptune, the soprano Amphitrite has been silent. Purcell now brings her forward in the most ravishing solo of the masque, the *da capo* aria 'Halcyon days'. An oboe announces the ingratiating melody, its four bars giving an idea of how much rhythmical variety Purcell can pack into a small space without a hint of fussiness. The

Amphitrite:

Hal-cyon days, now wars — are end-ing, You— shall find where e'er— you— sail.

enchantment of this song has been most nearly captured in words by Dr Anthony Lewis, who says that it 'manages to convey an impression of tranquil seas reaching into serene horizons of blue. The melodic flow is gently rippling, its liquidity seems to well forth with effortless ease. This is one of music's earliest and most memorable seascapes; certainly none since has been achieved with such economy of means. Ferdinand might well have said of it:

> This music crept by me upon the waters,
> Allaying both their fury and my passion
> With its sweet air.'[17]

The brightness of mood continues in the final bass solo, 'See, see, the heavens smile', the most concerto-like of the airs, full of instrumental ornamentation, vibrating with a vigorous thrust which sets it off from the tenderer Amphitrite. The lovers join in a lyrical duet, 'No stars again shall hurt you from above', taken up by the full chorus and strings. It is in the minor, one of the happiest strokes of the score, for it sidesteps that kind of bright noisy jubilation fine enough for *King Arthur* but jarring to the gentler joy associated with Ariel and the magical island. 'Hope shines through fear and uncertainty', says Dr Lewis, a touchingly suitable end to Purcell's score, perhaps, indeed, his valediction.

Shadwell's original finale was more flamboyant by a good deal:

[17] *Musical Times*, no. 1396 (June 1959), p. 322.

'Scene changes to the rising sun, and a number of aerial spirits in the air, Ariel flying from the sun advances towards the pit.' And there, suspended from his trapeze, the precariously balanced spirit warbled 'Where the bee sucks there suck I' in the graceful setting by Pelham Humphrey. After this, Ariel, 'hovering in the air', bade farewell to Prospero, and vice versa. Nothing remained except an epilogue telling the audience how expensive it all was to get up:

> To please you, we no art or cost will spare.

Such a startling ending once conceived would never have been sacrificed at Dorset Garden, so that although Purcell did not set 'Where the bee sucks' it is a virtual certainty that the curtain in 1695 came down with all the marvels still intact, Ariel carolling forth the earlier Humphrey tune. Art and cost paid off, for audiences continued to lay down money to see this extravaganza for well over a hundred years. The recent Purcell tercentenary revival at the Old Vic, even with nothing approaching the professionalism required by the music, showed how attractive an enterprise a performance of this work can be if the great score remains to embellish the text. With the help of imagination this revival confirmed one's notion of the eminently baroque quality of the whole in that its climax, the movement that gave it its stature, was the masque, a stately block composed of music, dance, and splendour of scene. The messy straggly effect of the play engendered by so many sets of such silly characters behaving in irresponsible ways suddenly vanishes as the clarion-voiced Neptune majestically imposes Purcellian order and dignity. The beauty of the work is in its confidence, its positiveness, its amplitude as it mingles rejoicing with a feeling for the grandeur as well as the serenity of the sea.

Conclusion

IN 1711 Alexander Pope, in a now famous passage of the *Essay on Criticism*, gave neatly pointed expression to a very generalized concept of Nature:

> First follow Nature, and your judgment frame
> By her just standard, which is still the same:
> Unerring Nature, still divinely bright,
> One clear, unchanged, and universal light,
> Life, force, and beauty must to all impart,
> At once the source, and end, and text of Art.

This is a concept formulated solely by the reason. That it was widely held is indicated, even if one knew nothing of the long train of Cartesian philosophers who developed it, by the instantaneous success of the poem. Pope had merely vocalized a strong if inarticulate public instinct, what oft was thought, or at any rate powerfully sensed and struggling towards thought, but ne'er so well expressed. In contrast to his later evolution the poet was at this stage in his career no innovator, but one who still lived by his own advice,

> Be not the first by whom the new is tried,
> Nor yet the last to lay the old aside.

He was a public spokesman. For many people Nature had become all but synonymous with reason, with conformity, with order, with common sense. The grandiose conceptions of baroque imagination were in some quarters coming to seem vulgar and faintly ludicrous. Extravagant individualism, the flaming spirit which shatters old forms and generates new, or which stretches an old form to the very limit as it seeks to cram it with new content, was giving way before an ideal simpler, more objective, more restful, and, regrettably, more standardized. To Dryden Nature had meant the higher pitch, not what was but what ought to be.

It was an ideal. To Pope Nature meant what reason and common-sense, added to his own observation, showed him to be true. It was not the dull average—no satirist was ever content with anything so limp and uninspired—but its voice, being subjected to rules, could be taught.

> Those rules of old discovered, not devised,
> Are Nature still, but Nature methodized;
> Nature, like Liberty, is but restrained
> By the same laws which first herself ordained. . . .
> Learn hence for ancient rules a just esteem;
> To copy Nature is to copy them.

Very occasionally Nature might throw up an exception. Pope speaks of certain supreme geniuses who could

> From vulgar bounds with brave disorder part,
> And snatch a grace beyond the reach of art.

But Dryden might possibly have said that this 'brave disorder' alone *was* art. The huge geniuses of his youth, and just before, were empyrean spirits who seemed unaware of anything so niggling as rules. Nothing that Rubens or Tintoretto achieved at the top of their bent could possibly be taught, nor did it conform to any rules outside itself. And though he received the poet's permission to 'tag' *Paradise Lost*, Dryden obviously recognized that Milton was an inimitable genius; during every day of Pope's lifetime, however, a pitiful host of eighteenth-century Miltonians from the author of *The Seasons* downwards seemed not to recognize it at all. Even Addison, the great popularizer of *Paradise Lost* in a famous series of essays in *The Spectator*, could only examine the poem in the light of certain supposed 'specifications' of the epic as derived from the examples of Homer and Virgil.

All this is another way of saying that the climate which had produced Purcell's masterworks was rapidly changing. A rarefied world of richness and beauty persisted, it is true, but its appearance was undergoing a transformation. Baroque outsize splendour was giving way to rococo refinement. Watteau, after all, is contemporary with *The Rape of the Lock*. Yet this vein is not the important or the central one. It is significant that Pope's great popular reputation was built not on this exquisite poem but, along with his Homer, upon the *Essay on Criticism* and later the *Essay on Man*, works of learning, of analysis, and of philosophy. Flamboyance was waning.

Nor was the climate very propitious for baroque heroes; those indomitable beings had run into heavy weather. To be sure, Addison in *The Campaign* had pictured the Duke of Marlborough in grandiose terms—

> So when an Angel by divine command
> With rising tempests shakes a guilty land,
> Such as of late o'er pale Britannia past,
> Calm and serene he drives the furious blast;
> And, pleased the Almighty's orders to perform,
> Rides in the whirlwind, and directs the storm.

—but he got the idea from *Macbeth*. Later in the century Johnson quotes Dr Samuel Madden's comment, which tells the whole story: 'If I had set ten schoolboys to write on the battle of Blenheim and eight had brought back the Angel, I should not have been surprised.'[1] The hero had become little more than a formula, an empty dummy—empty, that is, of everything but wind. The Addisonian ideal was the man of reason, no matter how he might be dressed. Neither Aurengzebe nor Almanzor any more than King Arthur or Dioclesian were men of reason, but Cato, alas, is nothing else. Paradoxically the heroic drama, though less reasonable, is far more intellectual than the serious drama of the eighteenth century. It is built around an idea, to exhibit the hero in a series of situations that will realize on the stage the magnificence of epic poetry. Since hyperbole is its normal language, its inevitable decline can be foreseen even at its zenith. A work like *Paradise Lost* is for poets a dead end (as Mr Eliot has noted), just as something like Rubens' Whitehall ceiling is for painters. After them the only direction for similar enterprises is downward. *Aurengzebe* and *The Conquest of Granada*, though of lesser stature, are analogous. The heroes protest too much. We here see the heroic ideal at the instant it is about to become formularized. In the next decade even Dryden himself has abandoned Almanzor and Almahide for Absalom and Achitophel, and Pope's master stands revealed.

It was a near-ruinous misfortune that Purcell should have

[1] *Life of Addison.*

settled himself upon a sinking ship. The kind of drama that Dryden wrote not only went out of fashion and never came back in, but, more serious, it embodies an attitude towards experience that has for us become wholly untenable. By the turn of the century the theatre public had outgrown the small rich coterie of the Restoration and was swelling with a semi-puritan middle class who wanted the drama to look like life, or at least in so far as life coincided with morality sentimentally presented. At their backs they heard the voice of Jeremy Collier, and it did not displease them. The spread of democracy, to say nothing of common sense, put an end to Almanzor for ever. To good Augustans he was all rant, and they could see through that. Though his own disappearance might cause no tears, along with him disappeared the stylization and formality which have always been indigenous to the greatest periods of drama. They have vanished permanently. In England the great literary models of the eighteenth century were of a very different kind—the *Spectator* papers, *Robinson Crusoe*, *The Seasons*, *Pamela*, Gray's *Elegy*. Merely to name them is sufficient commentary upon a changed world. An aristocratic society was no longer sole dictator to literature and art, as indeed these five works would at once suggest. To intellectual aristocrats like Swift and, in his later works, Pope, these books would all indicate a creeping taste for mediocrity which was a tidal wave of the future. Though they themselves might lash out with a *Dunciad* or *Tale of a Tub*, passionate cries for integrity of mind and clarity of vision, they could not stem the tide, but were drowned in the triumphant middle-class inundation of the meretricious. The novel-reading public had moved in.

Music was of course affected as well, even if the sudden rage for Italian opera early in the century might seem to belie such a proposition. High-flown unrealism could hardly be pushed farther than in these exotic flowers, but, as Burney's chronicles of their hectic fortunes reveal, they could capture no permanent audience larger than a small group of aristocrats and (not necessarily the same) connoisseurs. Handel's heroic struggle over nearly three decades to keep Italian opera afloat was most precariously and only intermittently managed, and even then only with constant royal patronage and the occasional emergence of a singer who became a popular passion. The true public taste was touched by *The Beggar's Opera* (1728) and finally, late in Handel's career, by the great oratorios written to English texts largely on Biblical themes.[2] At mid-century Rameau was still writing *pastorales* and *opéras à machines*, but the most popular operas in London were *Thomas and Sally* and *Love in a Village*.

Even the barely successful operas of Handel enjoyed an advantage which Purcell's did not. Sung throughout, and to Italian texts, which almost no one understood, their character bore little relation to the taste of the theatre-going public. The libretti might be allied to heroic plays, but for the audience they were merely skeletons upon which to hang a succession of arias in widely contrasting moods. Though static and incredible, the operas were acceptable as musical performances. Purcell's operas, the forgotten *Dido* excepted, were in altogether different case, because they were performed not in opera houses (as the King's Theatre had become) but as plays in ordinary playhouses. When the play became outdated and ceased to please, the music usually fell along with it. We have already seen that in actuality this is not quite what happened to Purcell. *The Tempest* is, of course, in a special category, and the *Fairy Queen* score was lost, but Purcell's music so transformed the other plays that they continued to have frequent revivals during the century, *King Arthur* even lasting well into the Victorian period. Yet to them all came that inevitable day when no Purcellian ravishment of the sense could woo an audience into accepting what it felt was nonsense, and the music accordingly sank into oblivion.

What to do with these plays is by no means the only obstacle in reviving Purcell's operas today, though it is surely the principal one. Merely presenting the music in concert form will not avail, as we have seen repeatedly, since the whole conception of the score was moulded by balletic, scenic, and dramatic considerations. And hearing a recording, exactly as with more familiar grand operas, is satisfying only after we have become fairly well acquainted with the work on the stage, so that our imaginations can readily supply what is lacking. The ideal would of course be

---

[2] I do not of course mean to imply that for oratorio there was a large paying public comparable to that of the theatres, but that the ordinary Englishman responded to oratorio with a feeling he could never muster for Italian opera.

to present the work as nearly as possible as it first appeared, with the extra advantage of modern lighting, accepting the radical differences in dramatic convention and making an effort to understand them. Failing this the best compromise would be that in which the play itself was cut down, always making sure to retain everything necessary to illuminate the musical scenes. In *King Arthur*, for example, the dialogue quoted earlier between Emmeline and her confidante with its conceit about jaundice could be profitably scrapped, but almost the whole of the last two acts with the temptation scenes and the balletic combat between the antagonists must be retained. By formal groupings and stylized gestures much of the dignity of the heroic concept could be suggested even with heavily curtailed dialogue. Any attempts at realistic or naturalistic performance would make nonsense of play and music alike. During the last few years revivals of *The Fairy Queen* at Covent Garden and *King Arthur* at Nottingham, even without resolving all the difficulties, have shown how much may be accomplished.

The other problems concern the music alone. One is the formidable professionalism of the vocal writing. Working during the rise of the instrumental concerto, Purcell like many of his contemporaries sometimes treated the voice as if it were an instrument. This is only one reason why the brave attempts of amateurs in the village musical society to put on a Purcell opera are liable to come to grief. Only the most professional singers who are able to manage florid music with dexterity will really suffice, and they are not very plentiful. Since they were still to be found in abundance throughout the eighteenth century, Purcell revivals caused no trouble then. The other problem is that of the male alto or counter-tenor for whom Purcell, himself an alto, wrote so much of his music. It is of course not a castrato, but is a higher voice than the tenor with a timbre of its own, rarer today than it used to be, and (to judge from contemporary practitioners) likely to be of insufficient power to hold its own in an ensemble. On the other hand it blends well with other voices, and can lend to ensembles a particular beauty unattainable by plummier voices alone. The most serious objection to this voice in operatic music, as Britten's recent *Midsummer Night's Dream* has glaringly revealed, is its pallid unshaded timbre, which to my mind is essentially undramatic in character. In Purcell the problem is fortunately not a very serious one since most of the solos do not involve a personality in the drama. In Handel's operas, on the other hand, the problem (whether of castrato or alto) is crucial and seldom admissible of a satisfactory compromise. For Purcell, if no counter-tenor is available, the music can usually be sung by a contralto, admittedly no very happy solution in a group of priests or warriors. To transpose the part so that it can be sung by a tenor upsets the key relationships of a scene (if it is a solo), and is obviously impossible in an ensemble. For a baritone to sing the music an octave lower is sometimes acceptable, though more often the particular character of the piece is injured; in an ensemble the balance of voices is thrown out completely. The contralto is usually preferable to the other compromises and is in many cases thoroughly satisfactory.

These difficulties of realizing the operas in stage performances may seem discouraging enough, but they dim before the compensations. For what can unroll before us is probably the richest vein in English culture of the baroque theatrical experience. The operas have much in common, of course, but each is in a distinct category with its own unique features so that taken all together the variety is astonishing. They might almost be said to present an anthology of baroque effects. From the very first, with *Dido and Aeneas*, Purcell displays his gift for incorporating any kind of material into a coherent whole. Witches, courtiers, sailors, and shepherds are all woven into the harmonious tapestry of song and dance which is dominated by the overpowering figure of Dido herself. The opera revolves around the two great *scenas* for the anguished queen, the supreme example in Purcell of an outsize heroic character whose dimensions both in majesty and suffering are fully explored in the music. She is reminiscent of one of the tortured figures of Bernini, the Saint Theresa or the *Beata Albertona*, dying in ecstatic pain, sculptured in a style both majestic and flamboyant, the perfection of high baroque. Purcell's genius at creating this kind of personality by musical means alone can be seen in the dramatic *scenas* of 'The Blessed Virgin's Expostulation' and 'Saul and the Witch of Endor', or in various of the mad songs. They are all in the violent baroque manner which makes *Lucia di Lammermoor* look a model of conventional propriety. Our only regret inspired by hearing *Dido* is at the waste of such operatic gifts in a theatre which was not yet ready for opera in the fullest sense.

King Arthur is an altogether different work in which the composer, attempting with Dryden to make a national opera, leaves the intimate world of Dido's grief for a public extrovert testimonial. Containing more seemingly disparate elements than any other of his works, it reveals one of the most thrilling aspects of the baroque artist, his masterful and masterly subjection of unruly material into a unified conception. The score flows on through religious ritual, fighting songs, bucolic pastorale, temptation scenes in a magical forest, and the irrelevant *tour de force* of the Frost Scene, all before the spacious patriotic masque of the close. Its success is partly Dryden's for his organizing power in putting all these together in a compulsive progressive movement. The two artists ideally complement one another. Yet the exaggerated rhetoric of Dryden's heroics could not really stand up (as a mere reading of the play will disclose) without the splendour of Purcell's score, which adds those elements of stylized elegance and grand yet sensuous formality that so elevate and enrich the colour of the whole. What results is a dazzlingly hued composition in a bold epic manner that puts one in mind of a ceiling by Rubens or Tiepolo—from the wrong angle it can look absurd, but viewed in the proper frame of mind its gusto sweeps all before it.

This high-flown exuberance is largely alien to the world of *The Fairy Queen*, a work not really to be judged like a play, but as an entertainment which might be described best as an apotheosis of the masque. In the second act it is the Masque of Night and Sleep rather than the quarrels of Titania and Oberon that constitutes the drama. Throughout the opera, in fact, it is the music surrounding Oberon, and not his speeches, which makes him impressive. Paradise itself appears in the final apotheosis. The masque, the most decorative of stage genres because pre-eminently visual, always appeals to Purcell's sense of stage picture and of pictorialism in musical style. The importance of formality is indicated by his closing the score with a giant chaconne, the strict musical form casting an imposing dignity upon some of the distracting frivolities that are collected together upon the stage at the end. The massive passacaglia movement accompanying the *King Arthur* temptation scene in the magic forest is another example of rock-like solidity giving direction to what might otherwise be romantic distractiveness.

Of the scores accompanying heroic plays—*King Arthur* stands apart from these, having been mapped out from the very start as an opera—*Dioclesian* and *Bonduca* belong to an earlier and less violent evolvement which I have described as the heroic romance. To give them visual realization we should want Veronese, for they are set in classical backgrounds in an aura of pseudo-history, and are acted out by statuesque figures in rich costumes who, assuming commanding postures as they pour forth their aggrandized sentiments, are like figures from a slow dance. The world of Tintoretto and Rubens is altogether too vehement. From the standpoint of technique no scores more quickly show Purcell off as the baroque virtuoso who delights in seemingly unending inventiveness at setting texts which appear to be indistinguishable. The masque in *Dioclesian* is the most elaborate example, though the ceremonial scene from the third act is as impressive as anything in Purcell as an object lesson in how pedestrian lyrics can be turned into a massive musical movement, the many pictorial touches taking their proper subsidiary place in a large formal structure. As for the ritual scene in *Bonduca*, we have seen how the composer, in returning to an almost identical layout of four years earlier in *King Arthur*, has discovered far more musical drama. Nothing is more characteristic of the baroque artist than this sense of delighted inventiveness at finding new treatments for a conventional subject.

The two largest scores of the last year place the crown upon Purcell's wide range. *The Indian Queen* is the most violent of exotics, an orientalized heroic play, while *The Tempest* weaves spells of delicacy and innocence or of marine magnificence around Shakespeare's magic island. In the former work it is the music which sheds the real splendour upon the design, gathering itself about the title character herself and making an imposing and even emotionally convincing figure of one who is otherwise a bizarre dummy. The world of dreams and visions is even more persuasively invoked than in *The Fairy Queen*, while 'I attempt from love's sickness to fly' delineates an eternal human dilemma that brings the Queen into immediate life. *The Tempest* is in complete contrast. After a number of charming incidental felicities it rolls to its close with a mighty diapason frankly Italian in manner, as if Purcell were doing homage to the birthplace of the baroque style. Neptune rises in opulent dignity, yet the prevailing spirit is joyousness. 'Fair and serene', he sings and Amphitrite replies,

> Halcyon days, now wars are ending,
> You shall find where e'er you sail!

This music winds happily around the words, spreading out in vistas of calm content. It is pleasing to remember that almost the last words Purcell set, and to music wherein wistfulness mingles with joy, were these:

> No stars again shall hurt you from above,
> But all your days shall pass in peace and love ...

for within a few weeks in Westminster Abbey he was receiving the ultimate tribute, one with which posterity has found no cause to quarrel: 'Here lies Henry Purcell, Esq, who left this life and is gone to that Blessed Place where only his harmony can be exceeded.'

A Selected Discography[1]

DIDO AND AENEAS   (1) Flagstad, Schwarzkopf, Hemsley, Mermaid Singers and Orchestra, conductor G. Jones.
HMV-1026 or RCA-Victor, LM-2019
(2) Houston, Leigh, Cummings, Stuart Chamber Orchestra and Chorus, conductor Gregory.   Period-546

THE FAIRY QUEEN   (1) Vyvyan, Morrison, Pears, St Anthony Singers and Boyd Neel Orchestra, conductor A. Lewis.   OL-50139/41
(2) (Selections) Margaret Ritchie, Ensemble Orchestral de l'Oiseau-Lyre, conductor A. Lewis.   OL-50029

THE INDIAN QUEEN   London Chamber Singers and Orchestra, conductor A. Bernard.   Record Society-1

KING ARTHUR   Harper, Morrison, Whitworth, Alan, Orchestra of the Philomusica of London, conductor A. Lewis.   OL-50176/7
OL Stereo-60008/9

THE TEMPEST   (Selections) Vyvyan, Herbert, Alan, Orchestra of the Philomusica of London, conductor A. Lewis.   OL-50171
OL Stereo-60002

TIMON OF ATHENS   (1) Sorrell, Manton, Woodhouse. (Arranged by Woodhouse for the Intimate Opera Company.)   Decca-4036
(2) (Selections) Margaret Ritchie, Ensemble Orchestral de l'Oiseau-Lyre.   OL-50029

[1] For a complete discography see G. L. Mayer: 'The Vocal Works of Henry Purcell—A Discography': *American Record Guide*, vol. xxv, no. 9 (May 1959), pp. 588 ff.

Index

217